MARKETING
AND
ENTREPRENEURSHIP

MARKETING AND ENTREPRENEURSHIP

Research Ideas and Opportunities

Gerald E. Hills

QUORUM BOOKS
Westport, Connecticut • London

Library of Congress Cataloging-in-Publication Data

Marketing and entrepreneurship : research ideas and opportunities /
    edited by Gerald E. Hills.
        p.   cm.
    Includes bibliographical references and index.
    ISBN 0–89930–765–5 (alk. paper)
    1. Marketing.   2. Marketing research.   3. Entrepreneurship.
    I. Hills, Gerald E.
    HF5415.M2969   1994
    658.8—dc20   93–6763

British Library Cataloguing in Publication Data is available.

Library of Congress Catalog Card Number: 93–6763
ISBN: 0–89930–765–5

First published in 1994

Greenwood Press, 88 Post Road West, Westport, CT 06881
An imprint of Greenwood Publishing Group, Inc.

Printed in the United States of America

The paper used in this book complies with the
Permanent Paper Standard issued by the National
Information Standards Organization (Z39.48–1984).

10 9 8 7 6 5 4 3 2 1

Copyright Acknowledgments

The editor and publisher gratefully acknowledge permission to reproduce the following copyrighted
material:

Figure 1.1 in this volume is reprinted from Donald Sexton, *The State of the Art of Entrepreneurship*.
Belmont, CA: Wadsworth Publishing Co., 1992.

This volume is dedicated with love to
Stela

Contents

A Definitional Debate

Identifying and Evaluating Opportunities

Research Opportunities and the Marketing Mix

A Broader Perspective

Tables and Figures

Tables

Figures

Preface

This is the first scholarly book dedicated to the interface between marketing and entrepreneurship and to providing numerous research opportunities on truly important issues. At a time when the marketing discipline is increasingly criticized for too little attention to important topics, this book offers a path for the researcher who wants to make a major impact. This is a pioneering book and it is hoped that it will one day be viewed a classic contribution to marketing and to entrepreneurship thought.

A spirit of entrepreneurship encompassed the conception and birth of this volume because it addresses a new and critically important subject area. The marketing discipline has, until recently, largely ignored entrepreneurship and new ventures. The growing entrepreneurship field has also devoted little attention to marketing.

Although there is considerable new knowledge in this volume, the primary focus is on questions, issues and variables that should stimulate added creativity. For the scholar, the sifting and sorting will be fruitful. The contents of this volume will be of value to the reader in search of ideas, concepts and research directions pertaining to marketing in new and/or growing ventures. The authors are leading scholars in the marketing and management disciplines.

The book begins with a rich collection of five articles on the nature of entrepreneurship and its relationship to marketing. This may be the single best array of definitional perspectives ever written, in part because leading contributors to the debate have returned to the task. The second section focuses on market opportunity, but rather than only look at market analysis and idea screening, there is also ground breaking work regarding entrepreneurial opportunity identification and opportunity recognition. Marketing strategy and each of the marketing mix areas are addressed in separate chapters with particular attention to the uniqueness of marketing in new enterprises as compared to mature, larger firms. The final section of the book may be the most intriguing, with attention to entrepreneurship in international markets and lesser developed countries, as well as the role of new and smaller enterprises in job generation. The primary audiences for this book include marketing, management and entrepreneurship professors, Ph.D. candidates, public policy makers, and intellectually curious business owners.

Generous support and mentoring from the Coleman Foundation provided me with the Coleman/Denton Thorne Chair in Entrepreneurship and the challenge to create a leading entrepreneurship program. Mrs. Jean Thorne, Mr. John Hughes, Mr. Trevor Davies, Mr. Michael Hennessy and their distinguished Board members have given generously of their time, ideas and monies to help me realize this goal. I cannot thank them too much.

Finally, there are many to thank for this volume. First, the contributing authors and my great friends deserve credit for climbing onto a new learning curve, some recently and some years ago, and then sharing their knowledge in these pages. At Quorum Books, I thank Mr. Eric Valentine and Ms. Sally Scott for their encouragement and guidance. In the UIC College of Business Administration, I thank Dean Paul Uselding, someone who intellectually understands the critical importance of entrepreneurship, new ventures, and family-owned businesses and is leading the entire College in support of this economic reality. Also in the College my continuing gratitude and appreciation go to Dr. Chem Narayana, head of the Marketing Department, for his ongoing support and leadership. In the UIC Institute for Entrepreneurial Studies, I thank my team members, Ms. Elaine McCall, Ms. Beverly Parker, and Ms. Lynn Ann Thomas, without whom this volume would not exist. As IES Administrative Secretary, Associate Director, and Manuscript Editor, respectively, they played a critically important role at every stage. Thanks also go to our student research assistants, Amy Jacobs, Anil Mahajan, Ilyne Rothschild, Van Simios, and Rich Wilson, who also carried out major steps in bringing this volume to completion. And, most importantly, my family, Stela, Douglas, Eduardo, Renee and Sylvia, who make all things possible.

Gerald E. Hills

Introduction

Market opportunities and marketing may be the two most important elements underpinning successful business creation, but scholarly attention to this interface has occurred only in recent years. This book attempts to define and conceptualize this interface, assess the status of the subject in the marketing discipline, and review relevant knowledge.

In the mid-1980s it was observed that because the importance of new ventures was well documented, one might expect marketing scholars to commonly enter "stage of the business life cycle" and "firm size" variables into marketing studies (Davis, Hills, and LaForge 1985). The evidence, however, suggested that marketing academicians had almost entirely neglected such investigations. A review of the *Journal of Marketing* from 1936 to the present failed to identify any titles directed wholly toward marketing and new ventures or firm size. Rarely did any of the articles even include these subjects as a secondary focus. A similar review of the *Journal of Retailing* since 1927 identified only four articles dealing with these subjects, the most recent published in 1952.

A review of the sources of entrepreneurship literature over more recent years identified four articles (two percent of the total number of articles) in which marketing was the major field of orientation. Articles "mentioning" marketing totaled seventeen (Hisrich 1989).

In 1983, proceedings were published as the result of a research meeting on marketing and entrepreneurship, cosponsored by the American Marketing Association (AMA) and the International Council for Small Business (Hills, Barnaby, and Duffus 1983). The primary value of this publication was the identification of important research issues, although it was clear at that time that few in the marketing discipline were interested. Four years later a second symposium was held, and this time it met with a new level of interest among established researchers in the marketing discipline (Hills 1987). Subsequent meetings have provided an outlet for research and an AMA Task Force on Marketing and Entrepreneurship has been created. As of this writing, a total of six symposia on marketing and entrepreneurship have been held, resulting in published proceedings including 135 articles (Hills 1987; Hills, LaForge, and Parker 1989; Hills, LaForge, and Welsch 1990; Hills and LaForge 1991, 1992, 1993).

The AMA Task Force is now in its sixth year of existence, serving an interest group of more than 300 professors with a quarterly newsletter. As this book goes to press, approval was received from the AMA to form an interest group of equal status to more traditional marketing groups. This is part of the new AMA Academic Council reorganization led by Gerald Hills last year.

In 1989, an entrepreneurship session track was included at the Academy of Marketing Science World Congress in Singapore. In 1990, 1991, and 1993, entrepreneurship tracks were included in the AMA Educators' Conference. Leaders of the discipline are recognizing the value of the subject, and a growing number of scholars are devoting attention to it. Yet the subject is still not institutionalized and, compared to the management discipline, the subject is still at the early growth stage (Hoy 1987). However, interest is growing rapidly. David Gardner (1991) observed that the next major "school of thought" in the marketing discipline may well develop from the interface of entrepreneurship.

The purpose of this book is to assist professors, Ph.D. candidates and others who have a scholarly research interest in marketing and entrepreneurship. It provides a "school of discovery" based collection of important research ideas that, if pursued, could truly make a difference in existing knowledge about new venture formation and growth and the role of marketing.

The first section of the book offers the richest statements ever written on defining entrepreneurship and the interface with marketing. The second section focuses on evaluating opportunities and, for the first time in the marketing discipline, on identifying new venture ideas. The reader will obtain new insights into the critically important subject of identifying new ideas for creating a new enterprise. The third section of the book addresses research opportunities regarding entrepreneurship and the marketing mix and marketing strategy. Finally, special attention is drawn to entrepreneurship internationally, its role in job creation, and the existing knowledge base in the entrepreneurship field. This book is but a beginning, but with luck, an important beginning.

REFERENCES

Davis, C. H., G. E. Hills, and R. W. LaForge. "The Marketing/ Small Enterprise Paradox: A Research Agenda." *International Small Business Journal* (Spring 1985): 31–42.

Gardner, D. M. "Exploring the Marketing/Entrepreneurship Interface." In *Research at the Marketing/Entrepreneurship Interface*, edited by G. E. Hills and R. W. LaForge; 3–21. Chicago: University of Illinois at Chicago, 1991.

Hills, G. E., ed. *Research at the Marketing/Entrepreneurship Interface.* Chicago: University of Illinois at Chicago, 1987.

Hills, G. E., D. J. Barnaby, and L. R. Duffus. *Marketing and Small Business/ Entrepreneurship: Conceptual and Research Directions.* Washington, DC: International Council for Small Business, 1983.

Hills, G. E., and R. W. LaForge, eds. *Research at the Marketing/Entrepreneurship Interface.* Chicago: University of Illinois at Chicago, 1991, 1992, 1993.

Hills, G. E., R. W. LaForge, and B. J. Parker, eds. *Research at the Marketing/ Entrepreneurship Interface.* Chicago: University of Illinois at Chicago, 1989.

Hills, G. E., R. W. LaForge, and H. P. Welsch, eds. *Research at the Marketing/ Entrepreneurship Interface.* Chicago: University of Illinois at Chicago, 1990.

Hisrich, R. D. "Marketing and Entrepreneurship Research Interface." In *Research at the Marketing/Entrepreneurship Interface*, edited by G. E. Hills, R. W. LaForge, and B. J. Parker, 3–17. Chicago: University of Illinois at Chicago, 1989.

Hoy, F. "Entrepreneurship in the Management Discipline: Coming of Age." In *Research at the Marketing/Entrepreneurship Interface*, edited by G. E. Hills, 283–86. Chicago: University of Illinois at Chicago, 1987.

A DEFINITIONAL DEBATE

1

Marketing and Entrepreneurship: The Domain

Gerald E. Hills

There is growing evidence that entrepreneurship should be treated as a major conceptual dimension within the marketing discipline. Marketing journals, programs, and associations are structured around: (1) different marketing functions such as product development and advertising; and (2) types of markets and firms such as consumer and industrial, services, health care marketing, and retailing. The time has come to also study firms at their inception and in the early stages of the business life cycle.

To illustrate the potential, following are four conclusions drawn from an in-depth, exploratory survey of expert opinion. Hisrich (1989) and Wortman, Spann, and Adams (1989) each cited this study as the first to examine the marketing/entrepreneurship interface. Although the study results are based on interviews with only fourteen venture capitalists, the venture capitalists had dealt with hundreds of sophisticated entrepreneurs and collectively financed and guided more than 200 new ventures (Hills 1984):

1. Venture capitalists rated marketing management at 6.7 on a 7.0 scale as important to the success of new ventures.

2. Venture capitalists overwhelmingly agreed that venture failure rates could be reduced, perhaps as much as 60 percent, through better preventure market analysis.

3. Three-quarters of the venture capitalists felt that entrepreneurs tend to be biased toward their venture idea, ignore negative market information, and resist obtaining in-depth market information due to their prior commitment to the venture idea.

    4. Venture capitalists agreed on several unique marketing-related challenges that face entrepreneurs, such as the inability to spread advertising costs, poor access to good quality distributors, and lack of access to retail shelf space.

It was clear that these new venture observers perceived marketing as a critically important part of entrepreneurship and, importantly, as different in some significant ways from marketing in mature firms. Further, Hisrich (1989) and a number of others have observed that surveys of entrepreneurs in the United States as well as throughout the world reveal that the two biggest problem areas are marketing and finance.

MARKETING

In order to study the marketing/entrepreneurship interface, it is important to make definition issues explicit. Marketing can be defined in a variety of ways and, in general, the proper domain and boundaries of marketing are not fully known (Sheth, Gardner, and Garrett 1988). Historically, there have been several schools of thought in the marketing discipline; such as the commodity, functional, institutional, buyer behavior, macromarketing, and managerial perspectives. But the implicit focus in all of them is on exchange and transactions.

The managerial perspective was adopted by Kotler (1972) when he proposed a generic concept of marketing concerned with how transactions are created, stimulated, facilitated, and valued. More recently it was noted that the main purpose of marketing is to create and distribute values among the market parties through the process of transactions and market relationships (Sheth, Gardner, and Garrett 1988). It is rather striking that substitution of the word entrepreneurship for the word marketing could yield a defensible definition as well! In both cases, there is win-win market behavior.

To move to a more operational level, the American Marketing Association has defined marketing as the process of planning and executing the conception, pricing, promotion, and distribution of ideas, goods, and services to create exchanges that satisfy individual and organizational objectives. Marketing management is the process of scanning the environment, analyzing market opportunities, designing marketing strategies, and then effectively implementing and controlling marketing practices (Cravens, Hills, and Woodruff 1987). In this book, we are addressing research at the *interface* of marketing and entrepreneurship, and we will primarily use the latter definition.

ENTREPRENEURSHIP

The study of new venture development and entrepreneurship *as a process*, and the study of the early stages of the business life cycle, belong as much or more to marketing than to any other business function. Indeed, some argue that the very term management may be somewhat in definitional conflict with the term entrepreneurship. Further, if we address the entrepreneurial spirit, it can be hypothesized that marketing is the organizational function most dominated by boundary agents; by open interactive systems; and by truly entrepreneurial activity. Market opportunity analysis, new product development, the diffusion of innovation, and marketing strategies to create growing firms are at the heart of both marketing and entrepreneurship. These also represent the most relevant, existing marketing literature bases.

Entrepreneurship as defined by Stevenson and Jarillo-Mossi (1986) focuses on opportunity and is therefore particularly relevant to the marketing interface; it is the process of creating value by combining resources to exploit an opportunity.

Finally, what is the role of small business in entrepreneurship research? In academic research, small business is quite simply the *size* variable, with focus on the lower end of the scale. Although the very term "small business" often conjures images of mediocre research and stagnant, nongrowth firms, this prejudice can make potentially exciting research issues seem unimportant. The research issue is quite clear: should we incorporate the size variable, business life cycle stage, and other related variables when we do organizational research on marketing?

THE INTERFACE

Marketing definitions vary greatly. Yet the relationship to several concepts such as innovation, growth, and uniqueness attributes is clear, as well as to organization creation and the creation of value. In an earlier essay, Hunt et al. (1987) defined marketing as a *social process* and entrepreneurship as wealth creation and expressed skepticism that marketing is any different for entrepreneurs than for anyone else. But from a managerial viewpoint, Figure 1.1 illustrates relationships between marketing management and entrepreneurship. Although the exact placement of some of the entrepreneurship descriptors is arbitrary, others fit logically. Venture idea identification, innovation, and exploiting opportunities seem to fit naturally between environmental scanning and market opportunity analysis. Team building becomes critical as the implementation stage is approached and the venture is launched. The business plan is partially comprised of market feasibility analysis and marketing strategy.

Figure 1.1
Marketing Management and Entrepreneurship

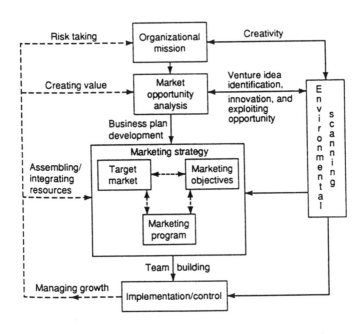

Following the initial sales generation, managing growth becomes relevant, and creating value ultimately depends on customer feedback and a constant reappraisal of customer needs relative to the product or service offered. Risk taking and creativity permeate the entire process most fundamentally at the business mission level. It is readily evident that the interface between marketing and entrepreneurship is extensive.

In defining the research interface, it may be important to look beyond narrow definitions of entrepreneurship and seek to evaluate the importance of other factors or variables. Related variables often include few, if any, economies of scale, severe resource constraints, a limited geographic market presence and limited market image, little brand loyalty or market share, little specialized management expertise, decision making under even more imperfect information conditions than in larger firms, a marked scarcity of time per major management task, a scarcity of professional managers, and a mixture of personal, non-maximizing financial goals. Just as a child is not a little adult, a new venture or smaller firm is not a little Fortune 100 firm. In firms where several of these conditions exist, one could expect that the marketing function would be both *viewed* differently and *performed* differently from marketing functions in mature firms. Although the basic definition of marketing remains intact, new venture marketing could join the ranks of other specialized areas; such as international marketing, industrial marketing, and services marketing. Finally, a study of the inherent definitional and conceptual similarities between marketing and entrepreneurship supported the hypothesis that more entrepreneurial firms should also be more marketing oriented (Morris and Paul 1987). Perhaps marketing *is* the home for entrepreneurship.

REFERENCES

Cravens, D. W., G. E. Hills, and R. B. Woodruff. *Marketing Management.* Homewood, IL: Richard D. Irwin, 1987.

Hills, G. E. "Market Analysis and Marketing in New Ventures: Venture Capitalists' Perceptions." In *Frontiers of Entrepreneurship Research,* edited by K. Vesper, 167–82. Wellesley, MA: Babson College, 1984.

Hisrich, R. D. "Marketing and Entrepreneurship Research Interface." In *Research at the Marketing/Entrepreneurship Interface,* edited by G. E. Hills, R. W. LaForge, and B. J. Parker, 3–17. Chicago: University of Illinois at Chicago, 1989.

Hunt, K., J. C. Huefner, C. Voegele, and P. B. Robinson. "The Entrepreneurial Consumer." In *Research at the Marketing/ Entrepreneurship Interface,* edited by G. E. Hills, R. W. LaForge, and B. J. Parker, 175–84. Chicago: University of Illinois at Chicago, 1989.

Kotler, P. "A Generic Concept of Marketing." *Journal of Marketing* 36(2), (1972): 46–54.

Morris, M. H., and G. W. Paul. "The Relationship Between Entrepreneurship and Marketing in Established Firms." *Journal of Business Venturing* 2 (3), (Summer 1987): 247–59.

Sheth, J. N., D. M. Gardner, and D. E. Garrett. *Marketing Theory: Evolution and Evaluation.* New York: John Wiley & Sons, 1988.

Stevenson, H., and J. C. Jarillo-Mossi. "Preserving Entrepreneurship as Companies Grow." *Journal of Business Strategy* 7 (1986): 10–23.

Wortman, M. S., M. S. Spann, and M. Adams. "The Interface of Entrepreneur-
    ship and Marketing: Concepts and Research Perspectives." In *Research
    at the Marketing/Entrepreneurship Interface,* edited by G. E. Hills, R.
    W. LaForge, and B. J. Parker, 117–37. Chicago: University of Illinois
    at Chicago, 1989.

2

Defining and Conceptualizing Entrepreneurship: A Process Approach

Neil C. Churchill and Daniel F. Muzyka

THE DEFINITION OF ENTREPRENEURSHIP

Entrepreneurship is a concept that has been discussed for many years, since the time of Cantillion in 1700 (Carland, Hoy, and Carland 1988). In this century, there has been considerable discussion over the exact definition of entrepreneurship, although there is general agreement that entrepreneurs perform the function in society of identifying opportunities and converting them into economic value—Schumpeter (1934), Gartner (1988); Carland, Hoy, and Carland (1988); Gartner (1990); and Baumol (1991) are just a few of the authors who have written on the subject. Much of the argument over the definition of entrepreneurship revolves around the factors considered *necessary* for entrepreneurship to take place and, derivatively, what constitutes an entrepreneur. The factors that are most commonly cited for entrepreneurship to take place are:

1. An individual
2. An act
3. Innovation and opportunity
4. An organization
5. Risk

The Individual

There is virtual unanimity that entrepreneurship necessitates at least one motivated individual. Even those who view entrepreneurship as an economic phenomenon emanating primarily from large, complex organizational systems, do not ignore the role of the individual.

Although there is agreement that there is an essential role for the "entrepreneur" in "entrepreneurship," there is some disagreement as to whether the entrepreneur is a single individual or may, in fact, be representational of the collective action of a "team." Researchers with considerable experience and knowledge of high-technology ventures focus on the entrepreneur *and* the "management team." This may be a due to the milieu in which they have conducted their research. High-technology ventures are usually comparatively sophisticated undertakings with many complex elements, and often considerable up-front financing by venture capitalists. In these "jump-started" enterprises, the process of value creation may require the formation of a true management team to bring the product to market or even to develop the opportunity. Biotechnology is a good example of a high-technology entrepreneurial arena where collective management action is required.

Supporting the idea of entrepreneurial teams is the work of those individuals doing research on corporate entrepreneurship or "corporate venturing," for example, MacMillan and Day (1987) and Covin and Slevin (1991) who have a tendency to speak more of teams than individuals. Again, this may be a result of the setting under examination. Where the entrepreneurial ventures are born of large complex organizations, there is a high probability that the venture will begin with an intact team that mirrors the process and beliefs of the parent organizations. In addition, when these ventures cross a beginning threshold, they, like venture-capital backed firms, receive considerable financing from sophisticated backers and experienced managerial advice. The typical entrepreneurial venture, on the other hand, begins with an entrepreneur, or a partner or two, and builds the management team slowly as the company grows in size, complexity, and the ability to use and, most importantly, afford a managerial organization.

The Act

Although everyone agrees that entrepreneurship involves an action, there is considerable difference of opinion as to exactly what this action must involve. Indeed, it may not always be *an* action because current research (Baumol 1991 and Van de Ven 1991) shows that a series of actions often takes place in the production of an innovation.[1] Further, as we shall see in the following section, there are differences of opinion as to what constitutes an "entrepreneurial innovation." Some scholars view only acts that involve the creation of an organization as entrepreneurial, others consider only acts that produce an economic innovation, and still others believe that to be entrepreneurial, an act must involve both an innovation and a new organization.

Innovation and Opportunity

Although entrepreneurship requires innovation, not all innovation is entrepreneurial. There is an extensive body of knowledge on creativity in science and the arts that does not involve "the commercial or industrial application of something new—a new product, process, or method of production; a new form of commercial, business, or financial organization."[2] There is also considerable research on innovation and the management of research and development that deals with an end product of ideas or objects whose ability to deliver economic value has yet to be tested. In the entrepreneurship literature, innovation is coupled with its ability to create economic value.

Whether done by an individual or a team, there is general agreement that entrepreneurship involves an act by a motivated individual who innovates by creating value through recognizing (or developing) an opportunity and converting it into a viable product or service. That is, innovating in a way that produces net economic value.

Although most scholars agree that innovation is a necessary condition for entrepreneurship, there are differences of opinion on the extent and type of innovation that makes an act entrepreneurial. As we have seen, Schumpeter defines entrepreneurship as dealing with innovative acts that create economic value *for society* and not just for the individual. An alternative point of view considers an entrepreneurial act as one that only produces economic value for the individual. This distinction in entrepreneurship is analogous to Herbert Simon's discussion of the two senses of artistic and scientific creativity: *creativity in the larger or social sense* is an act that "produces something that is novel and that is thought to be interesting or to have social value"—and *creativity in the weaker or individual sense* is an act that "possesses these characteristics for the individual but not for society" (Simon 1984).[3] A similar distinction is used by Baumol (1991) when he contrasts *firm-creating entrepreneurs* from *innovating entrepreneurs*, describing the first as "someone who creates and then, perhaps, organizes and operates a new business firm, whether or not there is anything innovative in these acts" and the latter as individuals "who transform inventions and ideas into economically-viable entities whether or not in the course of doing so, they create or operate a firm."

This contrast between innovation in the large, or societal, sense and innovation in the small, or individual, sense lies at the heart of the different definitions of entrepreneurship. It also highlights the question, posed by Baumol (1991) as to whether there is as much to be gained from research on firm-creating entrepreneurs as there is from focusing on the *innovating entrepreneurs* whose actions are so important to society.

The Organization

As far back as Cantillion and Say, there has been a school of thought that considers the creation of an organization as a necessary condition for entrepreneurship. Some individuals with this view go so far as to state that an individual acting to form a new organization is not only a *necessary* but a *sufficient* condition for entrepreneurship. William Gartner articulates this view as follows: "Entrepreneurship is the creation of organizations. What differentiates entrepreneurs from non-entrepreneurs is that entrepreneurs create organizations, while non-entrepreneurs do not" (1988, 11). Schumpeter, on the other hand, implies that the existence of an organization is not necessary stating, "Entrepreneurship is broader than business management because not all entrepreneurs operate established businesses. It is narrower than business management because not all managers, immersed as they are in the routine calculation of the circular flow, engage in entrepreneurial activities, that is, innovations" (1934, xxi).

With almost all scholars believing, with Schumpeter, that economic innovation is at the core of entrepreneurship, perhaps the critical difference between those who view organization creation as either a necessary or a sufficient condition is their view of the innovative act. For many, starting a business is by itself, innovative (from an *individually innovative* point of view), and hence, sufficient to be termed entrepreneurial. For them, the opening of a franchise by someone who has never done such a thing before is entrepreneurial because it creates value for the individual. For others, a socially innovative act must be present. We suggest that this is at the heart of matter and at the basis of the distinction often made between small business and entrepreneurship.

Another element that complicates the linkage between entrepreneurial activity and organization creation is "What exactly constitutes an organization?" The recent focus on entrepreneurs and entrepreneurial organizations has produced a considerable amount of literature on networks and networked organizations. Many successful entrepreneurs have built what can be termed "extended organizations" by renting and borrowing from individuals in other organizations on an "as needed" basis (Stevenson, Roberts, and Grousbeck 1985). Thus, particularly at start-up, it is often difficult to distinguish the limits to the entrepreneur's true organization. Some entrepreneurs have even gone to the extreme of building a firm with a very small, concentrated staff by leveraging the efforts of other individuals or organizations by putting in place a "contract organization."

Risk

As Carland, Hoy, and Carland (1988) pointed out, risk has been considered an important, and even a necessary part of entrepreneurship at least since Mill's writings in 1848, and it is still part of the definition in most dictionaries. Indeed, because entrepreneurs venture out into the unknown, there are almost always factors of indeterminable impact that can not be accounted for. On the other hand, the entrepreneur may encounter nothing that gets in the way of a perfectly successful economic innovation that no one else has chosen to undertake. The difference between the presence of uncertainty, as distinguished from that of risk, has been dealt with by economists since Frank Knight (1971). Although uncertainty is unavoidable, successful entrepreneurs go to great lengths both to reduce uncertainty by research and to reduce risk by passing it on to others whenever they can. Thus, rather than saying entrepreneurship involves risk, we should say that entrepreneurship involves uncertainty. Few, if any, entrepreneurs get up in the morning, look in the mirror, and say, "What risks can I take today?" but any number would get up and evaluate a potentially profitable opportunity that involves some uncertainty. Thus, we believe that it is considerably more accurate to say that entrepreneurship *involves uncertainty* and, almost always, the *management of risk*. In summary, it can be said that entrepreneurs manage risks and do not worry about the unknowable.

Summary

Definitions are important for communication and, although no one wishes to legislate definitions in a rapidly developing field, it is important to know what is held in common and what is held in disagreement. Fortunately, as our knowledge of entrepreneurship is increasing, so too are we gaining consensus on what is meant by the term. The differences are not about what economically innovative organizations do but rather the conditions that are necessary if we are to call them entrepreneurial. We can do a great deal of useful research while still trying to settle our lexical differences, which are the following: to be entrepreneurial,

1. Is it or is it not necessary for a new organization to be formed?
2. Is it or is it not necessary for innovation to occur?
   a. If so, is it sufficient for this innovation to occur only in an individual sense?
   b. If so, is it necessary for innovation to occur in a societal sense?

We have general agreement that three conditions are *necessary* for entrepreneurship to occur: (1) an individual, (2) who performs an act, (3) that involves innovation—properly defined. We have substantial disagreements about (1) the nature (or amount) of the innovation that is *necessary*—including whether the creation of an economic entity is sufficiently innovative to be entrepreneurial and, (2) whether the creation of an economic entity is a necessary *condition* of entrepreneurship.

AN OPERATIONAL CONCEPTUALIZATION OF ENTREPRENEURSHIP

Although definitions are important for communication, arguments over what is and what is not entrepreneurship should not get in the way of understanding the entrepreneurial phenomena. Rather than attempting to adjudicate between the differing views of entrepreneurship or putting forth a new definition of the subject, we believe it is useful to focus on the process that produces entrepreneurial results. In doing this, we need to look at both entrepreneurs and entrepreneurial activities in order to better understand, teach, and do research into this important phenomenon. Such a look is particularly relevant at this time because the writings and research into entrepreneurship to date have come almost exclusively from observation of the phenomenon in relatively similar Western socioeconomic environments. Our characterization of entrepreneurship is:

> A *process* that takes place in *different environments* and settings that causes changes in the *economic system* through *innovations* brought about by *individuals* who generate or respond to *economic opportunities* that *create value* for both these individuals and society.

It should be noted that we do not consider creation of a new organizational entity as a necessary part of the entrepreneurial process but rather something that often occurs, for practical reasons, in the form of a brand new firm or a new entity within an existing organization. Before looking further at the nature of the *process* itself, it is useful to examine the other components of this characterization.

COMPONENTS OF THE ENTREPRENEURIAL PROCESS

Environments

Entrepreneurship can occur in different economic, social, and political environments. These can be Western market-based economies, Eastern and Central European countries coming out from under central economic planning, or emerging and Third-World economies. It is clear from emerging research (Abell and Kollermeier 1992; Brandsma and Muzyka 1992) that certain aspects of the Western economic environment are lacking to greater or lesser degrees in developing economies. These are the relative availability of resource slack; a strong business support infrastructure; reasonably predictable regulatory structures; and relatively stable, although evolving, product markets. Thus, the Western model of entrepreneurship is not totally applicable to developing economies where the problems faced by the entrepreneur and the solutions required for successful innovation can be considerably different. Economic innovation can, and does, occur in all of these environments; the fundamental entrepreneurial process can be seen at work, but in different ways and in greater or lesser degrees. Our understanding of entrepreneurship must broaden to encompass these differences.

Settings

Within a given economic, social, or political environment, entrepreneurship can take place in a number of different settings: new ventures; existing small or medium-sized enterprises (SMEs); large-scale businesses; not for profit enterprises; or, as Osborne (1992) has so vividly described, governmental organizations. The exact nature of the entrepreneurial process may vary in these different settings, as will the problems faced and the solutions required, but economically innovative acts that create value for individuals and society can still take place. It is the act and its outcome, not the environment nor the setting, that is the essence of entrepreneurship.

Innovations, Individuals, Opportunities, and Value

Innovations, by definition, create something new. If this creation does not involve economic well-being, no matter how important the creation may be in a physical, social, or cultural sense, the innovation is not entrepreneurial. If, however, either the creating individual or someone else sees an opportunity to apply this creation in a way that adds economic value to society and then implements this vision, then this individual is an entrepreneur. As stated earlier, many people consider creating value for the individual alone is sufficient to be considered entrepreneurial. Others, including the authors, believe that to be entrepreneurial, something that is of net economic value must be created for society as well. Individuals who add value to themselves by swindles or other socially distasteful acts are not helping society and, hence, are not entrepreneurs in our eyes. Even if an enterprise makes a profit by, for example, selling drugs to schoolchildren, it has not met the test of adding value to society.

THE ENTREPRENEURIAL PROCESS

The Rational

In looking at entrepreneurial process in action, in developing research programs into its nature, and in responding to queries of "Can you *really* teach entrepreneurship?" we have developed the categorization, shown next, which separates the entrepreneurial process into components that we have found to be useful in teaching entrepreneurship, in planning and conducting research into the subject, and in explaining this discipline to others within the university community and without.

Components

1. Create (or recognize) and develop an opportunity
2. Evaluate its desirability—its economic potential and the personal and financial risks involved
3. Marshal the resources needed to exploit it:
    •Financial
    •Managerial
    •Technical
    •Physical
4. Possess the will or tenacity to see the innovation through— to "do it"
5. Manage the launch, including
    •Competitive and cooperative relationships with others
    •Networks
6. Manage the downstream realization of the value of the opportunity, including:

•Creation of value for the entrepreneur and society
•Capture of new opportunities
•Harvest or family succession for the entrepreneur

Teaching

To demonstrate the usefulness of this process approach, the following is a brief description of how we use it, in responding to questions about whether or not it can be taught. Further, if entrepreneurship is a process, we should be able not only to acquaint newcomers with the nature of the process but also to focus on the elements of the process that need further illumination.

Creation or recognition of opportunities

We don't believe that you can really teach people to be "creative" in either making or recognizing economic opportunities, but you can sensitize them to the process through examples of others; give them an understanding of what encourages people to come forward with innovations they have discovered; give them some heuristics to aid them in recognizing opportunities; and, perhaps most importantly, open up their minds to the nature of opportunities and the economic potential in even those that appear at first glance to be quite small.

Evaluation of the desirability and risks of the opportunities

There is a considerable body of knowledge dealing with what constitutes a good opportunity and how to evaluate both its potential and its risks. This is an area where we can do quite a reasonable job in equipping our students for this task. One caveat, however, current research suggests that we may need to develop a better understanding of the dynamic elements of economic opportunity because our largely static economic models do not provide much insight into time-related opportunities.

Marshaling the necessary resources

This is an area where we can contribute greatly. The availability of resources, their structures, and the processes of managing them are largely man-made and can, therefore, be relatively well described.

Possessing the will or tenacity to "do it"

This is a quality of the individual and it probably cannot be "taught," as such. We can, however, expose the potential entrepreneur to a number of situations where this quality was, and is, necessary and make sure that they understand that good opportunities are those that others do not yet see and hence will probably be met with a good bit of skepticism—including a probable reluctance by others to lend more than moral support to the innovative endeavor. Further, through the example of others who tried and succeeded and by providing a clear understanding of the reasons for failures, we can try to provide individuals with the confidence they require in themselves and their ideas. Although perhaps not teaching tenacity, we certainly can teach about its nature and usefulness.

Manage the launch

This is also a fairly well-understood process. Here the nature of the enterprise, its funding, technology, and initial size and strategy are all important factors. We can teach this and do so with an increasing understanding of the complex factors involved.

Managing the downstream capture of value

We can also help the would-be entrepreneur by providing a clear understanding of the problems and opportunities they are likely to encounter in managing the growth of their entrepreneurial enterprise. There is now a reasonable and consistent body of knowledge that will, if nothing else, help them to anticipate problems, alter their strategies as the company grows and their goals mature, structure their support systems, and manage in a more intelligent fashion.

Research

As the preceding examination of what can and can not be well taught demonstrates, there is ample room for further research. We believe that this categorization has helped us in identifying some fruitful areas and in communicating the results of our efforts to date. We believe that this categorization also points out what entrepreneurial scholars can do by themselves—to explore, for example, the factors involved in managing the launch. It also points out what entrepreneurial scholars can only effectively do, if at all, in conjunction with scholars from other fields—exploring creativity, innovation, and the knack for recognizing opportunities.

From this brief examination of the nature and definition of entrepreneurship a number of factors emerge. First, it is clear that even after many years of work, there is not one precise (read predictive) model of entrepreneurship or the entrepreneur. Entrepreneurship is something that can occur in many different environments and settings, and the process can take many forms. We should, therefore, not fall into the trap of attempting to characterize this complex process by defining it on the basis of only one factor.

Second, we are still in the early stages of understanding the phenomenon. There is much we can learn from practitioners at this point. We should not take great confidence in our limited data base to the point where we turn inward in our thoughts as so many other academic disciplines have done (Kuhn 1962).

Third, we may wish, for a time, to move away from studying the structural artifacts of entrepreneurship (example the exact characteristics of entrepreneurs) and move to building a greater understanding of the process involved. Particularly, we may wish to better understand what instills entrepreneurship, what fuels it, and what factors limit or force its demise. Furthermore, in this time of economic turbulence and changing opportunity sets, we may wish to better understand how to rekindle entrepreneurship for the sake of the many stagnant, bureaucratic processes that our socioeconomic system has fostered.

Finally, because entrepreneurship is a complex process that cuts across disciplines, we need to overcome some of the artificial barriers that restrain researchers. Particularly, we may wish to borrow not only theories but also research methods and perspectives that can provide insight across the organization.

NOTES

1. What is increasingly clear is that quite often these innovations come about by the incremental efforts of a number of individuals often acting quite independently until one of them makes the "quantum leap," ignores existing market logic, and produces an economic discontinuity. Who does it is unpredictable and unique, making such an act difficult for economists to study or even to recognize how important it is, because each act is a unique and non-recurring phenomena.

2. The complete quote is, "The strategic stimulus to economic development is innovation defined as the commercial or industrial application of something new—a new product, process, or method of production; a new form of commercial, business, or financial organization. Innovation involves (1) the commercial application of (2) any new idea" (Schumpeter 1934, xix).

3. That is, an independent discovery that employs the same process as did the original. Simon cites, as an example, young Gauss finding for himself the formula for the sum of the first N integers even though it was well known to trained mathematicians of the day.

REFERENCES

Abell, D., and T. Kollermeier. *Dynamic Entrepreneurship in the New Europe.* Brussels: European Foundation for Entrepreneurial Research, 1992.

Baumol, W. "Entrepreneurial Theory: Existence and Inherent Bounds." Paper presented at the Entrepreneurial Theory Conference at the University of Illinois, 1991.

Brandsma, J., and D. F. Muzyka. "Opportunity Development and Perception in Economies in Transition." *Frontiers of Entrepreneurship Research.* Wellesley, MA: Babson College, 1992.

Carland, J. W., F. Hoy, and J. A. C. Carland. "Who is an Entrepreneur? Is the Wrong Question." *Entrepreneurship Theory and Practice* 12(4), (1988): 33–39.

Covin, J. G., and D. P. Slevin. "A Conceptual Model of Entrepreneurship as Firm Behavior." *Entrepreneurship Theory and Practice* 16(1), (1991): 7–25.

Gartner, W. B. "What Are We Talking About When We Talk About Entrepreneurship?" *Journal of Business Venturing* 5(1), (1990): 15–36.

Gartner, W. B. "Who is an Entrepreneur? Is the Wrong Question." *Entrepreneurship Theory and Practice* 12(4), (1988): 11–32.

Knight, F. H. *Risk, Uncertainty and Profit.* Chicago: University of Chicago Press, 1971.

Kuhn, T. S. *The Structure of Scientific Revolutions.* Chicago: University of Chicago Press, 1962.

MacMillan, I. C., and D. L. Day. "Corporate Ventures into Industrial Markets: Dynamics of Aggressive Entry." *Journal of Business Venturing* 2(1), (1987): 29–39.

Osborne, D. "Government that Means Business." *New York Times Magazine* (April 1992): 20–28.

Simon, H. A. "What We Know About the Creative Process." Paper presented at the 2nd International Conference on Creative and Innovative Management, Miami, FL, 1984.

Schumpeter, J. *Economic Development* (1934). Translated by Redvers Opi with a new Introduction by John E. Elliott. New Brunswick, NJ: Transaction Books, 1983.

Stevenson, H. H., M. J. Roberts, and H. I. Grousbeck. *New Business Ventures and the Entrepreneur.* Homewood, IL: Richard D. Irwin, 1985.

Van de Ven, A. "A Systems Framework for Studying the Process of Entrepreneurship." Paper presented at the Entrepreneurial Theory Conference at the University of Illinois, 1991.

Zaleznik, A., and M. Kets de Vries. "Myths and Realities of Entrepreneurship." In *Enterprising Man,* edited by Collins and Moore. Lansing, MI: MSU Business Studies, 1964.

3

Where's Entrepreneurship? Finding the Definitive Definition

William B. Gartner

This chapter uncovers some ideas about entrepreneurship that seem to have gotten lost in the ongoing search for the definitive definition. If one were to take an outsider's view on the debate in the academic community about the nature of entrepreneurship (Brockhaus and Horwitz 1986; Carland, Hoy, Boulton; and Carland 1984; Carland, Hoy, and Carland 1988; Carsrud, Olm and Eddy 1986; Covin and Slevin 1991; Gardner 1991; Gartner 1988, 1990, 1991; Hills 1987; Low and MacMillan 1988; Sexton and Smilor 1986; Wortman 1986; 1987), the quest for an entrepreneurship definition seems to take on the characteristics of the search for Waldo in *Where's Waldo?* (Handford 1987). For those readers not familiar with *Where's Waldo?* (and its sequels *Find Waldo Now* [Handford 1988] and *The Great Waldo Search* [Handford 1989]), one should imagine a book filled with pages of illustrations depicting a tangled hoard of hundreds of individuals at various locations (e.g., on the beach, at sea, a museum, the railway station). The purpose of each Waldo book is ostensibly to find Waldo (illustrated as a fellow wearing glasses dressed in a red and white striped sweater and hat) in each conglomeration of people. In exploring each illustration, the search for Waldo engages different senses of discovery. In some illustrations, Waldo immediately stands out from the crowd. In other illustrations, one needs to systematically cover every square inch of a page to find him. Part of the adventure of searching for Waldo is in discovering individuals engaged in all kinds of interesting and amusing activities. In fact, on the endpaper of the book are checklists of "Hundreds more things for Waldo watchers to watch out for!"

Much like the search for Waldo, it *is* difficult to locate entrepreneurship within the larger context of other human activities. If it seems that some new definition of entrepreneurship "pops up" in every journal article and book on the subject, or that one finds it difficult to discover how an author has identified and described the entrepreneurs used in a study of entrepreneurship, it is with good reason. Entrepreneurship is difficult to define, and entrepreneurs and entrepreneurial activities are often difficult to identify and study because the phenomenon, itself, is complicated, equivocal, and "large."

This chapter describes how these three issues (complication, equivocality, and "largeness") comprise some of the reasons for why entrepreneurship is both an obvious idea *and* a confusing concept to make specific and concrete. One's own definition of entrepreneurship seems obvious, yet in application and discussion with others, one's own definition often becomes abstruse.   Arthur Cole's definitional dilemma bears repeating:

> My own personal experience was that for ten years we ran a research center in entrepreneurial history, for ten years we tried to define the entrepreneur. We never succeeded. Each of us had some notion of it— what he thought was, for his purposes, a useful definition. And I don't think you're going to get farther than that (1969, 17).

Taking Cole's advice to heart, I thought it would be more valuable to those individuals searching for a definition of entrepreneurship to explore reasons why it is so difficult to generate an entrepreneurship definition that everyone might agree on.

As a way of illustrating how these three issues work to enhance the paradox of defining entrepreneurship, I will focus my comments on the definition of entrepreneurship used in Chapter 2:

> Entrepreneurship is a *process* that takes place in *different environments* and *settings* that causes changes in the *economic system* through *innovations* brought about by *individuals* who generate or respond to *economic opportunities* that *create value* for *both* these individuals and society.

ENTREPRENEURSHIP IS COMPLICATED: THEREFORE SIMPLIFY

There is no one specific and easy way to get one's hands around entrepreneurship. It is multi-level and multi-disciplinary (as Herron, Sapienza and Smith-Cook [1991] indicated in their edited two-volume series *Entrepreneurship: Theory and Practice* on interdisciplinary perspectives on entrepreneurship). A focus on one particular approach or perspective to defining entrepreneurship is inadequate. The chapter 2 definition addresses this complicated "multi-reality." Entrepreneurship "takes place in different environments and settings...innovations brought about by individuals...that create value for both these individuals and society." In this definition, the locus of activity in entrepreneurship occurs at the level of individuals, settings, and societies in environments. Different levels are inextricably tied together. We look for individuals in entrepreneurship and the search takes us to organizations and environments.

A solution to a complicated view of entrepreneurship is to narrow one's field of vision—simplify. Instead of seeing a multi-level process, one sees entrepreneurship as solely the product of a few factors from a single discipline. For example, entrepreneurship can be solely explained by psychological factors, or economic factors, or _____ (fill in the blank with your favorite discipline). Herron, Sapienza, and Smith-Cook (1991) were confronted with this desire to simplify one's view of entrepreneurship, rather than seek a more complicated understanding, when they hosted their conference:

> The original intention of the conference was to examine various disciplines had viewed entrepreneurship, how they had examined it, what they had contributed to it, and how the disciplines themselves had been affected by the action. One interesting observation that emerged from this exercise is that each discipline has its own unique way of viewing entrepreneurship which remains relatively unaffected by the perspectives of other disciplines. In other words, we see evidence that many "uni-" rather than one or more "multi-" disciplinary views of our field currently exist (1991, 7).

This is the trade-off we are faced with. By simplifying entrepreneurship to a unidimensional phenomenon, one invariably loses sight of all of the other factors that might be involved. Yet, in order to come to grips with entrepreneurship, one needs to simplify, otherwise, the phenomenon of entrepreneurship becomes so complicated that it defies any possibility of understanding it. What the reader should be watching for in reading other chapters in this book is discovering how the authors coped with this problem. Did they recognize marketing as one of many dimensions of factors that characterize entrepreneurship, or did they attempt to characterize entrepreneurship solely by using marketing ideas and terminology? There is no right answer to this question, yet how one sees entrepreneurship determines "what and who" one will find.

ENTREPRENEURSHIP IS EQUIVOCAL: THEREFORE SPECIFY

A word that has taken a significant role in defining the nature of entrepreneurship is the concept of "opportunity." For example, Bygrave and Hofer define the entrepreneur as "someone who perceives an opportunity and creates an organization to pursue it" (1991, 14). Stevenson and Gumpert (1992) suggest that entrepreneurs first ask "Where is the opportunity?" Chapter 2 describes the process of entrepreneurship as involving "individuals who generate or respond to economic opportunities that create value for both these individuals and society." Yet, the definition of opportunity (from *Webster's*, "a favorable juncture of circumstances") suffers from the same vagueness as entrepreneurship. What is a favorable juncture of circumstances?

> I believe that the nature of "opportunity" involves taking an optimistic view of equivocal events. An equivocal event is an event that can be interpreted in a number of different ways. The problem of equivocality for a recipient is that, given an output, the receiver can't decide what input generated it. Two or more possible inputs are implied in that single output message, and the recipient faces the question of which of those possible meanings are the appropriate ones (Weick 1979, 180).

In other articles (Gartner 1991; Gartner, Bird, and Starr 1992; Gartner and Low 1990; Gartner and Starr 1992), we have suggested that entrepreneurship is a form of Weick's social psychology of organizing (1979) in that organizing reduces equivocality.

> In emerging organizations, entrepreneurs offer plausible explanations of current and future equivocal events as non-equivocal interpretations. Entrepreneurs talk and act "as if" equivocal events were non-equivocal. Emerging organizations are elaborate fictions of proposed possible future states of existence (Gartner, Bird, and Starr 1992, 17).

Entrepreneurs are optimists. Successful organizing involves generating trust from other individuals so that this optimism is warranted (Gartner and Low 1990).

The problem with equivocal events is that an individual has little foreknowledge of subsequent interpretations. Whether an opportunity is indeed an opportunity can only be known after the opportunity has occurred. The conundrum one faces in using the Chapter 2 definition is that one cannot determine "economic opportunities that create value" until after the fact.

A way of addressing the amorphousness of equivocality in entrepreneurship is to specify characteristics of the event as well as to determine appropriate interpretations of the outcomes of these events. For example, researchers typically determine that certain individuals are entrepreneurs in an entrepreneurial setting (e.g., the owner/managers—the founding team) whereas other individuals are not (i.e., employees, investors, suppliers, buyers). Yet the contributions of these other individuals, such as the role of pioneering buyers (von Hippel 1988), are often extremely important to the viability of a new venture. Who is more entrepreneurial, the founding team or the first buyer of an unproven product?

The process of entrepreneurship is equivocal, yet to understand this phenomenon, one must offer an interpretation of what has occurred. This is the paradox, equivocality described in non-equivocal terms. Invariably, something (maybe everything) about the equivocal aspects of entrepreneurship escapes in specifying its characteristics. Yet, specificity is necessary.

ENTREPRENEURSHIP IS "LARGE": THEREFORE MAKE IT SMALLER

Entrepreneurial activity comprises a wide range of human endeavors. In the Chapter 2 definition, entrepreneurship "changes the economic system through innovations that create value." The kinds of activities that induce change in an economic system are innovative and create value, are "large" activities. I want to evoke a broad sense of scope in using the word large. Returning to the Waldo books as an example, each illustration of a particular location (e.g., the beach) is "large." Each illustration describes hundreds of individuals engaged in the kinds of activities one would find at that location. "At the beach" involves various kinds of activities: sun bathing, eating, swimming, fishing, making sand castles, volleyball, walking, and the like. A list of "at the beach" activities can be very lengthy. The same sensibility of "large" can be found in entrepreneurship. A perusal of the literature on entrepreneurship would show that entrepreneurship can comprise a wide range of activities: starting a new independent business venture, starting a corporate venture, reorganizing an existing business, buying an existing business, downsizing a large business, the rapid growth of a small business, changing government practices, and modifying a country's economic policies. I am sure that many other activities can qualify as situations where the economic system is changed through an innovation that creates value. The dilemma with a "large" view of entrepreneurship is that nearly every important human activity can be subsumed underneath it. For example, the act of teaching can be entrepreneurial if it is innovative and results in economic value. The "larger" the domain of entrepreneurship becomes, the less power it poses to answer questions about itself. If entrepreneurship moves toward "everything important that everyone does" then entrepreneurship, as a field of study, becomes nothing more than what everyone else is looking at. The cast of characters increases. Waldo becomes much more difficult to find (but the search can still be very interesting and amusing).

A solution to this trend to increase the scope of entrepreneurship to include larger and larger chunks of human activities is to make entrepreneurship "smaller." My campaign to specify entrepreneurship as the creation of organizations (Gartner 1988) should be viewed as an attempt toward smallness. I am not suggesting that other activities are not entrepreneurial; rather, I am, for my own purposes as a researcher, attempting to find a domain of human activities that can be studied and, hopefully, understood.

There are trade-offs in the quest for smallness. As one moves down in scale from the creation of value to the creation of organizations to the creation of independent for-profit businesses, the importance of entrepreneurship as a social phenomenon may seem less important and critical. Describing how an individual starts a corner grocery store may pale in significance compared with describing how individuals generate economic opportunities that create value for society.

CONCLUSIONS

Definitions help focus one's attention on essential qualities. A definition should clarify and enlighten. But, all definitions do not necessarily need to be simple, specific, or small, in order to be useful. The goal of generating a definition is that it be understood by others. Understanding involves an ability to grasp the significance of something. Understanding involves comprehension. But, it is possible, in fact, likely, that a definition will be ambiguous if what is being defined is inherently ambiguous. This is the problem of generating a definition of entrepreneurship. The phenomenon, itself, is inherently complicated, equivocal, and "large." Simplifying, specifying, and making small, help us to hold on to parts of the problem. But, they do not solve the problem. Entrepreneurship will not yield to a definition agreed to by all.

In reading various publications that have referenced my article on the meanings that entrepreneurship academics have about entrepreneurship, "What are we talking about when we talk about entrepreneurship?" (Gartner 1990), I have been jarred with how often readers have misinterpreted the gist of this article. The thesis of the article is that no generalizable definition of entrepreneurship exists, and that entrepreneurship academics vary in their beliefs about the importance of eight different characteristics used to describe entrepreneurship. The eight characteristics were not dimensions of entrepreneurship that all respondents agreed on, but issues with significant disagreement. For example, for the "Innovation" dimension, the article described some individuals that believe that innovation is an important characteristic of entrepreneurship, whereas other individuals passionately disagreed that innovation was important. What readers should have taken from this article is this important lesson: You should not assume that when you say "entrepreneurship" that other individuals will understand what you are talking about.

If you are going to talk about entrepreneurship, offer a definition. Yet, recognize that a definition can never be definitive. At best, each of us should have a definition of entrepreneurship that should be useful for helping others see the "Waldos" we are studying.

REFERENCES

Brockhaus, R. H., and P. S. Horwitz. "The Psychology of the Entrepreneur." In *The Art and Science of Entrepreneurship,* edited by D. L. Sexton and R. W. Smilor. Cambridge, MA: Ballinger, 1986.

Bygrave, W. D., and C. W. Hofer. "Theorizing about Entrepreneurship." *Entrepreneurship: Theory and Practice* 16(2), (1991): 13–22.

Carland, J. W., F. Hoy, W. R. Boulton, and J. C. Carland. "Differentiating Entrepreneurs from Small Business Owners: A Conceptualization." *Academy of Management Review* 9(2), (1984): 354–59.

Carsrud, A. L., K. W. Olm, and G. G. Eddy. "Entrepreneurship: Research in Quest of a Paradigm." In *The Art and Science of Entrepreneurship* edited by D. L. Sexton and R. W. Smilor. Cambridge, MA: Ballinger, 1986.

Cole, A. H. "Definition of Entrepreneurship." In *Karl A. Bostrom Seminar in the Study of Enterprise,* edited by J. L. Komives, 10–22. Milwaukee: Center for Venture Management, 1969.

Covin, J. G., and D. P. Slevin. "A Conceptual Model of Entrepreneurship as Firm Behavior." *Entrepreneurship: Theory and Practice,* 16 (1), (1991): 7–26.

Gardner, D. M. "Exploring the Marketing/Entrepreneurship Interface." In *Research at the Marketing/Entrepreneurship Interface,* edited by G. E. Hills and R. W. LaForge, 3–21. Chicago: University of Illinois at Chicago, 1991.

Gartner, W. B. "Aspects of Organizational Emergence." Paper presented at the Conference on Entrepreneurship Theory, University of Illinois at Urbana-Champaign, October 1991.

Gartner, W. B. "What are We Talking About When We Talk About Entrepreneurship?" *Journal of Business Venturing* 5 (1), (1990): 15–28.

Gartner, W. B. "Some Suggestions for Research on Entrepreneurial Traits and Characteristics." *Entrepreneurship: Theory and Practice* 14 (1), (1989): 27–38.

Gartner, W. B. "Who Is an Entrepreneur? Is the Wrong Question." *American Journal of Small Business* 12 (4), (1988): 11–32.

Gartner, W. B., B. J. Bird, and J. A. Starr. "Acting as if: Differentiating Entrepreneurial from Organizational Behavior." *Entrepreneurship: Theory and Practice* 16 (3), (1992): 13–32.

Gartner, W. B., and M. B. Low. "Trust as an Organizing Trope." Paper presented at the National Academy of Management Meeting, August 1990.

Gartner, W. B., and J. A. Starr. "The Nature of Entrepreneurial Work." Paper presented at the Second Annual Global Entrepreneurship Research Conference, March 1992.

Handford, M. *Where's Waldo?* Boston: Little, Brown, 1987.

Handford, M. *Find Waldo Now*. Boston: Little, Brown, 1988.

Handford, M. *The Great Waldo Search*. Boston: Little, Brown, 1989.

Herron, L., H. J. Sapienza, and D. Smith-Cook. "Entrepreneurship Theory from an Interdisciplinary Perspective: Volume 1." *Entrepreneurship: Theory and Practice* 16 (2), (1991): 7–12.

Hills, G. E. "Marketing and Entrepreneurship Research Issues: Scholarly Justification?" In *Research at the Marketing/Entrepreneurship Interface*, edited by G. E. Hills, 3–15. Chicago: University of Illinois at Chicago, 1987.

Katz, J., and W. B. Gartner. "Properties of Emerging Organizations." *Academy of Management Review*, 13(3) (1988): 429–41.

Low, M. B., and I. C. MacMillan. "Entrepreneurship: Past Research and Future Challenges." *Journal of Management* 14(2), (1988): 139–62.

Sexton, D. L., and R. W. Smilor. "Introduction." In *The Art and Science of Entrepreneurship*, edited by D. L. Sexton and R. W. Smilor. Cambridge, MA: Ballinger, 1986.

Stevenson, H. H., and D. E. Gumpert (1992). "The Heart of Entrepreneurship." In *The Entrepreneurial Venture,* edited by W. A. Sahlmand and H. H. Stevenson, 9–25. Boston, MA: Harvard Business School, 1992.

von Hippel, E. *The Sources of Innovation*. New York: Oxford University Press, 1988.

Weick, K. E. *The Social Psychology of Organizing*. New York: Random House, 1979.

Wortman, M. S. "A Unified Framework, Research Typologies, and Research Prospectuses for the Interface Between Entrepreneurship and Small Business." In *The Art and Science of Entrepreneurship*, edited by D. L. Sexton and R. W. Smilor. Cambridge, MA: Ballinger, 1986.

Wortman, M. S. "Entrepreneurship: An Integrating Typology and Evaluation of the Empirical Research in the Field." *Journal of Management*, 13(2), (1987): 259–79.

4

Marketing/Entrepreneurship Interface: A Conceptualization

David M. Gardner

INTRODUCTION AND RATIONALE

Marketing, as a discipline, has often been labeled and sometimes criticized as interdisciplinary, borrowing here and there, continually searching for new inputs, all in an attempt to better understand and carry out the objectives of the marketing concept. In recent years, the discipline of marketing has been heavily influenced by the behavioral and quantitative sciences. As the discipline has and continues to absorb these influences, a question arises. The question, addressed by this chapter is: is there yet one more influence on marketing thought and practice, poised to challenge the accepted patterns—the accepted way of viewing and understanding things? This chapter explores a likely candidate for the next interdisciplinary influence on marketing by examining the interface of entrepre-neurial behavior and marketing.

Entrepreneurial behavior, as used in this chapter, is in the context of Austrian economics. The definition used here is broad and goes well beyond the limited definition of "one who is in business for himself." Rather, the definition used here is attributed to Savitt who argues that, "The entrepreneur works toward the disruption of any tendency toward equilibrium. Entrepreneurial behavior is disruptive. It challenges accepted behavior patterns. It introduces, often volatile, change" (1987, 311).

Entrepreneurial behavior is a potential candidate to significantly influence marketing thought and practice because it deals directly with a key concept in marketing: bringing innovation successfully to market. Although the basic concept of bringing innovation to market and the concept of diffusion of innovation is not unknown within the discipline of marketing, it is an area of thought and practice that is relatively undeveloped in comparison to managing products in mature markets. It is *not* important to argue whether entrepreneurial behavior is part of management science, behavioral science, strategic planning or policy, or not even a part of any science or body of thought or literature. What is important is to recognize that, for a variety of reasons, innovation, which is the central value of entrepreneurial behavior as well as a key concept in marketing, is increasingly important. It is important because innovation is disruptive, the product life cycle continues to shorten, more products are in the early stage of the product life cycle, and many successful products, for all practical purposes, do not make it into traditional maturity before being replaced with newer innovation. Furthermore, much of the thrust of innovation comes not just from established, process-orientated, new product development (NPD) environments, but from entrepreneurs "outside the system," intrapreneurs, and entrepreneurial organizations. A careful review of existing literature combined with numerous interviews with entrepreneurs and intrapreneurs, clearly indicates that both the quantity and quality of accumulated knowledge about markets created by innovation and the marketing of innovation, as well as other entrepreneurial activity directly dependent on marketing, is relatively scarce and in comparison with other areas, deficient.

The scarcity and deficiency of accumulated knowledge can not be attributed to a single cause. However, three causes may partially explain the situation as it exists today. The first is the strong marketing discipline preoccupation with managing in mature markets. It should be clearly noted, of course, that most product markets are mature. The largest revenue streams and profit lie in maturity. Consequently, most current marketing texts are, at least implicitly, primarily focused on issues centered in the environment of maturity and the strategies of market leaders and challengers. And similarly, much of the portfolio management literature, although recognizing the need for new products, offers virtually no perspective on innovation. Modern marketing management is often more "brand" orientated than "product" or innovation orientated. The focus on maturity, however, is not unique to either marketing managers or marketing academics—both are guilty. However, with the increasingly turbulent environment (Ansoff 1984) and the shorter product life cycle, this focus, of necessity, will have to change.

The second cause, however, is primarily due to a perspective underlying much academic thought and associated publications. If academics are to be a major force in understanding and developing concepts to drive both practice and theory, then the approach to science that underlies the academic approach to the discipline is critical. The logical positivism approach to science, the primary approach taken by the majority of marketing academics, is a mixed blessing. The rigor and logic demanded by this approach is essential in the move toward marketing theory. However, this same logic and rigor have the potential to seriously discourage the development of totally new ideas that are not already rooted in strong logical positivism, as were the social and quantitative sciences that have so heavily influenced marketing thought and practice. The net result is that—with particular reference to entrepreneurial behavior—as a discipline, marketing's concern with justification, associated with theory development, has often resulted in a lack of openness to issues of discovery. Consequently, issues of market formation through innovation and the disruptive influences of innovation have received less attention than issues of maturity.

The third cause is the largely descriptive nature of the vast majority of entrepreneurial literature. With only a few notable exceptions, the entrepreneurial behavior literature is highly descriptive. It does not have a substantial theoretical base. Consequently, there is little basis for a "predictive" approach to the interface with marketing, or for that matter, any other business function.

Fortunately, however, there is a positive side. If, in fact, entrepreneurial behavior has the potential to influence marketing thought and practice, it is logical to assume that marketing may, conversely, influence the understanding of entrepreneurial behavior. One way to approach this potential interaction is in terms of the *interface* between these two streams of literature, thought and practice. The definition of interface[1] that guides the development of the issues discussed in this chapter is:

> that area at which any two systems or disciplines share the same concepts, objectives, and goal-orientated behavior.

Examples of this definition are consumer behavior in which marketing and the behavioral sciences share a focus on the individual consumer in a purchase/consumption decision framework. Marketing management is another example.

In specific reference to the interface between marketing and entrepreneurial behavior their interface is defined as:

> that area where innovation is brought to market.

From this definition, we propose a paradigm that allows us to examine the interface for the potential influence of entrepreneurial behavior on marketing and vice versa.

ASSUMPTIONS AND DEFINITIONS

To explore this interface, certain assumptions are necessary to ensure that the boundaries of the interface are as clearly demarcated as possible. None of what follows is intended to be a comprehensive review of the associated literatures. Rather, it seems appropriate to indicate very basic, and skeletal assumptions that are perceived as the core of these two areas.

Marketing

The marketing literature is vast and reasonably well developed. It is not the purpose of this chapter to develop and argue for yet another definition of marketing. However, for the purposes of this chapter, marketing is defined as:

The application of the technology of market assessment and positioning to achieve a sustainable competitive advantage.

Marketing thought and practice is premised on the "marketing concept" and is built on a largely standard set of assumptions and practices about the major variables of price, product, promotion, and distribution. Marketing is highly contingent in its orientation, which allows marketing to be applied in a wide variety of situations and environments. However, all marketing activities *focus on the market* and are organized around generally accepted:

1. concepts
2. tools
3. infrastructure

Examples of concepts would be segmentation, the product life cycle, the marketing concept, the four P's and matching. Tools unique to marketing fall into the categories of market and marketing research as well as special applications of behavioral and quantitative approaches. Channels of distribution and the knowledge of how they function would be the main example of infrastructure, but advertising agencies and research houses are also part of the infrastructure of marketing. Using concepts, tools, and infrastructure, the objectives and goals of marketing are to enhance and understand the marketing concept with its emphasis on delivery of desired products and services to the consumer at a profit.

Entrepreneurial Behavior

Contrasted with marketing, the literature of entrepreneurial behavior is less well developed. The literature is rapidly developing, however, primarily in three broad areas: entrepreneurship, intrapreneurship, and entrepreneurial organizations. These terms are not universally agreed upon, but generally tend to focus on, respectively, the independent entrepreneur, the intrapreneur in a structured organization, and organizations that behave or desire to behave entrepreneurially, that is, actively seeking change (Ansoff 1984). The term "entrepreneurial behavior" is used in this chapter as the broad term that includes entrepreneurship, intrapreneurship, and entrepreneurial organizations.

In all categories of entrepreneurial behavior, however, there appear to be consistent and common elements all focused around bringing innovation to market successfully. Critical to the position taken in this chapter is the view of Casson who argues that an entrepreneur (intrapreneur and/or entrepreneurial organization) is "someone who specializes in making judgmental decisions about the coordination of scarce resources" (1982, 23). Casson argues, in support of this definition, that:

1. Entrepreneurship appears as a personal quality which enables certain individuals to make decisions with far-reaching consequences (1982, 11).

2. The entrepreneur has better—or at least more relevant—information than other people (1982, 157).

3. The entrepreneur believes that he is right, while everyone else is wrong. Thus the essence of entrepreneurship is being different—being different because one has a different perception of the situation (1982, 14).

4. The entrepreneur has often to create an institution to make markets between himself and other transactors (1982, 17).

In other words, entrepreneurial behavior is a characteristic way of responding/behaving to situations that Naisbitt describes as the "confluence of both changing values and economic necessity" (1980, 183).

Ansoff (1984) contrasts entrepreneurial behavior of the organization with the more typical incremental behavior of the organization. He argues, "Rather than seek to preserve the past, the entrepreneurial organization strives for a continuing change in the status quo" (1984, 180). He also observes that many of these organizations behave entrepreneurially continuously in a deliberate search for growth through change.

Invention versus Innovation

Also critical to this chapter is the contrast between invention and innovation. Inventions are ideas that have little or no commercial value until someone finds an application and takes the idea to market. Burgelman and Sayles suggest, at least in the industrial context, that:

> *Invention* refers to a company's seeking technical perfection and allied new ways of production as ends in themselves. *Innovation* refers to a company's efforts in instituting new methods of production and/or bringing new products or services to market. The criteria of success are "technical" for invention, but "commercial" for innovation. The link between invention and innovation is the "entrepreneurial capability of an individual and/or organization" (1986, 10).

Davis, in his insightful biographical review of various innovators, makes a similar distinction:

> The inventor produces ideas; the innovator makes new things happen. Many talented people do both, but someone who is good at inventing is not necessarily good at turning his concept into a viable commercial proposition. Many inventors are more interested in the idea as such, and in the challenge it represents, than in the business of making it into a marketable—and profitable—product or service, with all the difficulties and hazards which that involves (1987, 1).

In both instances, the authors clearly recognize the link between innovation and marketing as well as the close relationship between innovation and entrepreneurial behavior.

Given the centrality of innovation to the interface between marketing and entrepreneurial behavior, it is important to clarify what is meant by the term "innovation." Successful innovation meets a market need. Innovation is the adding of appropriate attributes to an existing idea or invention such that the product and/or service is consistent with the needs and perceptions and uses of a viable customer segment. In other words, *innovation is successfully taking an idea or invention to market.* The key difference is that to be labeled an innovation, the idea or invention must meet the test of market success.

There are at least three ways to classify innovation: type, level of technology, and perceived behavioral response. For instance, Capon and Glazer organize technology into three types or sources of know-how:

1. Product technology
2. Process technology
3. Management technology (1987, 2)

Classifying innovation by the level of technology is represented by the classification of Ansoff (1984). His classification is based on the assumption that "technology can serve as a major and powerful tool through which a firm can gain and maintain competitive preeminence" (Ansoff 1984, 101). Central to his understanding is the belief that technology plays a central role in creating turbulence in the environment in which organizations must function. The three points on a continuum defined by Ansoff are:

1. *Stable* long-lived technology which remains basically unchanged for the duration of the demand life cycle.

2. *Fertile* technologies. The basic technology is long-lived, but products proliferate, offering progressively better performance, and broadening the field of application.

3. *Turbulent* technologies. In addition to product proliferation, one or more basic technology substitutions take place within the span of the demand life cycle (1982, 102-104).

One of the most useful and well-researched constructs focusing on purchaser behavior is diffusion of innovation. This construct is of particular interest because of its focus on new products. Central to that large body of literature is the work of Robertson (1967, 1971). Based on a thorough analysis of the introduction of touch-tone telephones into Chicago in the 1960s, he found that innovation can be classified not only by changes in technology, but by perceived changes in consumer behavior patterns. Robertson (1967) defined three types of innovations:

A *Continuous Innovation* involves an extension of existing products with little change in technology which require relatively minor change in consumer behavior patterns.

A *Dynamically Continuous Innovation* is a new product representing minor technological advances. It requires some moderate level of change in existing consumer behavior patterns.

A *Discontinuous Innovation* is a major technological advance involving the establishment of a new product and the acquisition of new consumer behavior patterns.

However, the literature of entrepreneurial behavior is only implicitly about innovation. Much of the literature seems to avoid a discussion of the peculiarities of taking innovation to market successfully. Maybe the literature of entrepreneurial behavior is too influenced by the "small business" literature, which often is specifically not dealing with innovation. Consequently, the focus of the literature of entrepreneurial behavior is twofold: the behaviors that drive entrepreneurs and the necessity of organizational change to produce entrepreneurial organizations. Whether or not discussions of taking innovation successfully to market are included is problematic.

TOWARD A PROPOSED PARADIGM

One way of understanding the interface between marketing and entrepreneurial behavior is through the development of a paradigm. A paradigm is usually thought of as an example or representation of an idea or process. As a first step in the development of such a paradigm to increase our understanding, the diagram in Figure 4.1 shows that the interface is really where entrepreneurial behavior and the market intersect. For our purposes, the market is both the structure of the market and all the elements of supply and demand. The remainder of this chapter explores this intersection.

Table 4.1 represents the sources of entrepreneurial behavior. The understanding of entrepreneurial behavior is complicated by the fact that it can occur either inside or outside the boundaries of a structured organization. And within the structured organization, it can occur primarily due to one person, that is, the intrapreneur, or it can occur because the organization itself has taken on many of the characteristics that encourage the members of the firm, and hence the firm itself, to behave entrepreneurially. However, it is contended here that entrepreneurial behavior has similar characteristics that are not dependent on the location of the entrepreneurial behavior. Entrepreneurial behavior is vision-based. It is based on a vision of the particular innovation satisfying a market need in a more satisfactory or less costly manner than existing solutions. And behind this vision lies a strong action orientation and belief structure that seemingly impels the individual and/or organization to work and build and to become single minded until success has been achieved.

Figure 4.1
The Marketing/Entrepreneurship Interface

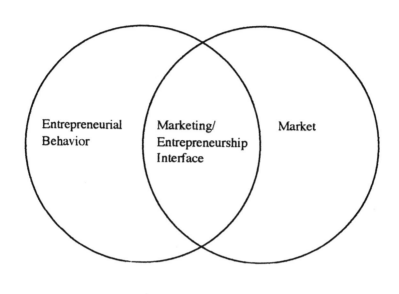

Table 4.1
Sources of Entrepreneurial Behavior

- Individual Entrepreneur

- Intrapreneur

- Entrepreneurial Organizations

Unfortunately, the vision of the entrepreneur, the intrapreneur, and even the entrepreneurial organization may often be limited and/or incorrect. Entrepreneurial behavior often results in common marketing mistakes:

- Inadequate market assessment resulting in defining the market too narrowly or too broadly
- Failure to practice segmentation as the market grows
- Pricing that ignores competing technology and needs of the potential market
- Failure to understand purchasing requirements of the potential market
- Failure to understand distribution channel requirements
- And countless other mistakes.

And, in addition, Peter Drucker adds, it is very common to find customers in markets that, "no one thought of, for uses no one envisioned when the product or service was designed, and that it will be bought by customers outside its field of vision and even unknown to the new venture" (1985, 191-192).

The Market

The activities of entrepreneurial behavior are ultimately directed toward a market. Although, as noted above, the market may not be fully understood, it is indeed the market that determines the success or failure of entrepreneurial behavior. Although it is not the purpose of this chapter to fully explore the role of markets in determining the success or failure of entrepreneurial behavior, it is appropriate to suggest our understanding of markets. The concept of a "market" is elusive primarily because a market has many dimensions. At a minimum, it has geographical place, type of products, type and number of buyers, type and number of sellers, market rules, and time, as relevant dimensions.

If we accept the central role of the exchange relationship in marketing as argued by Bagozzi (1979), we can then safely assume that there must be some intersection where the behaviors of buyers and sellers, facilitated by some form of institutional framework, come together to consummate exchange. That intersection point is commonly understood to be a market.

The market is important for entrepreneurial behavior. It is important because competition for ideas, product adoption, and sales momentum occur in the context of a market. It is in the context of the market that exchange takes place, and the results of that exchange is what determines the success or failure of entrepreneurial behavior. It is in the market where buyers determine how to allocate resources in a manner that allows resources to flow to some enterprises and not to others. However, as suggested by Casson:

> Markets work quite differently from the way neo-classical theory suggests. Transactors require a great deal of information in order to effect a trade. This information is very costly to the average transactors and somewhat less costly to the entrepreneur. The entrepreneur requires information not only about the contract of trade itself, but about the specification of the product and the personal characteristics of those with whom he trades. Even with this information he may have to provide additional services to his trading partners so that trade can proceed (1982, 158).

Information

From our perspective, it appears that the key and principle variable to understand the marketing/entrepreneurial interface is *information*. From Alderson (1965, Chapter 2), we believe that all markets are, at their most basic level, characterized by *both* product and information flows. For instance, Alderson (1965) argues that markets are cleared by information. Borrowing heavily from the arguments of Casson (1982) we join his observation that:

> In the case of technological innovation, the entrepreneur needs to synthesize technical information on the new method of production with information about the scarcity of factors of production in order to assess whether the new technique, besides its technical virtues, will also reduce costs of production. In the case of product innovation, the entrepreneur needs to synthesize information about buyer's preferences for product quality with information about the production costs of the new design of goods (1982, 146).

In addition, Casson makes three points about the use of information by those engaged in entrepreneurial behavior:

1. The entrepreneur does not necessarily possess any single item of information that no one else does. His advantage lies in the fact that some items of information are complementary, and that his combination of complementary items of information is different from everyone else's. This

suggests that the key to successful entrepreneurship is not to have more specialized or detailed knowledge than anyone else, but simply to have right sort of coverage of information.

2. Another point to emphasize is the diversity of the information synthesized by the entrepreneur. Many different types of information have to be synthesized, including information on preferences, technology, factor supply, transport services, tariffs, and any other forms of restriction on the reallocation of resources. This diversity of information means that the entrepreneur must be a generalist, capable of assimilating information of many different kinds.

3. The successful entrepreneur is the one who is first to achieve the synthesis of information, and so no entrepreneur can afford to be slow in gaining access to new information. Imperfections in communication cause lags to information filtering through to secondary and tertiary sources. To maintain his information up to date, the entrepreneur needs to be in contact with primary sources wherever possible (1982, 147).

Without further elaboration, I believe that the key element in understanding the marketing/entrepreneurship interface is the role of information in entrepreneurial behavior. The manner in which information is treated is one of the most critical components in the determination of entrepreneurial success or failure. For instance, it is my view that the misunderstanding or misuse of market information is the prime cause of entrepreneurial failure. Conversely, for whatever reason, successful entrepreneurial behavior is almost always built on solid, and often unique, market information. Some of that information may be intuitive, but it is, nonetheless, market information that is superior to that held by others. When this superior information is combined with other information and acted on, it then leads to a high probability of entrepreneurial success.

Concepts

The concepts, tools, and infrastructure of marketing are brought to bear on a market opportunity by entrepreneurial behavior. Table 4.2 shows the major

Table 4.2
Important Interface Concepts

- Marketing Concept

- Market Segmentation

- Time, Place & Possession Utility

- Product Life Cycle

- Strategic Planning

---

concepts that are necessary to plan for, acquire, and process the information critical for entrepreneurial success. Although information is the key variable, it is these concepts that guide successful information usage. However, it is also necessary to incorporate the specific marketing tools used to implement information strategies. Discussion of these tools will follow after a brief discussion of five concepts.

The first major concept is what has long been identified as the marketing concept. Although there have been critics of the marketing concept, there is no escaping the absolute necessity of understanding the needs and problems, in fact, the entire range of issues affecting the market reaction to the particular product and/or service introduced by entrepreneurial behavior. In particular, the marketing concept suggests a thorough familiarity with the purchaser/user of one's product.[2]

The second concept is that of market segmentation. This concept is closely related to the marketing concept in that it directs entrepreneurial behavior toward specific, identified groups of purchaser/users. From this concept, the insights and tools are available to recognize the specific degree of homogeneity or heterogeneity in a particular market. Furthermore, from this concept come the recognition that segments evolve over the life of the product and may be different for innovations at different stages of development.[3]

The third concept is the creation of time, place, and possession utility. All marketing activity is ultimately directed toward getting the product and its associated attributes in the hands of the intended purchaser/user at the correct time and place. This approach to the creation of utility has direct implications for price, promotion, and distribution as well as the attributes added to the product itself.

The fourth concept is the product life cycle. The underlying logic of the product life cycle is that products have a limited life, their sales history follows an S curve, and that consequently, the various marketing tools have varying elasticities throughout the life of the product. (See Day [1986] and Gardner [1987] for extensive discussion of this concept.)

Certainly common to both entrepreneurial behavior and marketing is the concept of strategic planning. Although strategic planning is a broad concept, that part dealing specifically with anticipating the growth of demand and competition is of critical importance to achieving sustained market success that originates with innovation.

Although there are undoubtedly other concepts that could be included here, the exact specification is not as important as the realization that there are concepts that define the marketing/entrepreneurship interface. For these to be valid concepts, they must truly be consistent with entrepreneurial behavior in its role of taking innovation successfully to market as well as marketing thought and practice.

Tools

Tools by themselves have only limited usefulness. For the best results, tools need to be used correctly and in a manner consistent with some overall objective. Concepts provide the guidance needed to decide not only what tools to use, but when to use them and at what time in the life of a product or service.

It would be inappropriate to discuss the exact tools that are consistent with the marketing/entrepreneurship interface. The task would be well beyond the scope of this chapter. However, it is appropriate to mention that tools developed in support of market research, product design, pricing, and promotion are particularly relevant to taking innovation successfully to market. In addition, the many tools developed over the years in support of marketing management, such as sales management and location analysis. Likewise, the various behavioral and quantitative tools that have become so valuable are also appropriate.

Infrastructure

Although not all products and services introduced by entrepreneurial behavior would be characterized by the market structure of emerging industries, a large majority are so characterized. Consequently, it is important to note Michael Porter's (1980) observation that for this type of industry, there is often an absence of infrastructure. The result not only creates further entrepreneurial opportunities, but also potentially serious limitations if not properly understood and/or dealt with appropriately. Admittedly, the issue is complex. For as Casson states, "The fact that the entrepreneur has often to create an institution to make markets between himself and other transactors extends the range of issues about which the entrepreneur has to make judgments" (1982, 17). It is often the case that channels of distribution need to be created or existing channels substantially modified to properly match the offering of entrepreneurial behavior and the market. Likewise, new support services may be needed as well as research services, new installation, maintenance services, and the like.

THE PARADIGM

A proposed entrepreneurship/marketing interface paradigm is shown in Figure 4.2. This is not a flow chart. Rather it is designed to show that the interface of entrepreneurial behavior and marketing is that area where innovation is brought to market. It is furthermore designed to show that information is the single most important variable within the interface. Also, within the interface, several concepts that are common to both entrepreneurial behavior and marketing are noted, especially in the context of bringing innovation successfully to market.

IMPLICATIONS

For Entrepreneurial Behavior

The clear implication of this proposed interface is that successful entrepreneurial behavior must incorporate a wide range of marketing concepts. These concepts are centered around the principle of information that links this behavior with the market. To the extent that these concepts are ignored or violated, the probability of unsuccessful innovation rises. To ignore these concepts and move directly to tools puts entrepreneurial behavior at risk because correct concepts are the guide to selection and deployment of the correct tools.

For Marketing

Marketing's role in innovation, then, is to provide the concepts, tools, and infrastructure to close the "gap" between innovation and market positioning to achieve sustainable competitive advantage. It is, furthermore, marketing's responsibility to recognize differences between marketing of products and services in

Figure 4.2
Entrepreneurial Behavior/Marketing Interface Paradigm

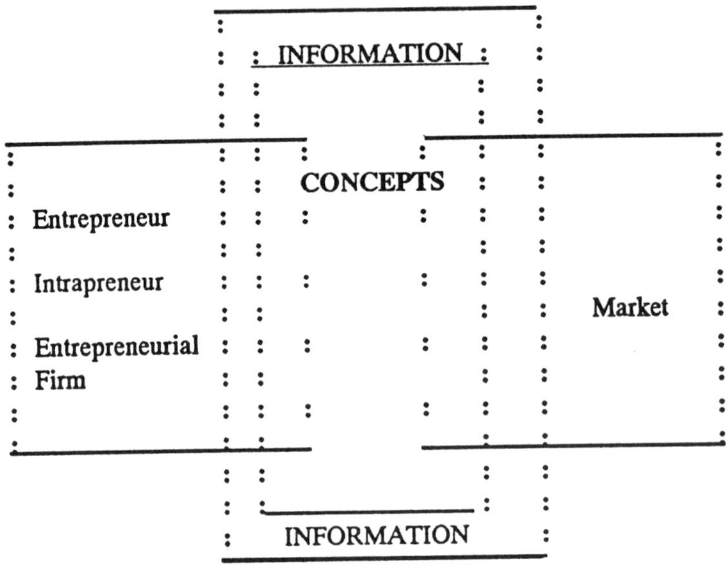

maturity versus marketing for products in early stages of the product life cycle. Likewise, it is also incumbent on marketing to realize that in many cases, markets may not even exist for innovations.

And a further warning: marketing must be careful not to become too focused on efficiency issues, but to understand effectiveness issues. Marketing thought and practice needs to adopt the stance of "what should be" versus the more narrow stance of improving today's performance.

For Markets

Opportunities arise for a variety of reasons. Some are primarily driven by an unfulfilled need, others are primarily driven by the discovery of a new or novel solution to an existing problem. Yet others are driven by new technology in search of an application. The key, however, *must be* information. Only then can proper positioning and strategy issues be addressed. Otherwise, in Aldersonian terms, "the market will not be cleared."

DYNAMICS OF THE INTERFACE

The message contained in this discussion of the interface between entrepreneurial behavior and marketing is deceptively simple. Yet, the popular press contains many references to those who have violated this simple message. Likewise, the files of venture capital organizations are also full of firms who ignored this simple message. The message is that innovation must be matched with the market in all its dimensions.

However, a secondary but imperative message is that the interface is, and must be, dynamic. It is not static! Two factors account for the dynamic nature of this interface. The first is the obvious nature of the product life cycle and the entrepreneurial response to those changes. As innovation proves successful, it attracts imitation, competition, all accompanied by the demands of growth and further opportunity.

The second factor is the very turbulence of the market itself. Drucker (1988) argues that we live in the age of discontinuity. Ansoff (1984) similarly argues that the level of turbulence faced by most firms is increasing. And as turbulence increases (often caused by entrepreneurial behavior), the familiarity of events becomes more novel and discontinuous, with weak signals, and the response time of the organization is often slower than changes in the environment (Ansoff 1984, p. 12).

The key to dealing with the dynamics of this interface is to understand the critical factors for success at each and every stage of the life cycle of the innovation and to acquire the flexibility and capability to be able to anticipate and evolve in the often rapidly changing environment. The critical success factors that are at the interface of entrepreneurship and marketing will be related, in some way, to the concepts listed in Table 4.2.

A WARNING

This exploration of the entrepreneurial behavior/marketing interface is not designed to explore the entire range of entrepreneurial issues. It is *only* designed to explore the important, but somewhat narrow, range of issues where entrepreneurial behavior and marketing share common ground.

TOWARD A THEORY OF NEW PRODUCT INTRODUCTION AND GROWTH

Much of what often passes for new product planning and marketing is really only "new" in a very limited sense. It uses accepted and stable technology, it does not require customers to change usage habits or perceptions and existing markets are the target. In fact, many of the target markets are mature and the nature of the "new" products is very incremental. There is nothing wrong with new styles of cookies sold through supermarkets. There is nothing wrong with new flavors of toothpaste or even toothpaste with new therapeutic properties.

However, both sides of this interface offer much toward a new theory of new product introduction and growth. From entrepreneurial behavior comes the propensity to challenge the "accepted" understanding of the currently available information, and then, to move toward closing the gap given a set of unique information. From marketing comes the concepts and tools to implement the strategies to successfully take innovation to market. But, although entrepreneurial behavior needs to learn to address the issues of the market, marketing needs to develop concepts that allow it to better understand the early stages of the life cycle where most entrepreneurial behavior takes place.

NOTES

This paper originally appeared in *Research at the Marketing/ Entrepreneurship Interface,* edited by Gerald E. Hills and Raymond W. LaForge. Chicago: University of Illinois at Chicago, 1991.

1. Interface is defined as (1) "a plane or other surface forming a common boundary of two bodies or spaces" or (2) "the boundary between two phases in a heterogeneous physical-chemical system" in *Webster's Ninth New Collegiate Dictionary.*

2. See Houston (1986) for a discussion of the marketing concept.

3. For discussion and review of the concept of segmentation, see Bonoma and Shapiro (1983) and Beane and Ennis (1987).

REFERENCES

Alderson, W., *Dynamic Marketing Behavior*. Homewood, IL: Richard D. Irwin, Inc., 1965.

Ansoff, H. I. *Implanting Strategic Management*. Englewood Cliffs, NJ: Prentice-Hall, 1984.

Bagozzi, R. P. "Toward A Formal Theory of Marketing Exchanges." In *Conceptual and Theoretical Developments in Marketing*, edited by O. C. Ferrell, Stephen W. Brown, and Charles W. Lamb, 431–47. Chicago: American Marketing Association, 1979.

Beane, T. P., and D. M. Ennis. "Market Segmentation: A Review." *European Journal of Marketing* 21(5), (1987): 20–42.

Bonoma, T. V., and B. P. Shapiro. *Segmenting the Industrial Market*. Lexington, MA: Lexington Books, 1983.

Burgelman, R. A., and L. R. Sayles. *Inside Corporate Innovation: Strategy, Structure, and Managerial Skills*. New York: The Free Press, 1986.

Casson, M. *The Entrepreneur: An Economic Theory*. Oxford: Martin Robertson and Company Ltd., 1982.

Davis, W. *The Innovators: The Essential Guide to Business Thinkers, Achievers and Entrepreneurs*. New York: American Management Association, 1987.

Day, G. S. *Analysis for Strategic Market Decisions*. St. Paul, MN: West Publishing Company, 1986.

Drucker, P. *The Age of Discontinuity: Guidelines to Our Changing Society*. New York: Harper and Row Publishers, 1988.

Drucker, P. *Innovation and Entrepreneurship: Practice and Principles*. New York: Harper and Row, Publishers, 1985.

Gardner, D. M. "The Product Life Cycle: A Critical Look at the Literature." In *Review of Marketing 1987*, edited by Michael J. Houston, 162–94. Chicago: American Marketing Association, 1987.

Houston, F. "The Marketing Concept: What It Is and What It Is Not." *Journal of Marketing* 50 (April 1986): 81–87.

Naisbitt, J. *Megatrends: Ten New Directions Transforming Our Lives*. New York: Warner Books, Inc., 1980.

Porter, M.E. *Competitive Strategy*. New York: Free Press, 1980.

Robertson, T. S. "The Process of Innovation and the Diffusion of Innovation." *Journal of Marketing* 31 (January 1967): 14–19.

Robertson, T. S. *Innovative Behavior and Communication*. New York: Holt, Rinehart and Winston, 1971.

Savitt, R. "Entrepreneurial Behavior and Marketing Strategy." In *Philosophical and Radical Thought in Marketing*, edited by A. Fuat Firat, Nikhilesh Dholakia, and Richard P. Bagozzi, 307–22. Lexington, MA: Lexington Books, 1987.

5

Broadening the Concept of Entrepreneur: The Entrepreneurial Consumer

Jonathan C. Huefner and H. Keith Hunt

INTRODUCTION

A key issue in the continuing debate in academic research on entrepreneurship concerns the definition of entrepreneur and the essence of entrepreneurial behavior. Although virtually all entrepreneurship research has focused on the creation and growth of new business ventures, researchers have agreed on little else. What exactly is entrepreneurship and the essence of the entrepreneurial spirit? What approach will provide us the key to unlock this puzzle? We propose that focusing solely on entrepreneurship in a business context is constraining.

Gartner, using a Delphi technique, identified eight major issues and concerns that constitute entrepreneurship as a field of study. The eight themes he identified are:

> *The Entrepreneur*: The entrepreneur theme is the idea that entrepreneurship involves individuals with unique personality characteristics.

> *Innovation*: The innovation theme is characterized as doing something new as an idea, product, service, market, or technology in a new or established organization.

> *Organization Creation*: The organization creation theme described the behaviors involved in creating organizations.

> *Creating Value*: This theme articulated the idea that entrepreneurship creates value.

Profit or Nonprofit: The profit/nonprofit theme is concerned with whether entrepreneurship involves only profit-making organizations.

Growth: At issue in this theme is the importance of growth as a characteristic of entrepreneurship.

Uniqueness: This theme suggested that entrepreneurship must involve uniqueness.

The Owner-Manager: This theme suggested that entrepreneurship involves individuals who are owners and managers of their businesses (Gartner 1990, 16).

It is noteworthy that of the eight areas only the last, the owner-manager theme, is limited solely to business applications. Although all the other themes can be applied in a business setting, it takes little imagination to apply them to other areas of human behavior as well.

We propose that what the business world and business scholars call entrepreneurship is really only the business manifestation of the entrepreneurial spirit or of entrepreneurial behavior. The entrepreneurial spirit and behavior can be found in many, if not all, aspects of human involvement, not just in business. The purpose of the research presented here is to present the possibility that entrepreneurship is a general human behavior rather than just a business behavior.

An example of non-business entrepreneurship is Peter Ueberroth's organization of the Los Angeles Olympics in 1984. Before Ueberroth was asked to be the president of the Los Angeles Olympic Organizing Committee (LAOOC), he had started his own travel business and had grown it into a very successful venture. He became president of the LAOOC in 1980 and sold his business one year later, serving the remaining three years of his term as a volunteer (Kao 1991, 83). The LAOOC was not a business venture for Ueberroth, yet in both his travel business and in the LAOOC his activities and impact were substantially the same. In each venture, Ueberroth was highly entrepreneurial and is recognized as such. Ueberroth's story provides a clear example of how some individuals approach life in an entrepreneurial way.

Our attempt to broaden the use of entrepreneur to non-business contexts is similar to what Kotler and Levy (1969) did when they broadened the concept of marketing by identifying the underlying dimensions of any and all marketing. Those underlying dimensions brought greater understanding of what we were seeing in commercial marketing and allowed us to do conceptually richer research than was previously possible.

Based on the field's diversity in approaching entrepreneurship and the exemplary work of Kotler and Levy, our objective has been to verify that entrepreneurial behavior does exist in non-business contexts. In line with our primary research interests in consumer research and social psychology, we chose to first examine this broadened concept of entrepreneurship in a consumer context.

CONSUMER ENTREPRENEURSHIP: TWO STUDIES

Study One

Due to the ground-breaking nature of our research, we tried to approach the topic with as few preconceptions as possible (Hunt, Huefner, Voegele, and Robinson 1989). We gave subjects descriptions of both entrepreneurial behavior and consumer behavior and asked them to think of any actual experiences they or someone they knew had that involved both types of behavior. This resulted in a specific entrepreneurial consumer story from each respondent. Some subjects had almost instant recall of entrepreneurial consumer episodes from their own experience.

We used independent expert judges to rate how entrepreneurial a consumer episode was. The stories were judged on a five-point scale ranging from "not at all entrepreneurial" to "highly entrepreneurial." The averaged score across judges was an individual's consumer entrepreneurism score.

People for whom we had a specific story about consumer entrepreneurial behavior were sent a questionnaire which included Robinson's EAO (1987), and a set of questions about demographics and traditional business entrepreneurship activities.

Robinson's EAO is based on an attitude approach to the measurement of entrepreneurship rather than a personality characteristics approach (Robinson et al. 1991). Robinson's research demonstrated that an attitude approach enjoys greater predictability than the personality approach (Robinson 1987). The EAO is also based on the tripartite model of attitude. The tripartite model says that an attitude has three component parts: (1) a cognitive component, (2) an emotional or affective component, and (3) a conative or action tendency component. Thus, for an aspect of entrepreneurship such as innovation, the cognitive, affective, and conative dimensions of one's attitude on this dimension are measured. The EAO has demonstrated both reliability and predictive validity in discriminating known groups of entrepreneurs and non-entrepreneurs.

Contrary to our expectations, we found that the EAO, which is very business specific, failed to adequately predict entrepreneurial activity in the consumer domain as defined by our judges' ratings. In hindsight, this is not surprising in light of arguments that attitude scales need to be context specific (Mischel, Zeiss, and Zeiss 1974). This suggested to us the need to develop an entrepreneurial attitude scale specific to the context of consumer behavior.

Study Two

The thrust of this research was to see if there was a core of entrepreneurial behavior common to both business and consumer contexts (Huefner, Hunt, and Robinson 1991). It is impossible at such an early stage in a research endeavor to specify exactly which dimensions of entrepreneurial behavior should be included in such a research project. Based on Study 1 and their usage in current literature we chose the following five dimensions: (1) innovation, (2) personal control, (3) achievement, (4) opportunism, and (5) charlatanism. As with Robinson's EAO used in the first study, each of these five dimensions was measured as an attitude. Continuing our basis in tripartite attitude theory, there were equal numbers of statements from each of the three component parts of attitude. We created three separate scales based on these five dimensions and three attitude components: a business entrepreneur scale, a consumer entrepreneur scale, and a general entrepreneur scale. Each item on each scale matched with a similar item on each of the other scales with only enough wording changes to make the item clearly consumer, business, or general.

After fully explaining what we meant by entrepreneurial consumer behavior, we found that subjects could nominate persons they knew well as being either highly or not at all entrepreneurial consumers. Each of the nominated individuals completed all three scales. Subjects also answered questions about their previous business entrepreneurial activity and demographic information.

For the entrepreneurial consumer behavior discriminant function, thirteen of the seventy-eight items from the consumer-specific scale entered into the discriminant function with a perfect hit rate (100 percent). For the entrepreneurial business behavior discriminant function, twenty of the seventy-eight items from the business specific scale entered into the discriminant function with a 77 percent hit rate.

Remember that the three scales had matching items. The items included in the discriminant function for entrepreneurial consumers were substantially different from those items included in the discriminant function for business entrepreneurs. However, there were four items that discriminated in both areas:

1. I enjoy creating opportunities for myself.
2. I make a conscientious effort to get the most out of my resources.
3. I often sacrifice in order to take advantage of opportunities.
4. I always find myself adapting to circumstance.

One way of summarizing these four items is as an individual's efforts and willingness to sacrifice to take advantage of available resources and opportunities and to adapt to circumstance. It is our view that this may constitute one essential part of entrepreneurship in a general sense.

DISCUSSION

We feel there is sufficient behavioral evidence to support the view that entrepreneurial behavior exists in more than just the business context. We find the implication that entrepreneurial behavior exists in many aspects of life very exciting. For the social scientist it shows that all the positive benefits of entrepreneurial behavior can exist across all dimensions of life, not just in the narrow sphere of business.

Because so much of our thought and research in this area has been exploratory, there have been some real shortcomings to our methodological approach. We realized from our first study that a single story from an individual's behavior can in no way be an adequate measure of their consumer behavior in general. It was because of this that we also focused on the variety and ease with which subjects could give us their examples of consumer entrepreneurial behavior. We feel it is a much better approach, as done in the second study, to ask people who know the subjects well to nominate those who are clear examples of a given behavioral tendency. With adequate instructions, such nominations are much more likely to be based on a range of behavior over both time and situation.

We would like to suggest some potential areas for the study of entrepreneurship other than business and consumerism. At the beginning of this chapter we used the story of Peter Ueberroth's LAOOC involvement as an example of entrepreneurial behavior in a non-business context. Another example of this is Robert Moses' organization of the New York World's Fair. In our local area, a woman organized and personally sponsored a storytelling festival simply for the benefit of the community. Storytellers were brought in from across the nation for this two-day event. Each of these "public entrepreneurs" challenges the notion that entrepreneurship involves a profit motive. Becker (1963) uses the term "moral entrepreneur" to describe someone who crusades to change the values and rules of society. He gives the American temperance movement as an example. We are familiar with a playwright/actor who calls himself a playwright entrepreneur because he writes and stages material outside the style accepted for established theater.

It is our reasoned belief that only through acknowledging the existence of non-business entrepreneurs and studying them as carefully as we study business entrepreneurs will we discover the essence of entrepreneurship, the entrepreneurial spirit, or whatever it is that exists in entrepreneurs and/or leads an individual to engage in entrepreneurial behavior.

REFERENCES

Becker, H. S. *Outsiders: Studies in the Sociology of Deviance.* New York: Free Press, 1963.

Gartner, W. B. "What Are We Talking About When We Talk About Entrepreneurship?" *Journal of Business Venturing* (1990):15–28.

Huefner, J. C., H. K. Hunt, and P. B. Robinson. "Cross-Validation of the Entrepreneurial Consumer." In *Research at the Marketing/ Entrepreneurial Interface,* edited by G. E. Hills and R. W. LaForge, 333–51. Chicago: University of Illinois at Chicago, 1991.

Hunt, H. K., J. C. Huefner, C. Voegele, and P. B. Robinson. "The Entrepreneurial Consumer." In *Research at the Marketing/Entrepreneurial Interface,* edited by G. E. Hills, R. W. LaForge, and B. J. Parker, 491–92. Chicago: University of Illinois at Chicago, 1989.

Kao, J. J. *The Entrepreneur.* Englewood Cliffs, NJ: Prentice Hall, 1991.

Kotler, P., and S. J. Levy. "Broadening the Concept of Marketing." *Journal of Marketing* 33 (1969): 10–15.

Mischel, W., R. Zeiss and A. Zeiss. "Internal-External Control and Persistence: Validation and Implications of the Stanford Preschool Internal-External Scale." *Journal of Personality and Social Psychology* 29 (1974): 265–78.

Robinson, P. B. *Prediction of Entrepreneurship Based on an Attitude Consistency Model.* Ph.D. Dissertation, Brigham Young University, 1987.

Robinson, P. B., D. V. Stimpson, J. C. Huefner, and H. K. Hunt. "An Attitude Approach to the Prediction of Entrepreneurship." *Entrepreneurship: Theory and Practice* 15 (1991): 13–31.

IDENTIFYING AND EVALUATING OPPORTUNITIES

6

Conceptualizing Entrepreneurial Opportunity Identification

Peder Smed Christensen,
Ole Ohlenschlaeger Madsen,
and Rein Peterson

INTRODUCTION

Opportunity identification is the starting point of new entrepreneurial activities. Surprisingly little entrepreneurship and marketing research has focused on this important stage. In the marketing literature, opportunity identification is usually presented either as a matter of environmental scanning techniques (e.g., Porter 1980) or creativity enhancing techniques (see Kotler 1980) like lateral thinking (De Bono 1978). Admittedly, environmental scanning and creativity-enhancing techniques may play a very important role in improving the chances of identifying opportunities. But, they provide only an incomplete picture of the opportunity identification process.

It has been argued in the marketing literature that we do not really know how entrepreneurs identify opportunities (Stasch 1990). Furthermore, the development of appropriate market research techniques has been rated as a priority research issue in entrepreneurship research by experts in the field (Hills 1987).

We believe that both the marketing and entrepreneurship fields would benefit from more research on opportunity identification. In this chapter, we provide a conceptual framework for such research.

A number of propositions on entrepreneurial opportunity identification will be presented. Of particular interest in the entrepreneurial opportunity identification process will be the role of entrepreneurial *behavior.* We do not define entrepreneurship as a matter of inherited personality traits nor as small business ownership. Rather we see it as learned *management behavior that is opportunity driven without regard for the resources currently controlled* (see also Stevenson and Jarillo 1990). Specifically we define entrepreneurship as:

> opportunity driven, with an ability to make rapid commitment
> to opportunities that arise in a multi-stage decision mode, often

using other people's resources, managing through networks of
personal relations, with the expectation that one will be re-
warded in direct proportion to the new value created (Peterson
and Stevenson 1987).

All factors influencing entrepreneurial opportunity identification are of course
important, but from a practical management perspective, we need to determine
whether operational management behaviors that facilitate opportunity identification can be identified.

In the marketing and entrepreneurship fields, the term opportunity is
frequently used, but rarely defined. It seems to include, for example, the entry
of new markets, introduction of new products, or the start of new independent
businesses. Conceptually these are all very different. We have, therefore,
decided to start with a discussion of the concept of opportunity at some length,
because it is necessary to have an explicit understanding of opportunity in order
to conceptualize the *process* of opportunity identification. Then, we will present
propositions relating to entrepreneurial opportunity identification and management behavior. Third, the entrepreneurial opportunity identification process will
be conceptualized, and finally, suggestions for further research will be made.

THE CONCEPT OF OPPORTUNITY

General Perspectives

In general, the term "opportunity" refers to a favorable chance. More
precisely an opportunity can be defined as a *desirable* future state that is
different from the current state and that is deemed *feasible* to achieve (Stevenson
and Gumpert 1985; Stevenson and Jarillo 1986; Stevenson and Sahlman 1987).
An opportunity, therefore, involves feasible change, in a favorable direction, to
reach a desired future state. Feasible refers to technical and economic factors,
whereas desirable involves more subjective preferences. Opportunity is clearly
a relativistic concept: what is desirable or feasible for one person or company
may not be desirable or feasible for other persons or companies. Some writers
on marketing and entrepreneurship have explicitly discussed the economic
content of opportunities in a similar vein.

From a marketing perspective, Kotler defined an opportunity as "A company
marketing opportunity is an attractive area of relevant marketing action in which
a particular company is likely to enjoy a differential advantage" (1980, 81).

In economics, an opportunity has been viewed as an innovation or a market imperfection. Schumpeter (1935) equated opportunity and innovation, and distinguished between five different types of innovations:

- New products
- New production or organizational methods
- New markets
- New sources of input
- New market structures (e.g., breaking a monopoly)

Schumpeter's definition makes sense from an economic development perspective.

Kirzner (1979, 1982), working in the tradition of the Austrian school of economics, saw an opportunity as a market imperfection. He looked at the problem from the perspective of information: "Entrepreneurial profit opportunities exist where people do not know what it is that they do not know, and do not know that they do not know it. The entrepreneurial function is to notice what people have overlooked" (Kirzner 1982, 273). That is, the entrepreneur is not necessarily an expert, but "is better informed than everybody else—he knows where knowledge is to be obtained and how it can be usefully employed" (Kirzner 1982, 273). Accordingly to Kirzner, an opportunity is a market imperfection, which is exploited by entrepreneurs, thus bringing the market closer to equilibrium.

In the entrepreneurship field, an opportunity is often defined as the possibility to start a new venture (see, for example, the Frontiers of Entrepreneurship Research, Proceedings from the Babson Entrepreneurship Research Conference, 1980-1991). Again, the term "venture" is used imprecisely to refer to such different situations as new products, new markets, new companies, or even an acquisition, and all are conceptually very different.

The above-mentioned perspectives on opportunity add to our insight. However, to further our understanding of opportunity identification, we will have to be more specific about the economics of the concept of opportunity. First of all, from a marketing and entrepreneurship perspective, an opportunity must be defined as having sustainable profit potential, beyond pure windfall profits, and "one-shot" deals. Second, an opportunity must be defined as a *market position*, that is, a field of activity in which a company is competitive beyond the short run, and able to reap a profit. A market position can be viewed both from its value context and from the perspective of competition.

Market Position in a Value Context

The economy can be viewed as a system in which value is added in steps during the process of transforming resources from their natural state to finished end user products and services. Porter introduced the concept of *value chain* and *value system*:

> The value chain displays total value and consists of value activities and margin. Value activities are the psychical and technologically distinct activities a firm performs. These are the building blocks by which a firm creates a product valuable to buyers (1985, 38).

The value chain is defined at the strategic business unit level, and explains how a company competes in a particular section of the product/market arena. The value chain in turn is a part of a value system: "A firm's value chain is embedded in a larger stream of activities that I term the value system. Suppliers have value chains (upstream value) that create and deliver the purchased inputs used in a firm's chain. A firm's products eventually becomes part of its buyer's value chain" (Porter 1985, 34).

Similarly Alderson introduced the concept of a transvection, which is:

> The unit of action for the system by which a single end product such as a pair of shoes is placed in the hands of the consumer after moving through all the intermediate sorts and transformations from the original raw materials in the state of nature a transvection is in a sense the outcome of a series of transactions, but the transvection is obviously more than this a transvection includes the complete sequence of exchanges, but it also includes the various transformations which take place along the way (1965, 86).

In Alderson's theory, the marketing problem is to find the shortest way from natural resources to finished products, that is, the optimal combination of sorts and transformations. The transvection is a useful concept in this respect, because it encompasses what is needed in the total marketing process disregarding ownership factors.

Therefore, in value terms, we define a position as an intersection of the value system. In Alderson's terminology, it could be a part of one or more transvections or maybe a whole transvection in the case of vertically integrated companies. In Porter's terms, a value chain is a position.

Market Positions and Competition

A market position is supported by a combination of resources, and obviously a market position is only sustainable if the underlying resource combination is competitive. From the perspective of strategic marketing, competition is normally seen as the domain of business strategy, that is, at the product/market (industry) level, because direct competition takes place at this level (see, for example, Porter 1980). The competitiveness of a position at the product/market level may, however, be dependent on other product/market areas.

Alderson (1965) used the concept of *enterprise differentiation*, where a firm presents an overall market posture based on a unique combination of goods and services reflecting the total marketing position of the firm. Similarly, Porter (1985) stressed the use of interrelationships between units as a means of achieving competitive advantage, that is, by exploiting the synergies in a corporate portfolio of strategic business units.

Interrelationships between business units have been recognized as important for some time. Interrelationships between business units from different firms is a relatively new topic and is being recognized as equally important for the achievement of competitive advantage. This is reflected in the network approach to marketing developed by the Uppsala School of Industrial Marketing (see for example, Hägg and Wiedersheim-Paul 1984). In their work, a network consists of one or more companies having long-term cooperative relationships with each other.

A network can be characterized on the following dimensions (Johanson and Mattson 1988):

- The distribution of labor among companies with specialized capabilities in the network
- The links in the network in terms of exchange of knowledge, legal arrangements, etc.
- The location of power in the network
- How extensively the firms are interrelated in the network.

According to the Uppsala School of Industrial Marketing *competitiveness is achieved through the development of good long-term relationships through marketing strategies.*

Transaction costs can be used to explain why a network can be an efficient form of industrial organization. In situations characterized by uncertainty, risk of opportunism, bounded rationality, and small-number exchange relations, it may be more efficient to network because the transaction costs to internalize these functions in the firm can be become very large. A network may be a more efficient way of organization, simply because it may involve less administration and overhead costs. Therefore, in some large firm situations it could even pay to *deintegrate* the activities of a firm, focusing only on strategically important activities (Jarillo 1986).

In sum, two important marketing issues related to opportunity identification are, first, how to position a firm in a network, and second, how to secure the competitive position of the network as a whole. This raises the question of effective network management.

Defining Opportunities at the Business Strategy Level

Profit potentials usually exist and are harvested on the business strategy level, and it is therefore natural to define the unit of analysis at this level when studying opportunities. An opportunity should not be understood only as the possibility to establish a new business unit. According to Porter, one could:

- Create a new strategic group
- Shift to a more favorably situated strategic group
- Strengthen the structural position of the existing group or the firm's position in the group
- Shift to a new group and strengthen that group's structural position (1980, 150).

Obviously a new profit potential is created if the position of an existing business unit is improved or if an opportunity to establish a new business unit is exploited. It is therefore natural to define an opportunity as either the possibility to:

- Establish a new business unit, or
- Improve the position of existing business unit.

In both cases, a new profit potential is created, and entrepreneurial behavior may be equally important in identifying both kinds of opportunities. According to this definition, setting up a new company may or may not involve one or more opportunities, and pursuing an opportunity may not necessarily involve setting up a new company.

Using this definition of an opportunity, and using the business unit as the unit of analysis, we researched entrepreneurial opportunity identification in the field. A case field study was carried out at four smaller entrepreneurial Danish electronics companies, and propositions characterizing entrepreneurial opportunity identification were identified (Christensen 1989). Subsequently survey questionnaire data from seventy five Danish industrial firms representing a broad intersection of Danish industry were collected in order to see whether more general support for these propositions could be generated. The questionnaire data basically confirmed the propositions from the case field study (Christensen, Madsen, and Peterson 1989). The conclusions are discussed in the following together with highlights from supporting empirical evidence and from the literature.

SOME PROPOSITIONS REGARDING OPPORTUNITY IDENTIFICATION

Environmental Factors

The availability of opportunity is often contingent on environmental change opening windows of opportunity:

Proposition 1: Opportunity availability is contingent on environmental change.

Often exogenous technological progress or changes in market structures create opportunities that can be exploited through entrepreneurial behavior. One of the case companies studied in our field study was a manufacturer of VHF radios, navigation systems, and mobile telephones. The company saw the opportunity to establish itself in the mobile telephone business at a time when the large public mobile cellular telephone network in Denmark was about to be upgraded, creating a bigger market for mobile telephones. This basic technological change (beyond the firm's control) was very important in making opportunities available. Similarly, this firm now believes that the European internal market will change the structure of many markets during the 1990s, resulting in opportunities for entrepreneurial firms. Everyone in the firm has been placed on an alert to possible openings for the firm's capabilities to exploit.

The importance of environmental change in making opportunities available has also been noted by other researchers. Porter suggested that "Technological changes or evolution often open up possibilities for entirely new strategic groups" (Porter 1980, 150). Alderson (1965) argued that the availability of opportunities depend on the level of activity, and as activity expands opportunities proliferate. So our first proposition demonstrated empirically a previously postulated principle in the literature.

Firm Specific Factors

Environmental change in itself is not sufficient to make opportunities feasible. Entrepreneurial individuals also have to be capable of perceiving opportunities.

Proposition 2: Opportunity identification is contingent on profound technological and market knowledge.

The presence of profound technological or market knowledge is in many cases a prerequisite for the ability to identify specific opportunities. The abovementioned manufacturer of VHF radios, navigation systems, and mobile telephones already had a strong market presence in VHF radios and navigation systems when the opportunity to enter the mobile telephone business was identified. The knowledge accumulated through the other two businesses was an important factor behind the identification of the mobile cellular telephone business.

This proposition is also supported by Stevenson and Sahlman (1987) who suggest that opportunity identification is dependent on a profound knowledge of product and market factors. The fact that ideas often arise out of former employment is also an indication of this (See Vesper 1980). One reason for the importance of profound knowledge may be that it can be an important condition for creativity. Simon, studying creativity, thus argued that "Expertness is the prerequisite to creativity" (1988, 16).

Related to proposition 2, it was found empirically that the pursuit of opportunities involved a learning process enabling people to perceive new opportunities that could not be predicted at the outset.

Proposition 3: Opportunity identification is contingent on learning.

In the case field study, this was particularly well illustrated in one company, where the opportunities were identified incrementally. Through the pursuit of an initial opportunity, the company learned about new potential applications and product developments based on its core technologies. This, in turn, led to further development of existing business units and establishment of new business units.

The learning aspect of opportunity identification also finds some support from other researchers. Stevenson and Sahlman (1987) stressed that an essential aspect of entrepreneurship is learning. Ronstadt (1988) suggested that entrepreneurship is often a dynamic multi-venture process in which the entrepreneur moves down an opportunity "corridor" allowing him to identify new opportunities that could not have been perceived from the outset. This learning effect from opportunity pursuit makes it extremely important which opportunities are selected for pursuit.

Entrepreneurial Management Behavior

Environmental changes play an important role in the creation of opportunities, and profound knowledge and learning influence the perception of opportunities as desirable. However, two specific entrepreneurial management behaviors are essential factors for opportunities to be realized.

Proposition 4: Opportunity identification is contingent on the ability to use external resources.

External resources are not owned, nor under the direct control of a person or firm, but may be used by a person or firm. In the entrepreneurship field, this is considered an essential entrepreneurial management skill (e.g., Birley 1985; Stevenson and Gumpert 1985; Jarillo 1986; Klofsten et al. 1988). In one of the case companies, a new business unit was established in such a way that the whole production process was essentially farmed out to suppliers and the marketing rights were given to an agent. Within the company itself, there remained only the research and development function and some limited administrative functions. Apparently, the resource requirements in a start-up phase can be limited by using external resources in this way. The ability to use external resources also tends to expand the opportunity space by making more opportunities feasible. Personal networks often play an important role in making external resources available. In this connection, it has even been argued that it is not so important what you know, but *who* you know (Aldrich and Zimmer 1986; Peterson and Ronstadt 1987). Furthermore, Koller (1988); Long and Graham (1989); and Christensen, Madsen, and Peterson (1989) also found that informal contacts themselves are often the source of new opportunities.

Although external resources and networks are important, the practical ability to overcome unsatisfactory situations and to solve problems is essential.

Proposition 5: Opportunity identification is contingent on the ability to turn problems into opportunities.

In entrepreneurship research, it is considered essential to be able to turn adverse situations into positive situations. It has, thus, been found that entrepreneurial ventures often have their launch in an adverse situation (Shapiro 1971; Peterson 1977; Brockhaus 1980; Vesper 1980; Peterson and Weiermair 1988). One case study company had a print shop specializing in the printing of business forms. At the beginning of the 1970s, the pre-press process of preparing a film for the actual printing process was time consuming, inflexible, dirty, and costly. As a response to this problem, the company developed a computerized pre-press system to overcome this unsatisfactory state of affairs. This new system, in turn, formed the basis for the establishment of a new business unit. An operational problem thus became the source of new opportunities. Similarly, von Hippel (1978, 1986) has suggested that lead users are often a source of new product ideas.

Strategic Thinking and Formal Strategic Planning

By strategic thinking we mean the intuitive ability to understand the dynamics of market structures, competition, customer needs, timing, synergies, and the like. It is an ability to proceed with tentative, incomplete information, always leaving one's options as open as possible, waiting for the right moment. Strategic thinking is a craft skill that is honed by repeated use and hands-on experimentation. Strategic thinking plays an extremely important role in opportunity identification, because it enables companies and persons to understand the dynamic nature of an evolving opportunity and when it can best be exploited.

Proposition 6: Opportunity identification is contingent on the ability to think strategically.

The companies in our case field studies were very good at understanding the timing, competition, and the changing overall focus of the company. Strategic thinking was very important in opportunity identification, for example, in understanding where it was feasible and desirable to use external resources.

The importance of strategic thinking can lead one to expect that strategic planning was found to be extremely important in the opportunity identification process. This proved not to be the case. We found strategic planning to be very useful, but only in the evaluation and implementation stages of opportunity pursuit, especially before and after an opportunity had been identified.

Proposition 7: Formalized strategic planning plays its primary role in setting priorities, on selection of opportunities to pursue, and in implementing new opportunities over time.

Formal strategic planning (with its emphasis on analysis) was only used in two of the case companies and only in the later stages in the life cycle as a matter of setting priorities and securing coordination. Formal strategic planning has been strongly criticized in the literature. Mintzberg (1978, 948) argued, for example, that "contemporary prescriptions and normative techniques of analysis and planning seem unable to address the complex reality of strategy formation" Peters and Waterman (1982, 49) found that formal strategic planning leads to "paralysis induced by analysis." Similarly we found that formal strategic planning was useful in the evaluation of opportunities, setting priorities, and implementation, but not at the creative stage of identifying opportunities.

CONCEPTUALIZING ENTREPRENEURIAL OPPORTUNITY IDENTIFICATION

Each of the propositions are in themselves important, but it is when they work together that they are most powerful. Entrepreneurial behavior in itself will not be enough, that is, behaving entrepreneurially in the way we have described is not a universal formula for identifying opportunities. Rather we found that it is only when an environmental change is combined with the presence of profound knowledge, entrepreneurial behavior, and strategic thinking, that opportunities become identified. Combining this with the notion of opportunities as having to be deemed desirable as well as proven feasible, we have the entrepreneurial opportunity identification process conceptualized in Figure 6.1.

Further Research Opportunities

This chapter points to several opportunities for further research. Each of the above-mentioned propositions needs to be examined further. The learning of entrepreneurial behaviors identified along with strategic thinking need to be explored further. Are strategic thinking and entrepreneurial management behaviors culture and industry specific? How can one change an organization that is poor at opportunity identification? What role can marketing play? How do individuals learn to use external resources? How do you preserve opportunity pursuit by individuals as organizations grow?

Opportunity identification is still a little understood process. The marketing and entrepreneurship fields need a better understanding of opportunity identifica tion to make useful prescriptions for practitioners and students for what to do in order to increase the chance of identifying opportunities.

Figure 6.1
Conceptualizing Opportunity Identification

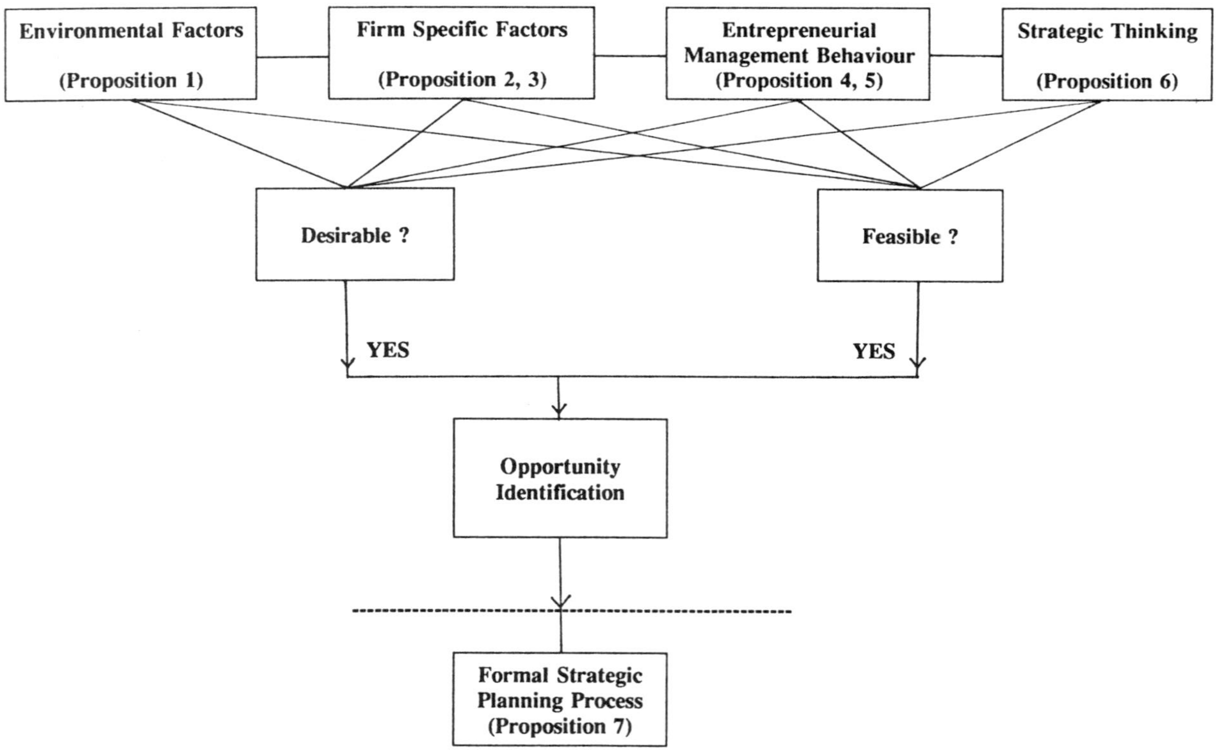

REFERENCES

Alderson, W. *Dynamic Marketing Behavior*. Homewood, IL: Richard D. Irwin, 1965.

Aldrich, H., and C. Zimmer "Entrepreneurship Through Special Networks." In *The Art and Science of Entrepreneurship*, edited by Donald L. Sexton and Raymond W. Smilor, New York: Ballinger Publishing Co., 1986.

Birley, S. "The Role of Networks in the Entrepreneurial Process." *Journal of Business Venturing No. 1* (1985). 1(1) 107–17.

Brockhaus, R. H. "The Effect of Job Dissatisfaction on the Decision to Start a Business." *Journal of Small Business Management* (January 1980) 18(1) 37–43.

Christensen, P. S. " Strategy, Opportunity Identification, and Entrepreneurship: A Study of the Entrepreneurial Opportunity Identification Process" Ph.D. thesis, Aarhus University Press, Aarhus University, 1989.

Christensen, P. S., O. Madsen, and R. Peterson. "Opportunity Identification: The Contribution of Entrepreneurship to Strategic Management" chapter presented at the Strategic Management Society conference, San Francisco, October 1989.

De Bono, E. *Opportunities*. Middlesex, England: Penguin Books, 1978.

Hägg, I., and F. Wiedersheim-Paul, eds. *Between Market and Hierarchy*. University of Uppsala. Sweden, 1984.

Hills, G. E. "Marketing and Entrepreneurship Issues: Scholarly Justification?" In *Research at the Marketing/Entrepreneurship Interface,* edited by Gerald E. Hills, 3–15. Chicago: University of Illinois at Chicago, 1987.

Jarillo, J. C. "Entrepreneurship and Growth: The Strategic Use of External Resources," Unpublished Doctoral dissertation, The Harvard Business School, 1986.

Jarillo, J. C. "On Strategic Networks" *Strategic Management Journal* (January-February 1988).

Johanson, J., and L.G. Mattson. "Internationalization in Industrial Systems—A Network Approach." In *Strategies in Global Competition,* edited by N. Hood and J. E. Valne. New York: Croom Helm, 1988.

Kirzner, I. M. *Perceptions, Opportunities, and Profit*. Chicago: University of Chicago Press, 1979.

Kirzner, I. M. "The Theory of Entrepreneurship in Economic Growth." In *Encyclopedia of Entrepreneurship*, edited by Calvin A. Kent, Donald L. Sexton, and Karl H. Vesper, 272–76. Englewood Cliffs, NJ: Prentice Hall, 1982.

Klofsten, M., P. Lindell, C. Olofson, and C. Wahlbin. "Internal and External Resources in Technology Based Spin Offs: A Survey." *In Frontiers of Entrepreneurship Research.* Wellesley, MA: Babson College, 1988.

Koller, R. H, II. "On the Source of Entrepreneurial Ideas." In *Frontiers of Entrepreneurship Research.* Wellesley, MA: Babson College, 1988.

Kotler, P. *Marketing Management: Analysis, Planning, and Control.* Englewood Cliffs, NJ: Prentice Hall, 1980.

Lorenzioni, G., and O. A. Ornati. "Constellations of Firms and New Ventures" *Journal of Business Venturing* 3(1), pp 41–57 (1988).

Long, W., and J. Graham. "Opportunity Identification Process: Revisited." In *Research at the Marketing/Entrepreneurship Interface*, edited by G. E. Hills, R. W. LaForge, and B. J. Parker 209–20. Chicago: University of Illinois at Chicago, 1989.

Mintzberg, H. "Patterns in Strategy Formation" *Management Science* (May 1978).

Peters, T. J., and R. H. Waterman, Jr. *In Search of Excellence.* New York: Harper and Row, 1982.

Peterson, R. *Small Business: Building a Balanced Economy.* Porcepic Press, 1977.

Peterson, R., and R. Ronstadt. "Developing Your Entrepreneurial Know-Who," Working paper. National Centre for Management Research and Development, University of Western Ontario. London, Canada, 1987.

Peterson, R., and H. H. Stevenson. "An Empirical Search for Entrepreneurship," Working paper. National Centre for Management Research, University of Western Ontario. London, Canada, 1987.

Peterson, R., and K. Weiermair. "Women Entrepreneurs, Economic Development and Change." *Journal of Economic Planning* (June 1988).

Porter, M. E. *Competitive Strategy.* New York: Free Press, 1980.

Porter, M. E. *Competitive Advantage.* New York: Free Press, 1985.

Ronstadt, R. "The Corridor Principle." *Journal of Business Venturing* Vol. 3, No. 3 (1988).

Schumpeter, J. *Theorie der Wirtschaftliche Entwicklung.* Duncker & Humblot. München and Leipzig, 1935.

Shapiro A. *An Action Plan for Entrepreneurship.* Multidisciplinary Research, Inc., Austin Texas, 1971.

Simon, H. A. "Understanding Creativity and Creative Management." In *Handbook for Creative and Innovative Managers,* edited by Robert L. Kuhn. Mew York: McGraw-Hill, Inc., 1988.

Stasch, S. F. "Identifying New Venture Ideas: What We Know and Don't Know." In *Research at the Marketing/Entrepreneurship Interface,* edited by G. E. Hills, R. W. LaForge, and B. J. Parker, 325–30. Chicago: University of Illinois at Chicago, 1990.

Stevenson, H. H., and D. E. Gumpert. "The Heart of Entrepreneurship" *Harvard Business Review* (May–June 1985).

Stevenson, H. H., and J. C. Jarillo. "Preserving Entrepreneurship as Companies Grow." *The Journal of Business Strategy* (1986).

Stevenson, H. H., and W. Sahlman. "Entrepreneurship: A Process not a Person." Working paper. Harvard Business School, 1987.

Stevenson, H. H., and J. C. Jarillo. "A Paradigm of Entrepreneurship: Entrepreneurial Management." *Strategic Management Journal* (Summer 1990).

Vesper, K. H. *New Venture Strategies.* Englewood Cliffs, NJ: Prentice-Hall, 1980.

von Hippel, E. "Users as Innovators." *Technology Review* (January 1978).

von Hippel, E. "Lead Users: A Source of Novel Product Concepts." *Management Science No. 7* (1986).

Williamson, O. E. *Markets and Hierarchies.* New York: Free Press, 1975.

7

Evaluating New Venture Ideas: Considerations from the New Product Development Process

Stanley F. Stasch

There is general agreement in the marketing literature that successful new product introductions are necessary for a firm's continued growth over the long run. Similarly, there is evidence that new businesses make an important contribution to the economy's long-term growth, because new businesses reportedly create more new jobs than do established businesses. Thus, successful new product introductions and successful new venture start-ups make important contributions to economic growth.

Over the last ten to fifteen years, much has been written about the new product development process (NPDP). The intention of those writings has generally been based on the notion that the more we know about the process whereby new products are developed and introduced, the more we should be able to foster successful new product introductions and avoid new product development efforts that are not likely to be successful. There seem to be many similarities between the process whereby new products are developed and introduced, and the process that entrepreneurs use to search out ideas and start new ventures.

Given that such similarities seem to exist, we can ask if the concepts employed within the NPDP can be applied to new ventures, in order to help foster more successful new ventures and to avoid starting up new ventures that are not likely to be successful. The purpose of this chapter is to describe the new product development process—with emphasis on the third and fourth steps of that process—in order to gain a better understanding as to if, and how, it might prove to be useful in helping entrepreneurs evaluate new-venture ideas.[1]

THE NEW PRODUCT DEVELOPMENT PROCESS

Probably one of the strongest contributors to our knowledge of the NPDP has been Booz, Allen, and Hamilton, Inc., which periodically surveys the "best practices in new product management" in a large number of companies. According to the most recent such survey, the new product development process consists of the following seven steps:

1. Identifying a new product strategy
2. Generating new product ideas
3. Screening and evaluating new product ideas
4. Business analysis of new product ideas
5. Developing the new product
6. Testing the new product
7. Commercializing the new product

This process, and its utilization by companies, is described in the 1968 and 1982 reports published by Booz, Allen, and Hamilton, Inc. The process has generally been so widely accepted that it, or some derivative of it, appears in almost every principles of marketing textbook.

This chapter is concerned only with the third and fourth of the seven steps listed above. The next section describes the theory underlying each of these two steps in more detail as they apply to the NPDP. Some comments are also made regarding the extent to which firms actually put into practice the theories related to these NPDP steps. The third section of the paper addresses the screening and evaluating step as it might apply to new venture ideas. The fourth section addresses the marketing aspects of the business analysis step as they might be applied to potential new ventures. The final section suggests potential future research topics.

SCREENING, EVALUATING, AND BUSINESS ANALYSIS

A new or established company wishing to grow through a strategy of new product introductions must first develop sources that generate ideas for new products. Then it must screen those new product ideas in order to identify the more promising ones. Following such a screening, the company will then do a business analysis to estimate the sales and profit potential associated with the more promising new product ideas. These later two steps are basically the third and fourth steps in the NPDP, and they are discussed more fully in the following.[2]

Screening and Evaluating New Product Ideas

The screening process consists of procedures designed to select, from a large pool of ideas, the ones that warrant further analysis.

Academic literature

A company's screening criteria form obstacles through which an idea must pass if it is to proceed to the next stage of the NPDP. In the screening stage, a company must attempt to avoid two types of error—continuing to evaluate an idea that will not succeed, or discarding an idea that might lead to a successful new product. The screening stage is used because costs rise substantially in the subsequent steps of the NPDP.

One of the two major approaches to screening involves checklists that are used by managers to judge the merits of a specific new product idea. The purpose of a checklist is to evaluate quickly and economically the many ideas generated in the previous step by using certain standards that have been developed by management. Checklists that consist of standards that are too rigid or too loose are likely to lead to one of the two types of errors mentioned.[3]

Checklists typically consist of one or more standards for each of a number of variables considered to be important in the evaluation of new product ideas. Variables commonly found on checklists include marketability, growth potential, product capabilities, availability of distribution channels, nature of competition, and others. Cooper (1979) listed 47 variables that can be used in screening new product ideas, and he proposed a model that can help managers identify the variables that should be used in their checklists.

The second major approach to screening employs concept tests, which provide consumer reactions to the new product idea.[4] On one hand, concept testing is more applicable to new products that will require a change in the consumer's purchasing behavior than it is for "me-too" products that require no change in buying habits. On the other hand, concept testing may not be applicable to true innovations, because consumers may have difficulty in understanding how the innovation could be used.

It is questioned whether concept tests should be used to predict future buyer behavior, repeat purchasing, or propensity to try the new product. Tauber (1975) suggested that concept testing has shown to be a good predictor of trial, but that it cannot be a good predictor of repeat purchasing or frequency of use, both of which are important determinants of new product success.

It is generally agreed that concept tests should perform a number of tasks, but there is less agreement as to what these tasks should be. Some tasks mentioned in the literature include (1) defining the relevant market for the new product idea, (2) identifying product or Zbenefit attributes that are probable describing the behavior of consumers toward the new product idea and predicting their behavior.

A number of specific marketing research techniques can be used in concept testing, including multi-dimensional scaling, factor analysis, and conjoint analysis. The first two of these can be used to produce a perceptual map comparing the new product idea with existing brands, whereas conjoint analysis can be used to identify the product attributes that consumers consider most important.[5]

The three above-mentioned techniques are highly structured and so they are appropriate for new product concepts where perceptual categories exist in the minds of consumers. Where no such perceptual categories exist, as might be the case in true innovations, unstructured methods such as sentence completion, word association, pictorial techniques, or focus groups are likely to be more appropriate.[6]

Practice

There is considerable evidence in the literature indicating that companies do a great amount of marketing research oriented toward new product development and introduction, and that a significant portion of such research addresses the screening of new product ideas. Booz, Allen, and Hamilton, Inc., report that companies have improved the efficiency of their new product development processes. Their 1968 study found that, on the average, companies had to consider 58 new product ideas for each new product that was successfully introduced. Their 1982 study reported that companies were able to introduce one successful new product for each seven new product ideas that were evaluated. Much of the improved efficiency seems to have occurred in the screening and evaluation step of the NPDP. However, not very much has appeared in the literature about the predictive capabilities of techniques for screening and evaluating new product ideas.

Business Analysis of New Product Ideas

In the business analysis step of the NPDP, new product ideas that have successfully passed through the screening step are further evaluated to see if they satisfy corporate requirements for initial estimates of sales, market share, profit, or return on investment. The requisites for this analysis include studies of markets, competition, and marketing plans, as well as costs and technical inputs.

Academic literature

The purpose of the business analysis step is to arrive at a concrete business recommendation as to whether further implementation of the new product idea is likely to be profitable.[7]

A business analysis basically involves two tasks: (1) compiling data on such things as demand for this type of product, the nature of competition, and any other factors that conceivably could enhance or deter the sales of the new product, and (2) establishing criteria or goals (e.g., profits, return on investment, market share, etc.) that the proposed new product must meet in order for it to be given further consideration. The first of these two tasks is undertaken typically for the purpose of making a sales estimate or sales forecast for the new product. The second is undertaken to see if the new product is likely to achieve the market share, profits, return on investment, or other goal needed to make the new product worthy of further development and testing.

Sales is the critical measure in a business analysis, and it can be estimated in five ways. One source of sales estimates is use of *judgmental estimates*, which can be obtained from various sources such as consumers, sales representatives, distributors, management, and other experts. Computer models have been developed to estimate sales and rates of return using judgmental sales estimates in combination with estimates of primary demand, the company's ability to exploit the opportunities, expected penetration, and saturation of the market.

A second source of sales estimates is use of *historical sales data*. Sales may be computed by estimating the size of the market and then estimating the share of the market the firm would hope to achieve with the new product.

Estimates of consumer behavior patterns can be used as a third source of sales estimates. For example, sales estimates of frequently purchased products can be based on estimates of trial, first repeat, adoption, and frequency of purchase (Tauber 1977).

A fourth source of sales estimates can be based on *models* designed to estimate the sales of frequently purchased goods. Such models attempt to combine the estimates of trial purchase rates with estimates of repeat purchase rates. The most well known of such models has been reported by Fourt and Woodlock, but several other models have also been reported.[8]

Diffusion of innovation theory might be useful for attempting sales estimates of infrequently purchased products. Many principles of marketing textbooks suggest that a rapid diffusion of innovation (i.e., high sales estimates) is likely to occur if the new product possesses five characteristics when compared with products already on the market: if it has relative advantages, it is compatible with current use, it is easier to use, it can be experienced on a trial basis, and it has benefits that are easy to communicate (Stanton et al., 1991).

Practice

It may not be unusual to find firms that do not conduct a separate business analysis step during their NPDP. One explanation for this is that some firms evaluate the results obtained at the conclusion of each NPDP step, and so they feel that there is no need for a separate business analysis step. Other reasons for bypassing the business analysis step are (1) the investment required for the new product's development is low, (2) the risk involved is small, (3) there is a pressing need either to lead or follow a competitor into the market, or (4) results from the screening and evaluating step are seen to be very positive.

Firms that are currently in the relevant market find their business analysis to be relatively routine when introducing a new product. An in-depth study of ten new product introductions showed that, for nine of the ten new products, the firms in question had previous, ongoing experience in the market (Lonsdale and Stasch 1986).

Often, judgmental estimates of sales are made by company management, and/or market data are purchased from outside suppliers (such as the A.C. Nielsen Company) or collected through market studies routinely conducted by the firm. Sales estimates based on the measures of trial, repeat purchase, adoption, and frequency of purchase are only occasionally found in practice, probably because of the expense involved and the difficulty of estimating adoption and frequency of purchase.

SCREENING AND EVALUATING NEW VENTURE IDEAS

A search of the literature did not uncover any published materials concerned with the application of NPDP concepts to new ventures. Yet, because many new ventures are based on the development and introduction of a new product, such new ventures are essentially synonymous with the new product, and so it would seem that NPDP concepts would at least apply to some new ventures.

The previous section suggested that probably not all new products are subjected to each of the steps of the NPDP. Companies developing new products that are new to the firm but not new to the marketplace, or that are only slight or moderate improvements over those currently available, may feel that it is not necessary to subject such new products to a thorough investigation within each step of the NPDP.

It would appear that similar reasoning could be applied to new ventures. Such reasoning might address the question: Are there any circumstances when an entrepreneur might have good reasons for not putting a new venture idea through a screening and evaluating exercise?

When Should New Venture Ideas Not Be Screened and Evaluated?

There seem to be three circumstances that can help an entrepreneur decide whether or not to subject a new venture idea to a screening and evaluation procedure.

1. Is there currently a market for the product or service that is associated with the new venture idea, and is that market being satisfied by current offerings?

2. Is the entrepreneur experienced and/or trained in such a way that he or she has a good understanding of, and knowledge of, the market, the competition, and how to market the product or service involved?

3. Relative to the competitive offerings already on the market, is the product or service involved in the new venture idea a "me too" version or a "new, improved" version? Or, is it a "new-to-the-world" product/service or a true innovation (e.g., lasers)?

The answers to these three questions can describe five different categories of market existence/entrepreneur's experience/newness of product or service, which suggest whether or not a new venture idea should be put through a screening and evaluating process (see Table 7.1).

According to category one in Table 7.1, if the market exists, and if the entrepreneur is well experienced with the market, and if the new venture's product/service is essentially similar to current offerings in the marketplace (i.e., it is a "me too" product or service), then there would appear to be little need to screen the new venture idea, as it is already being accepted in the marketplace. However, if the product/service is a "new, improved" version compared with current offerings, the new venture idea should probably be screened to see if the market wants and will welcome the "new, improved" characteristics (see category two in Table 7.1).

If the product/service is "new, improved" and the entrepreneur is not experienced in the marketplace, the new venture idea should definitely be screened in order to make up for the entrepreneur's inexperience as well as to test the acceptance by the marketplace of the "new, improved" characteristics (see category three in Table 7.1.).

If the new venture idea is based on a "new-to-the-world" product or service, then by definition it is unlikely that the entrepreneur will be experienced with the marketplace or how to market the product/service involved. Additionally, it may not be clear whether a market exists for the "new-to-the-world" thing or how

Table 7.1
Three Circumstances That Can Help Determine if a New Venture Idea Should be Screened and Evaluated

Category	Market Exists/ Is Being Satisfied?	Entrepreneur Experienced in the Market?	New Venture's Product Screening is:	Evaluation Needed?
1	Yes	Yes	Me Too	Probably Not
2	Yes	Yes	New, Improved	Probably
3	Yes	No	New, Improved	Definitely
4	Unclear	No	New To World	Definitely
5	Probably Not	No	An Innovation	Probably Not

well the marketplace is currently being satisfied. Under such conditions, it would appear that screening and evaluating the new venture idea would definitely be necessary (see category four in Table 7.1.).

Finally, if the new venture idea involves a true innovation, not only will the entrepreneur not be experienced in the market, it may not be possible for the marketplace to realistically evaluate the possible acceptance and use of the innovation (see category five in Table 7.1.). In such a case, as Drucker has pointed out, it may not be practical to use screening and evaluating procedures that involve the marketplace.

> Five years ago [fax machines] were found only in a few large offices. Today they are ubiquitous and are rapidly spilling out of the office and into the home. The fax machine is American in invention, technology, design and development. And U.S. manufacturers had fax machines all ready to be sold. Yet not one fax machine offered for sale in the U.S. today is American-made.
>
> The Americans did not put the fax machine on the market, because market research convinced them that there was no demand for such a gadget. But we have known for decades that one cannot conduct market research on something not in the market. All one can do is ask people: "Would you buy a telephone accessory that costs upwards of $1,500 and enables you to send, for $1 a page, the same letter the post office delivers for 25 cents?" The answer, predictably, will be "no" (Drucker 1990).

Screening and Evaluating New Venture Ideas in Practice

Nothing was identified in the literature regarding the screening and evaluating of new venture ideas by entrepreneurs. However, in order to shed some light on this phenomenon, this chapter will summarize the findings of two exploratory studies conducted by the author.

One study described the personal circumstances of ten entrepreneurs at the time they started new ventures, the sources of the ideas for the new ventures, and any other interesting or unusual events that occurred at the time of the new venture start-ups (Stasch 1991). All of the new ventures were reported in the business press in some detail. These 10 new venture start-ups were reviewed for the purpose of determining whether or not there was any evidence that the entrepreneurs involved subjected their new venture ideas to any kind of screening or evaluation.[9] The evidence from these start-ups was then compared to the three conditions listed in Table 7.1 to determine the extent to which actual screening and evaluating matched the normative guidelines presented in Table 7.1 and discussed in the preceding. The findings were as follows:

1. Five of the 10 start-ups were judged to belong in the first of the five categories shown in Table 7.1. There was no evidence in the materials reporting these start-ups that the entrepreneurs involved had subjected their new venture ideas to a screening and evaluation. This finding was in agreement with the guideline indicating that category one new venture ideas probably do not need to be put through a screening and evaluation.

2. Four of the other five start-ups were judged to belong in categories two, three, or four. Of these four start-ups, there was some evidence that three of the entrepreneurs made some attempts to screen and/or evaluate their new venture ideas. The fourth of these start-ups involved a foreign partner who had seen the new venture idea being successfully employed in his native country. In effect, the latter event may have constituted a screening and evaluation in the minds of the entrepreneurs involved. These findings appear to be in agreement with the theory which suggests that category two, three, and four new venture ideas should be screened and evaluated.

3. The tenth start-up was judged to belong in category three or four. There was no evidence that this entrepreneur used any kind of screening and evaluation device on the new venture idea. It should be noted, however, that the entrepreneur involved was extremely wealthy and this fact may well have influenced the situation.

4. None of the start-ups were judged to belong in category five of Table 7.1.

A second exploratory study was undertaken specifically for this chapter, in order to further investigate the subject phenomenon. In many of its monthly issues, *Inc.* magazine publishes a "profile of a start-up," which tends to be a lengthy description of the start-up of a new business. Twenty-one such start-ups were identified in the issues of *Inc.* magazine published in the period of early 1988 to early 1991. Regarding the reported use of screening and evaluating procedures by the entrepreneurs involved in these new ventures, the findings were as follows:

1. Two of the new ventures were judged to belong in category one, and in neither of these start-ups was there any evidence that the new venture idea was screened or evaluated in any way. This finding is in agreement with Table 7.1 regarding category one new ventures.

2. Seventeen of the new ventures were judged to belong either in category three or category four. Reports of four of these start-ups included evidence that the new venture ideas were screened or evaluated in some way. No evidence of screening and/or evaluating of the new venture idea was included in the reports on the other 13 start-ups. This finding suggests that quite possibly many new venture ideas falling into category three or four are not given a significant screening and evaluation.

3. The remaining two start-ups were like category one new ventures except that the entrepreneurs involved were not experienced in their respective marketplaces. One of these entrepreneurs reportedly screened the new venture idea; the other did not.

4. None of these new ventures were judged to belong either in category two or category five.

Of the 31 start-ups included in these two exploratory studies, 22 were judged to belong in categories two, three, or four. Of these 22 start-ups, only seven seem to have utilized screening and evaluation. Using only these 22 new ventures as a basis, it seems that perhaps somewhere between two-thirds and three-fourths of such categories of new ventures are started without the new venture idea having been formally put through some kind of screening and evaluation activity.

MARKETS, MARKETING, AND MARKET-SHARE ANALYSIS OF NEW VENTURE IDEAS

Along with marketing considerations, a thorough business analysis should include the four main marketing-oriented topics that should be part of a business analysis: (1) identifying and measuring the target market; (2) evaluating competition within the target market; (3) developing a marketing plan and evaluating its effectiveness vis-à-vis the target market and the competition; and (4) making a sales or market-share forecast based upon the target market, competition, and the effectiveness of the marketing plan. (In the remainder of the chapter these four topics will be referred to as "Marketing Analysis" for short.)

A Normative Marketing Analysis Process

Identifying and measuring the target market

All marketing textbooks and all successful marketers tend to agree that effective marketing requires knowledge of the target market, including its size, attitudes, opinions, interests, purchase behavior, where and how they buy, how the product/service is distributed, and more. If the new venture's product or service is "new, improved" or "new-to-the-world" or a true innovation, it is imperative that the entrepreneur have a good estimate of the percentage of the target market that might adopt the product/service and how quickly they might do so. Without an in-depth knowledge of the target market, it is not possible to arrive at the necessary estimates. Such estimates may also require knowledge of the expected rate of diffusion of the innovation (if appropriate), as well as any unusual behavior on the part of the customers or distributors involved.

Evaluating competition within the target market

With the possible exception of true innovations, a target market must pre-exist if the new venture idea is to succeed. If there is a target market, it is probably already partially satisfied by the offerings of one or more competitors. Who are these competitors? How do they compete? Are they strong, moderate, or weak competitors? How will they respond if the proposed new venture enters the market and tries to capture market share? Questions such as these can help entrepreneurs realistically estimate the percentage of the target market that might possibly switch their loyalties and purchases to the entrepreneur's new venture.

It is also necessary to include consideration of any other factors that might further reduce the market potential for a new venture's product or service. Examples of other factors include legal or environmental challenges championed by competitors, or possible conflicts that the new venture may encounter within the distribution system that traditionally services the target market. Such factors are likely to have a negative impact on the size of a new venture's market potential, and should be incorporated into this analysis of the portion of the target market that might be available to the new venture.

Developing a marketing plan and evaluating its effectiveness

After the preceding information is thoroughly evaluated, the entrepreneur should have a more realistic estimate of his or her market potential. In order to actually attain that market potential, the entrepreneur should develop a marketing plan to effectively attract the target market and persuade it to switch to the entrepreneur's new offering. Most marketing textbooks agree that a successful marketing plan must be directed at a well-defined target market, and it must offer a superior product/service relative to the competition. Or, if the new venture involves a "me too" product/service, it should be priced lower than the competition and/or offer some other obvious advantage to the target market. A successful marketing plan should also include a good promotional program and good "product positioning" (i.e., what is communicated about the product/service in order to make it more appealing to the target market than any of the competitors' offerings). Equally important to the success of the new venture is that the plan include a method of distribution that can effectively reach the identified target market.

If the entrepreneur has developed a marketing plan within his or her overall business plan, then the new venture has a reasonable chance of obtaining its market potential.

Making a sales or market-share forecast

After the entrepreneur has measured the target market, evaluated the competition, and developed a marketing plan, he or she should attempt to integrate these three components in such a way as to arrive at a realistic sales or market-share forecast for the new venture. The concept is to start with the size of the entire target market, and to realistically reduce that market size to reflect the number and effectiveness of competitors. The "more realistic market potential" arrived at should further be modified to reflect the effectiveness of the marketing plan. With a near perfect marketing plan, it may be possible for the new venture to achieve 80 to 90 percent of the "more realistic market potential." With a weak marketing plan, the new venture might achieve no more than 10 percent of the market potential.

Such forecasts cannot be very precise, but they can be realistic. If a marketing plan is expected to result in the new venture's product/service being distributed in only 60 percent of the outlets serving the target market, then only 60 percent of the "more realistic market potential" is likely to be available to the new venture. Further, if during the screening and evaluation of the new venture idea, only 40 percent of the members of the target market "liked the idea" associated with the new venture, then it would be expected that the new venture would be able to achieve no more than 40 percent of the above 60 percent of the "more realistic market potential," or only about 24 percent (60 times 40) of the "more realistic market potential."

Incorporating such expected results of the marketing plan into a market potential forecast can result in a more realistic estimate of the market potential that the new venture could achieve.

Market Analysis of New Venture Ideas in Practice

A search of the literature did not reveal any empirical studies regarding the application of marketing analysis procedures by entrepreneurs to their new venture ideas. However, Hills (1985) did report the perceptions that venture capitalists had of the market analysis portion of the business plans developed by entrepreneurs. The six most relevant findings from that exploratory study were

1. Entrepreneurs primarily rely on their intuitive "feel" for estimating market potential.

2. Entrepreneurs do not usually consider market potential analysis from professional marketing researchers to be worth the added cost.

3. Entrepreneurs are typically less systematic and professional in analyzing market potential than they should be.

4. Entrepreneurs typically underestimate what is actually required to market their products.

5. Entrepreneurs tend to under budget for marketing activities.

6. Almost two-thirds of the venture capitalists participating in the study felt that about one-half of all entrepreneurs could avoid failure by doing a more thorough market analysis.

The exploratory study of 10 new venture start-ups, mentioned previously, also included information regarding whether or not market analysis was undertaken for new venture ideas. The findings of that investigation were as follows:

1. In four of the start-ups, no evidence was presented to suggest that a marketing analysis might have been made. It seems quite likely that no such analysis was made in any of those start-ups.

2. In two other start-ups, although there was no evidence to indicate that marketing analyses were made, it was noted that the entrepreneurs were very knowledgeable about the markets, the competitors, and marketing. Because of their knowledge, perhaps the entrepreneurs performed informal or intuitive market analyses, rather than formal analyses.

3. Evidence suggested that in two other start-ups there was a significant chance that the entrepreneur did some kind of rudimentary market analysis.

4. Evidence from the last two of the 10 start-ups indicated that entrepreneurs probably did a market analysis for their new venture ideas.

The second exploratory study described earlier, the one undertaken specifically for this chapter, involved 21 new ventures. The descriptions of those start-ups were also studied with an eye toward identifying whether or not the entrepreneurs performed market analyses. The findings from this exploratory study were as follows:

1. The descriptions of seven of the start-ups included no evidence that the entrepreneurs performed market analyses on their new venture ideas. Again, it seems unlikely that a market analysis was performed in any of these start-ups.

2. In six of the start-ups, the evidence suggested that there was a fair chance that the entrepreneurs did some kind of rudimentary market analyses.

3. The evidence from the remaining eight start-ups indicated that the entrepreneurs involved probably performed market analyses on their new venture ideas.

On the basis of these three exploratory studies, it seems reasonable to estimate that at least one-half, and perhaps as many as two-thirds, of all new venture ideas are not subjected to a reasonably thorough market analysis.

FUTURE RESEARCH TOPICS

Based on the limited available literature, not very much is known about the extent to which entrepreneurs put new venture ideas through formal screening and evaluation procedures. And, according to one small sample of venture capitalists, entrepreneurs often do not formally evaluate the size and nature of the market for new ventures and do not prepare effective marketing plans or provide for an adequate marketing budget.

The foregoing discussions have argued that the third and fourth steps of the new product development process can be applied to new venture ideas. Because we know so little about current practices, we can only speculate that the concepts associated with those steps are not being widely used by entrepreneurs. This raises the question as to whether entrepreneurs are familiar with screening and evaluating concepts, and the concepts underlying the various aspects of marketing analysis. If entrepreneurs are not familiar with these concepts, what could be done to inform entrepreneurs about these concepts and encourage their use? Both of these questions would be good research topics.

Regarding screening and evaluating, the foregoing discussions suggest a number of possible research topics. Some of the more appropriate issues that might be researched are: What screening and evaluating procedures are being utilized currently, and under what circumstances? Under what circumstances should new venture ideas be screened and evaluated? How much screening and evaluating should be done on new venture ideas? What screening and evaluating procedures are the best ones to use, and under what circumstances?

Research questions may also be posed regarding market analysis. What kinds of market analyses are currently being utilized, and under what circumstances? Should all new venture ideas be subjected to a formal market analysis and, if not, which ones should not be subjected to an analysis? How much marketing analysis should be carried out under different circumstances? What marketing analysis procedures work best, and under what circumstances?

There are numerous, critically important research issues that uniquely relate to entrepreneurs and new ventures. It will also be important to learn from entrepreneurs' successes to determine if large, mature firms can benefit from the experiences of early stage ventures that often bring the most beneficial, major breakthroughs to society. Perhaps a different process is most appropriate for independent entrepreneurs.

NOTES

1. For recent books published on the subject, see Crawford (1991), Kuczmarski (1988), and Urban, Hauser, and Dholakia (1987). Pessemier (1982) and Urban and Hauser (1980) can also be useful references.

2. This section is based on the article by Chaterji, Lonsdale and Stasch (1981).

3. For discussions of such checklists, see Crawford (1991, 199–208), Kuczmarski (1988, 140–81, 207–18) and Urban et al. (1987, 51–54).

4. For general discussions of concept tests, see in Crawford (1991, Chapters 8 and 9) and Urban et al. (1987, 74–76).

5. See Boyd et al. (1989, Chapter 9 and 17) for discussions of these three techniques.

6. See Boyd et al. (1989, Chapters 4 and 9) for discussions of these techniques.

7. For discussions of the business analysis step, see Crawford (1991, Chapters 14 and 16), Kuczmarski (1988, 189–207), and Urban et al. (1987, Chapter 8).

8. See Fourt and Woodlock (1960), Claycamp and Liddy (1969), Massy (1969), Eskin (1973), and Silk and Urban (1978).

9. It should be noted that these reports of new venture start ups were taken from secondary sources. Therefore, if the secondary source did not specifically mention some kind of screening and evaluation of the new venture idea, that did not necessarily mean that some kind of screening and evaluation of the new venture idea absolutely did not occur.

REFERENCES

Booz, Allen, and Hamilton, Inc. *Management of New Products.* 1968.

Booz, Allen, and Hamilton, Inc. *New Products Management for the 1980s.* 1982.

Boyd, H. W., Jr., R. Westfall, and S. F. Stasch. *Marketing Research: Text and Cases.* 7th ed. Homewood, IL: Irwin, 1989.

Chaterji, C. S., R. T. Lonsdale, and S. F. Stasch. "New Product Development: Theory and Practice." In *Review of Marketing: 1981,* edited by B. M. Enis and K. J. Roering, 143–157. Chicago, IL: American Marketing Association, 1981.

Claycamp, H. J., and L. E. Liddy. "Prediction of New Product Performance: An Analytical Approach." *Journal of Marketing Research* (November 1969): 414–20.

Cooper, R. G. "Project New Product: An Empirically Derived New Product Screening Model." Paper presented at the Product Development and Management Association Conference, Washington, DC, 1979.

Crawford, C. M. *New Products Management.* 3rd ed. Homewood, IL: Richard D. Irwin, 1991.

Drucker, P. F. "Marketing 101 for a Fast-Changing Decade." *Wall Street Journal* (November 20, 1990): A14.

Eskin, G. J. "Dynamic Forecasts of New Product Demand Using a Depth of Repeat Model." *Journal of Marketing Research* (May 1973): 115–29.

Fourt, L. A., and J. W. Woodlock. "Early Prediction of Market Success for New Grocery Products." *Journal of Marketing* (October 1960): 31–38.

Hills, G. E. "Market Analysis in the Business Plan: Venture Capitalists' Perceptions." *Journal of Small Business Management* (January 1985): 38–46.

Kuczmarski, T. *Managing New Products.* Englewood Cliffs, NJ: Prentice-Hall, 1988.

Lonsdale, R. T., and S. F. Stasch. "In Search of a Better Approach to the Development of New Products." *The Journal of Consumer Marketing* (Winter 1986): 35–44.

Massy, W. F. "Forecasting the Demand for New Convenience Products." *Journal of Marketing Research* (November 1969): 405–12.

Pessemier, E. A. *Product Management: Strategy and Organization.* 2nd ed. New York: John Wiley & Sons, 1982.

Silk, A. J., and G. L. Urban. "Pre-Test Marketing Evaluation of New Packaged Goods: A Model and Measurement Methodology." *Journal of Marketing Research* (May 1978): 171–91.

Stanton, W., M. Etzel, and B. Walker. *Fundamentals of Marketing.* 9th ed. New York: McGraw-Hill, 1991.

Stasch, S. F. "Entrepreneurs' Circumstances and Sources of New Venture Ideas: An Exploratory Study." A paper presented at the American Marketing Association Summer Educators' Conference, San Diego, 1991.

Tauber, E. M. "Why Concept and Product Tests Fail to Predict New Product Results." *Journal of Marketing* (October 1975): 69–71.

Tauber, E. M. "Forecasting Sales Prior to Test Market." *Journal of Marketing* (January 1977): 80–84.

Urban, G. L., and J. R. Hauser. *Design and Marketing of New Products.* Englewood Cliffs, NJ: Prentice-Hall, 1980.

Urban, G. L., R. J. Hauser, and N. Dholakia. *Essentials of New Product Management.* Englewood Cliffs, NJ: Prentice-Hall, 1987.

8

Opportunity Recognition: Lessons from Venture Capital

Jeffry A. Timmons and Daniel F. Muzyka

INTRODUCTION

The venture capitalist's success in searching for potentially successful ventures is a key determinant of performance of the fund he controls. Venture capitalists have been largely unwilling or unable to articulate the detailed characteristics they associate with successful ventures, the specifics of any formal models or frameworks they utilize, and the very mechanisms behind the successful performance of venture funds (see Stevenson et al. 1986).

Why are the characteristics associated with successful ventures so difficult to uncover? Why can't we rely on formal models such as the competitive strategy models (Porter 1980; Hofer and Schendel 1978) to evaluate potential entrepreneurial ventures? Based on our research, a number of answers appear to be appropriate to these questions. First, systematic research into the characteristics of successful ventures has only begun, partly as a result of the unwillingness of venture capitalists to discuss them and partly as a result of the small database from which to generalize. Second, venture capitalists noted that they did not find the competitive strategy frameworks and other policy models to be directly and easily transferable to their environment.

Some of the difficulty experienced by venture capitalists might be associated with the underlying databases used by researchers. Research in industrial organization economics and strategic management has not focused on new venture development and performance. Most of the industrial organization studies have been based on firm and industry data related to large enterprises (e.g. the Fortune 500). Strategic management research, consulting, and practice have similarly provided few concrete guidelines for the use of venture capitalists identifying potentially profitable venture and have left underdeveloped the notions regarding new business creation and venturing.

Previous research in entrepreneurship has provided venture capitalists with some insights but is generally exploratory in nature and presents somewhat contradictory results. There have been several studies directed at determining what factors are used by venture capitalists to evaluate venture proposals and how venture characteristics relate to venture success. These studies (e.g., Wells 1974; Poindexter 1976; Tyebjee and Bruno 1981; MacMillan et al. 1985) are directed at determining what factors are used by venture capitalists in selecting ventures from the population of proposals they receive. They tend to support the traditional wisdom that the key evaluation criteria, and presumably the key success factor, were primarily related to the characteristics of the entrepreneur. Another stream of studies have attempted to link venture characteristics with venture performance (e.g., Hoban 1976; Sandberg and Hofer 1986). The research in this stream tends to support the notion that product-market character-istics were more directly related to venture success than the characteristics of the entrepreneur.

The new venture capital climate in the 1980s has been accompanied by both innovative investment practices and approaches, particularly in start-up and early stage investments (Timmons and Gumpert 1982). Building on this earlier research and cumulative practical experience, Timmons (1985, Chapter 3) introduced specific criteria and a framework for venture selection and evaluation. This framework provides a basis for the propositions developed here.

RESEARCH DESIGN

The purpose of our research was to try to develop a more complete under-standing, from the perspective of the venture capitalists, of the characteristics of "successful" ventures. It was our hope that we could (1) extend and link the work done by those reviewing deal selection criteria and the structure-strategy-performance link (2) develop a practitioner-originated list of the common characteristics of high-performing ventures; (3) provide researchers with as complete as possible a list of the possible factors leading to higher performance in entrepreneurial ventures; and (4) develop an initial list of characteristics for venture capitalists to use in their screening and selection of investment opportunities. He wished to seek operational definitions of the factors affecting venture success and, therefore, adopted relatively unstructured research methods.

We selected a sample of 47 sites for interview purposes. Included in the total sample of 47 firms and investors were 18 private investors, four internation-al venture capital firms, and 21 venture capitalists recognized as having highly innovative and diverse portfolios (see Timmons et al. 1984). The investors included in the sample represent a broad range of investment interests, orienta-tions, industry participants, and performance.

The research process was exploratory in nature. Unstructured interviews were conducted with principals of the venture capital firms. The characteristics for discussion and the definition of a "successful venture" were supplied by the venture capitalists being interviewed, because any pre-defined and exact performance standard might have introduced unwanted bias. A series of general and "fatal flaws" propositions were developed based on the information from the field interviews. The propositions discussed in the following section developed with a minimum of reliance on formal paradigms (e.g., Porter's [1980] competitive strategy paradigm). The propositions were, however, grouped by the authors into logical categories. No attempt was made to rank the characteristics or propositions because a major objective of the study was to outline a complete set of characteristics common to successful ventures across markets and industries. (As a general point, the term "industry" is used as in Porter [1980] to describe the group of firms producing products that are substitutes for each other [e.g., computer industry] and includes many [e.g., word processing work stations]). Finally, as a part of our research effort, we attempted to compile a list of "fatal flaws" or characteristics venture capitalists associated with ventures that had a high likelihood of failure.

RESEARCH FINDINGS

Five groups of characteristics were identified as a result of the interviews: product-market characteristics, competitive dynamics, business economics, business performance, and management. The propositions that follow were found to apply across venture industries.

PRODUCT-MARKET STRUCTURE

Venture capitalists note that a thorough and complete understanding of the product-market characteristics is an essential element of a proper evaluation of a venture opportunity. The first proposition is fundamental to the success of any venture—the identification of the true market for the venture's product. What venture capitalists have noted as more important than a "market" for the venture product is a well-defined notion of the actual customers, the customers' rationale for purchasing the new product or service, and benefits and economic payback realized by the customer (see Muzyka et al. 1986; Lilien and Kotler 1983).

Many individuals discussing the problems of applying the concepts organized under the title of competitive strategy (Porter 1980; Bogue and Buffa 1986; Hofer and Schendel 1978) have noted the problem of market definition.

Proposition 1: Ventures that will have a product/ service with a clearly identified and enthusiastic customer are more likely to succeed than ventures that have a vague or poorly-defined customer population.

Proposition 2: Ventures that will provide a product with a clear payback to the customer in less than 18 months are more likely to succeed than ventures with a product having ill-defined economic returns to the customer.

Another major product-market factor is simply the size of the market to be served by the venture. Markets that are too small appear to give little room for growth and competition. In many cases, venture capitalists note, venture plans that describe businesses addressing relatively small markets contain unrealistically high expectations for long-run market share.

Proposition 3: Ventures that are likely to serve a clearly defined market with an annual size of between $10 million and $100 million are more likely to succeed than ventures serving a very small or very large market.

Markets for proposed ventures that are too large appear to be an undesirable characteristic of a new venture for several reasons: (1) large expectations are the result of inadequate research or unbridled enthusiasm and (2) ventures that appear to have a potentially large market for their product tend to attract and end up competing with large corporations in their market. Major corporations, armed with the necessary market, financial, and technical information, can often rapidly transfer learning or experience from related businesses (Spence 1981) in order to be low-cost producers in a new market.

Another product-market characteristic that is of importance to the financial success of a venture is the market growth rate.

Proposition 4: Ventures that will serve a market with a potential growth rate of 30 to 60 percent are more likely to succeed than ventures serving markets with very slower high-growth rates.

As with market size, market growth rates that are too low do not provide enough opportunity for venture growth (and, therefore, return), which markets with excessive growth rates tend to attract many (sometimes too many as Sahlman and Stevenson [1985] noted) new entrants. Furthermore, markets with excessively high growth rates require that venture management not only manage the creation of a business but potentially madcap growth. Also, expected profits in potentially large, fast-growing markets may be sufficient for established industry competitors to overcome the risks of entry (Stonebraker 1976). The notion that fast growth is associated with markets served by successful or selected ventures can be found in both Sandberg and Hofer (1986) and MacMillan, et al. (1985).

The final point addressed by venture capitalists regarding product-market structure is the differentiation of the product vis-à-vis the competition.

> Proposition 5: Ventures that are based on a product that incorporates or is manufactured by a process that incorporates legally protected or highly unique technologies or features are likely to be more successful than ventures that rely on more generic product features or technologies.

Legal restrictions or key protected (either through patents or trade secrets) technologies can present a formidable barrier to market entry (see Waterson 1984). MacMillan, et al. (1985) identified this as a major consideration in the selection of new ventures.

A related issue is the distinctiveness of the features of the proposed product or service as compared to similar ones (close substitutes) that may exist in the marketplace.

> Proposition 5.1: Ventures whose product or service features can be served by similar products or services, or by the easy combination of similar products or services, are less likely to be successful than ventures involving a product or service with new features.

> Proposition 5.2: Ventures whose product or service can be duplicated by the relatively immediate extension of the product line of an existing competitor are less likely to be successful than ventures involving a product or service with unique features.

It has been shown (Brander and Eaton 1984; Schmalensee 1978) that existing competitors in a market can and will compete on the basis of an interlocking series of differentiated products. If existing competitors have a product line in place with products that have different groupings of features, existing customers may be well served by purchasing products with a bundle of features near those of the product proposed as part of the new venture. Also, the existing competitor may have a shared cost advantage from producing other similar products (Porter 1985; Bogue and Buffa 1986).

One of the most discussed dimensions along which a company can differentiate its product is quality (Waterson 1984). As the literature (Garvin 1983; Buzzell et al. 1981; Crosby 1979) would suggest, high product quality has a double benefit.

> Proposition 5.3: Ventures that produce products or services of higher quality than substitute or competitive products have a greater likelihood of success than ventures involving production of moderate-or low-quality goods.

Superior quality not only permits the business to differentiate its product but it also permits the total cost (direct production, service and warranty cost) of products to be lower in the long run.

COMPETITIVE DYNAMICS

Venture capitalists made a number of common points concerning the history and state of competition in the industry. The first major point made by the venture capitalists that we interviewed was that an assessment must be made of the reaction to new competitors in the marketplace.

> Proposition 6: Ventures that would face strong and vindictive competitors in their served market segment or adjacent market segments are less likely to succeed than potential ventures with limited or passive competition.

Research has shown that predatory behavior, albeit economically irrational at times, is a common and effective barrier to entry as noted by some researchers (Milgrom and Roberts 1982).

Another proposition developed from our interviews involved the basis of competition in the market for a proposed venture.

> Proposition 7: Ventures that compete in the marketplace on the basis of product differentiation and technological innovation are more likely to be successful than ventures which compete on price.

> Proposition 7.1: Ventures that compete on the basis of technological innovation or a differentiated product are more

successful if the technologies or products are not perceived to be threatening to the competitors or have an inherently long head time for competitive response.

Venture capitalists consistently made it clear that ventures that planned initially to compete strictly on the basis of price were less likely to succeed than those that relied on product differentiation and research and development. Venture capitalists also claimed that ventures that proposed to offer an existing product or service in a geographic area where it is currently not offered (focus strategy as defined by Porter [1980]) were less likely to succeed than those who adopted a "differentiation" strategy. This is consistent with Sandberg's and Hofer's (1986) findings regarding venture strategy.

In addition to the product-market characteristics noted in the previous section, venture capitalists we interviewed indicated that ventures that had a strong likelihood of achieving and maintaining a dominant position in the marketplace were more likely to succeed.

> Proposition 8: Ventures that have the potential to attain and maintain a dominant position (high relative market share) in the market are more likely to succeed.

> Proposition 8.1: Ventures that have the potential to acquire and sustain a market share (in a clearly defined market) in excess of 20 percent are more likely to be successful.

> Proposition 8.2: Ventures that are likely to exercise price leadership based on share position are likely to be more successful.

> Proposition 8.3: Ventures that can attain and maintain a low or the lowest cost position are more likely to be successful.

The wisdom from industrial organization economics (Waterson 1984), strategic management research (Buzzell et al. 1975), and practice (Henderson 1979), which relates market share, concentration, and profitability seems to hold true with regard to entrepreneurial ventures.

Another major concern of venture capitalists assessing competitive dynamics is the nature of the barriers to entry in the market place. As previous research would indicate, high barriers to entry permit competitors to realize higher profits (Bain 1972).

Proposition 9: Ventures that can grow in a market niche protected by extensive entry barriers are more likely to succeed than those competing in a market without protective barriers.

Proposition 9.1: Ventures with low barriers to initial entry, and therefore lower cost, are more successful.

A higher profit potential leads to a potential for more successful ventures. As noted by venture capitalists, these same barriers to entry take on another role when considering the initiation of a new venture in an existing market. It takes time, money, and energy, or a novel idea or concept, to surmount high barriers without a large expenditure of funds.

The discussion with venture capitalists regarding the strategic options faced by ventures contains many of the same elements as the literature on low market share companies following a "niche" strategy (Hamermesh et al. 1978; Woo and Cooper 1981). The suggestion has been made in our discussions and in the literatures on low-share firms that they should establish themselves within the confines of a protected market within an industry. In effect, there must be mobility barriers (Waterson 1984) that prevent existing industry competitors from competing in the specific markets served by the venture. The industry "U" (Porter 1980; Muzyka and Crittenden 1986) or "V" (Bogue and Buffa 1986) curve is consistent with this notion. What our research indicates is that successful ventures appear to have identified lucrative markets within an industry, found gateways to entry (Yip 1982) through the barriers protecting the markets, taken dominant share positions in the specific market while ensuring that their costs are the lowest of any competitor serving the specific market, and have attempted to grow and maintain barriers to protect the chosen market.

A final consideration under the category of competitive dynamics is the product line growth path for the venture. The data from investors with regard to successful ventures was that from the outset, they had a clear product line growth path.

Proposition 10: Ventures that rely on one innovative product with little or no possibility for expansion or extension are less likely to succeed than ventures that rely on a product concept that can lead to a product line.

An alternative issue with respect to growth is that the market opportunity, as seen by the entrepreneur, may not have been previously addressed for good economic reasons: growth behind the single product may not have been possible without resorting to another, completely new technology.

BUSINESS ECONOMICS

Venture capitalists identified a major set of comments we have organized under the title "business economics." The major groups of propositions included in this section are associated with the economic value created by the business. The first set of propositions are related to the determination of the "value-added" stream the venture will be part of.

> Proposition 11: Ventures with a clearly defined position in a value-added stream and a durable and high value added have a better chance of success than those with low value added.

> Proposition 11.1: Ventures that expect stable gross margins of between 20 and 50 percent have a greater chance for success than ventures with gross margins less than 20 percent or with volatile gross margins.

Venture capitalists confirm that it is important, particularly with regard to proposed ventures in industrial markets, to understand the nature, size, and durability of the value-added position of the venture (see Porter 1985; Bogue and Buffa 1986). Venture capitalists went on to note that ventures with low or volatile value added, and therefore low margins, were unlikely to be successful.

Low-margin ventures required efficiency as well as effectiveness on the part of management. Related propositions deal with the relationship and nature of the elements of the value-added stream adjacent to those addressed by the venture. Venture capitalists noted the real need to understand the value added of the proposed business vis-à-vis suppliers and buyers.

> Proposition 11.2: Ventures having clearly defined inputs, multiple factor inputs, and sources of supply for these inputs have a greater chance for success than those that must develop sources of supply or that must determine how to best manufacture or provide the product/service.

> Proposition 11.3: Ventures that have clearly defined, accessible, and established product distribution channels are more likely to be successful than ventures with poorly defined or non-existent product distribution channels.

> Proposition 11.4: Ventures that have an exclusive or unique relationship with suppliers and/or distribution channels are more likely to be successful.

Entrepreneurial ventures that were critically dependent on developing sources of supply, or were dependent on developing channels of distribution, appeared to be less successful. Those that had special relationships with suppliers and/or distributors appeared to be more successful. The issue that seems somewhat at variance with the literature is the wisdom that both supplier and buyer power should be absolutely weak (Porter 1976; Lustgarten 1975; Waterson 1984).

With regard to ventures, there would appear to be some intermediate, optimal level of supplier and buyer power.

The second set of propositions under the category of business economics are those related to the nature of the investment stream required to create the business. Ventures that required planned major, "lumpy" investments up-front were not usually successful.

> Proposition 12: Ventures that require multiple rounds of funding and have capital requirements between $300,000 and $1 million per round, tend to be more successful than ventures requiring only small or very large investments, or those with very irregular capital requirements (e.g., large funding up-front with little required in additional rounds).

> Proposition 12.1: Ventures that are planned, proposed and funded largely in a single investment stage are typically less successful than those segmented for both planning and funding purposes into smaller logical segments with discrete and measurable performance criteria.

Venture capitalists cited many problems with such ventures, including the fact that real monitoring of performance was difficult in ventures where there was major up-front investment.

In addition, venture capitalists related that highly asset-intensive ventures did not perform well.

> Proposition 12.2: Ventures that are asset intensive are typically less successful than ventures with moderate or low asset intensity.

Venture capitalists noted that this seemed true for two reasons: (1) ventures requiring major asset development put a major strain on potentially untried management, and (2) venture capitalists noted that the acquisition and development of assets such as plant and equipment provided little competitive advantage for new ventures.

The final value-related issue is the requirement of the venture capitalist to have mechanisms in order to capture the value created by the business.

> Proposition 13: Ventures with no clear exit path, be it an initial public offering (IPO) or sale to another firm, are typically less successful than ventures that have a clear economic value to another firm or that can be configured in such a fashion that they will have a clear and reasonable chance of operating as a separate entity.

> Proposition 13.1: Ventures that are funded with the expectation that the best exit option for the venture capitalist is a buy back by the management are less likely to succeed than ventures with an externally and independently apparent value.

The main issue for venture capitalists was that ventures could not, by definition, be successful if the economic value that was thought to be created in the business was not recognized by others. In essence, the value did not exist and the venture could not be successful if there was no market for the venture itself. These propositions are consistent with Tyebjee's and Bruno's (1981) and MacMillan's, et al. (1985) findings.

BUSINESS PERFORMANCE

In addition to the proposition already noted, venture capitalists outlined performance standards associated with successful ventures. The performance characteristics of a proposed venture are obviously related to the structure and conduct characteristics outlined previously. However, venture capitalists noted that they also contain certain additional information concerning management behavior and expectations and resource management.

The first set of performance standards identified as part of the research were time-related standards.

> Proposition 14: Ventures planned for final disposition, IPO, or sale to another company, within four to seven years are likely to be more successful than ventures with usual life cycles involving early sale or longer term disposition.

> Proposition 15: Ventures with a reasonably planned time break even of between 18 months (or less) and 36 months

are more likely to succeed than ventures with long or very short break-even periods.

> Proposition 15.1: Ventures with exceedingly short break-even periods are likely to serve product-market segments with few barriers to entry and are likely to be less successful.

> Proposition 15.2: Ventures with exceedingly long break-even periods are likely to have intrinsically risky and possibly unrealistic assumptions concerning long-term payouts, making them generally less successful.

Ventures with very short expected periods to IPO sometimes contained unrealistic assumptions concerning the difficulty of initiating the venture or overcoming industry entry barriers. Also, venture capitalists noted that some ventures with short periods to IPO are typically entering industries with few barriers to entry. These ventures have a low value at offering time because they can be easily replicated. Ventures with exceedingly long expected periods to IPO were generally identified as being very risky for a variety of reasons, including the threat of obsolescence of the underlying technology.

Venture capitalists interviewed indicated certain cash flow and profit plan standards that successful ventures generally met.

> Proposition 16: Ventures that have a reasonable chance of attaining durable after-tax profits in the 10 to 15 percent range are more likely to be successful than ventures with exceedingly low or exceedingly high expectations.

> Proposition 16.1: Ventures with long-term profit expectations of less than five percent are less likely to be successful than ventures with higher profit expectations.

> Proposition 16.2: Ventures with excessively high expectations are less likely to be successful in the long run due to heightened competitive interest in the product-market or unrealistic long-run expectations concerning the cost structure.

Venture capitalists noted that extraordinary profit expectations did not indicate a sound plan. Excessively high returns would attract competition to the industry, lowering the eventual returns for all competitors (Stonebraker 1976; Masson and Shaanan 1982; Caves, Fortunato, and Ghemawat 1984). On the other hand, low profit expectations left little "slack" in the financial statements to meet negative operating contingencies or variances from plan, making the management task more difficult.

The other clear cash flow and profit plan measure generally associated with successful ventures was the time until positive cash flow.

> Proposition 17: Ventures with planned positive cash flows beginning between 18 and 36 months after investment are more attractive than those that do not achieve positive cash flow for longer periods.

Ventures with long planned periods until positive cash flow were found to be too risky investments to be made with a new management team. The final category of performance measures indicated by venture capitalists were the "returns."

> Proposition 18: Venture plans that exhibit in the range of 10 times initial investment in five years are associated with more successful ventures.

> Proposition 19: All factors considered, ventures with an initial return on investment (ROI) expectation of 25 to 30 percent generally have the greatest chance of success. Ventures with ROIs less than 10 percent or excessively high proposed returns are less successful than ventures with more moderate returns.

Venture capitalists noted that ventures with higher planned returns were either the creation of an overly optimistic planning process or were likely to attract a great deal of competition (assuming low barriers to entry).

MANAGEMENT

Venture capitalists interviewed as part of this research uniformly noted that the most important factor that is a potential prior determinant of venture success is the management team. Just as many researchers in strategic management emphasize that the formulation of an effective corporate strategy can only lead to the realization of a successful corporate strategy if the implementation is successful (Hamermesh 1986), venture capitalists uniformly agree that venture success is critically dependent on implementation: a poor venture concept can sometimes be rescued by good management but a good venture concept will not rescue poor management.

The first proposition we state is one that was reiterated in each of our interviews: venture success is more likely if the management team works well together and has a proven track record in the proposed business area.

> Proposition 20:   Ventures with a proven, well-integrated management team with high integrity are more likely to succeed than those with a totally inexperienced management team with no proven track record.

> Proposition 20.1: Ventures with key management experience in the venture technologies, market, and/or products are more likely to succeed than ventures with management teams with limited or no experience in the key venture technologies or products.

> Proposition 20.2: Ventures that include one or more industry "superstars" (with prior profit and loss, marketing, and/or technological experience in the industry) in their top management teams are more likely to succeed.

The types of prior experience that venture capitalists noted as most important were (1) experience with general management in a start-up environment and (2) industry experience. In addition, the presence on the proposed management team of an industry "superstar" with extensive technical and/or operating experience appears to be a major contributor to venture success.

A second major and associated point is the integration and orientation of the management team.

> Proposition 21:   Management teams that can work in a complementary fashion toward achieving the overall objective are more likely to succeed than those composed of individuals with different objectives and/or only a limited ability to work together.

> Proposition 21.1: Management teams with a uniform orientation toward opportunity rather than resource control are more likely to be successful than management teams oriented toward control and/or management of acquired resources.

Venture capitalists associate a prior degree of understanding and a common set of objectives with regard to the business as the most important prior predictors of whether a management team will cooperate. Finally, venture capitalists indicated that managers who exhibit "trustee" behavior (see Stevenson et al. 1985) or an orientation toward acquiring and protecting assets are unlikely to foster an environment necessary to achieve success.

Certain general management skills appear to be most critical to venture success, including the ability to focus the venture organization's efforts on providing the organization with strong leadership (Zaleznick 1977); on dynamically manipulating incentives for employees and fellow managers; and on developing the minimal, essential administrative systems (Hamermesh 1984).

Those venture capitalists we spoke to stated that they were able to evaluate managers on their abilities in these areas by careful review of the venture objectives and plan review of the prior performance and career paths and discussions with the proposed management team.

> Proposition 22: Ventures with strong general management and appropriate general management incentives are more likely to succeed than ventures with "unfair" or poor incentives and mediocre general management.

> Proposition 22.1: Ventures with a general manager who is able to identify and maintain organizational and management focus on the factors key to the success of the venture are more likely to be successful.

> Proposition 22.2: Ventures with a general manager who exhibits strong leadership skills and projects a strong vision of the overall venture objectives are more likely to be successful.

> Proposition 22.3: Ventures with a general manager who understands how to manipulate incentives for fellow employees are more likely to be successful.

> Proposition 22.4: Ventures with a general manager skilled at configuring, implementing, and operating appropriate (and minimal) organizational systems for monitoring and resource allocation are more likely to be successful.

Of particular interest in our discussion with venture capitalists was the role of proper incentives. Consistent with the literature on agency theory, our data suggests that the proper alignment of personal and venture goals and expectations through realistic and reasonable incentives is a critical determinant of venture success (Pratt and Zeckhauser 1985; Jensen and Meckling 1976).

The conventional wisdom of the venture capital market is echoed in these comments regarding management: management and implementation are issues with a pervasive influence on venture success. In particular, our research would suggest that experience and the proven ability to apply it are two of the most important characteristics of the lead entrepreneur and the management team in general. Some studies (e.g., Sandberg and Hofer 1986) find little or no relationship between venture performance and entrepreneur or management characteristics. Our research would suggest that the definitions used in some studies to operationalize the entrepreneur's characteristics do not capture all of the dimensions associated with what venture capitalists perceive as "experience" and "ability" or the role of the management team as a group.

FATALLY FLAWED VENTURES

As indicated earlier, in the course of our research we also attempted to compile a list of "fatal flaws" individual characteristics often associated with ventures that fail. The fatal flaws were identified by asking what factors usually led to the ultimate failure of the venture (see Table 8.1) and should be considered in conjunction with the proposition outlined above. These fatal flaws are somewhat different than those presented by MacMillan et al. (1985), whose orientation was directed more toward what apparent factors would lead to rejection of a venture proposal.

IMPLICATIONS FOR PRACTITIONERS

There are a number of preliminary implications for practitioners from gained this research. The most important implication is that the identification of potentially successful ventures requires the careful consideration of a constellation of factors. It is clear from our interviews that venture capitalists felt that each of the elements discussed previously (i.e., product-market strategy, business economics, competitive dynamics, business performance, and management) constitute a multi-dimensional "venture screen." The notion that venture success is tied to the interaction of many economic and organizational factors runs parallel to the notions found in the business policy literature regarding successful business performance (e.g., Andrews 1980).

The competitive strategy literature notes that the creation of sustainable competitive advantage (Porter 1985; Bogue and Buffa 1986) is also the result of the alignment of a number of different factors. Our exploratory research findings are consistent with those of research into the factors leading to higher levels of performance in larger, established enterprises: successful performance is the

Table 8.1
Fatal Flaws (Leading to Venture Failure)

Product-Market Structures:

- Very small or very large market for the product or service

Competitive Dynamics:

- Overpowering competition and high cost of entry
- Inability to identify adjacent markets (or niches) in which to expand

Business Economics:

- Overwhelming financial requirements
- Inability to produce a product at a cost that will make it competitive
- Lack of influence and control over product development and component prices
- Inability to harvest the opportunity profitably

---

result of the interaction of many factors but most particularly, the quality and actions of management (Chandler 1977).

There are three additional findings. The second major implication for entrepreneurs and venture capitalists is a restatement of an often forgotten idea: good venture ideas (many venture plans are simply statements of ideas) do not equate with good venture opportunities. A sound product or idea is a necessary, but not sufficient, condition for launching, building, and eventually harvesting an economically successful venture. The third implication of our research for fund managers and investors is that a basic understanding of the target market for a potential venture's products and the value added to the customer of the products are essential. Venture capitalists should strive to understand the basic economics of the product and the business before investment. Our final key finding for practitioners is that the existence of a good concept and product-market strategy does not guarantee the existence of a good venture opportunity.

The entrepreneur and management team were the most critical elements for venture success and cited in our research. The top management of the proposed venture must demonstrate basic general management skills and the ability to manage under uncertainty.

IMPLICATIONS FOR RESEARCHERS

Our research challenge lies in the integration of these propositions with our understanding of competitive strategy and to further our understanding of competitive strategy as it applies to emerging businesses. Our objective should be to create a complete "structure-conduct-performance" framework for entrepreneurial ventures. We have attempted to begin the process here by providing researchers with propositions that can be useful in guiding future research efforts.

Our research would appear to have implications for the nature and type of research to follow. First, we would suggest that further work must be done to understand the link between the structural characteristics of funded ventures and their eventual performance. Extensive field research will be required to accomplish this because we cannot rely on the observations made by those who have done past work in linking structure, conduct, and performance—they have, for the most part, relied on aggregate computerized data from large established concerns (e.g., COMPUSTAT data). Second, the challenge for researchers in exploring the link between venture characteristics and venture success would appear to be avoiding the temptation to be "reductionist" in the search for the factors having the greatest influence on venture performance. Venture success appears to be related to an interrelated, multi-disciplinary set of dynamic factors, not a single static relationship.

REFERENCES

Andrews, K. R. *The Concept of Corporate Strategy.* Homewood, IL: Richard D. Irwin, 1980.

Bain, J. S. *Essays in Price Theory and Industrial Organization.* Boston, MA: Little, Brown, 1972.

Bogue, M. C., and E. C. Buffa. *Corporate Strategic Analysis.* New York: The Free Press, 1986.

Brander, J. A., and J. Eaton. "Product Line Rivalry." *American Economic Review,* 74 (June 1984).

Buzzell, R. D., B.T. Gale, and R. G. M. Sultan. "Market Share—A Key to Profitability." *Harvard Business Review* (Jan.–Feb. 1975).

Buzzell, R. D., and F. D. Wiersema. "Successful Share-Building Strategies." *Harvard Business Review* (Jan.–Feb. 1981).

Caves, R. E., and M. E. Porter. "From Entry Barriers to Mobility Barriers." *Quarterly Journal of Economics* (May 1977).

Caves, R. E., and M. Fortunato, and P. Ghemawat. "The Decline of Dominant Firms." *Quarterly Journal of Economics* (Aug. 1984).

Chandler, A. D. *The Visible Hand.* Cambridge, MA: Harvard University Press, 1977.

Crosby, P. B. *Quality is Free.* New York: McGraw-Hill, 1979.

Garvin, D. A. "Quality on the Line." *Harvard Business Review* (Sep.–Oct. 1983).

Hamermesh, R. G., M. J. Anderson, and J. E. Harris. "Strategies for Low Market Share Businesses." *Harvard Business Review* (May–June 1978).

Hamermesh, R. G. "A Note on Implementing Strategy." Harvard Business School Case #9383–015 (1984).

Hamermesh, R. G. *Making Strategy Work.* New York: John Wiley, 1986.

Henderson, B. D. *On Corporate Strategy.* Cambridge, MA: Abt Books, 1979.

Hoban, J. P. "Characteristics of Venture Capital Investments." Unpublished doctoral dissertation, University of Utah, 1976.

Jensen, M. C., and W. H. Meckling. "Theory of the Firm: Managerial Behavior, Agency Costs and Ownership Structure." *Journal of Financial Economics* 3 (1976).

Kotter, J. P. *The General Managers.* New York: The Free Press, 1982.

Lilien, G. L., and P. Kotler. *Marketing Decision Making.* New York: Harper and Row, 1983.

Lustgarten, S. H. "The Impact of Buyer Concentration in Manufacturing Industries." *Review of Economics and Statistics* (May 1975).

MacMillan, I. C., R. Siegel, and P. N. Subba Narashima. *Criteria Used by Venture Capitalists to Evaluate New Venture Proposals.* New York: New York University, 1985.

Masson, R. T., and J. Shaanan. "Stochastic-Dynamic Limit Pricing: An Empirical Test. *Review of Economics and Statistics* (Aug. 1982).

Muzyka, D. F., V. L. Crittenden, and W. F. Crittenden. "Segmentation in an Industrial Market: A Key to Strategic Marketing." *Proceedings of 1986 American Marketing Association Conference,* 1986.

Muzyka, D. F., and W. F. Crittenden. "An Exploratory Study of Growth Options: The Case of Low Market Share Companies." *Proceedings of 1986 Southern Management Association Conference,* 1986.

Poindexter, J. B. "The Efficiency of Financial Markets: The New Venture Capital Case." Unpublished doctoral dissertation, New York University, 1976.

Porter, M. E. *Interbrand Choice, Strategy and Bilateral Market Power.* Cambridge, MA: Harvard University Press, 1976.

Porter, M. E. *Competitive Strategy.* New York: The Free Press, 1980.

Porter, M. E. *Competitive Advantage.* New York: The Free Press, 1985.

Pratt, J. W., and R. J. Zeckhauser. *Principals and Agents: The Structure of Business.* Boston, MA: Harvard Business School Press, 1985.

Sahlman, W. A., and H. H. Stevenson. "Capital Market Myopia." *Journal of Business Venturing* (Winter 1985).

Sandberg, W. R., and C. W. Hofer. "The Effects of Strategy and Industrial Structure on New Venture Performance." In *Frontiers of Entrepreneurship Research*. Wellesley, MA: Babson College, 1986.

Schmalense, R. "Entry Deterrence in the Ready-to-Eat Cereal Industry." *Bell Journal of Economics* (Autumn 1978).

Spence, A. M. "The Learning Curve and Competition." *Bell Journal of Economics* (Spring 1981).

Stevenson, H. H., M. J. Roberts, and H. I. Grousbeck. *New Business Ventures and the Entrepreneur*. Homewood, IL: Richard D. Irwin, 1985.

Stevenson, H. H., D. F. Muzyka, and J. A. Timmons. "Venture Capital in a New Era: A Simulation of the Impact of Changes in Investment Patterns." In *Frontiers of Entrepreneurship Research*. Wellesley, MA: Babson College, 1986.

Stonebraker, R. J. "Corporate Profits and the Risk of Entry." *Review of Economics and Statistics* (Feb. 1976).

Timmons, J. A., and D. E. Gumpert. "Discard Many Old Rules About Getting Venture Capital." *Harvard Business Review* (Jan.–Feb. 1982).

Timmons, J. A. *New Venture Creation*. Homewood, IL: Richard D. Irwin, 1985.

Timmons, J. A., N. D. Fast, and W. D. Bygrave. "Seed and Venture Capital Investing in Technological Companies." In *Frontiers of Entrepreneurship Research*. Wellesley, MA: Babson College, 1984.

Tyebjee, T. T., and A. V. Bruno. "Venture Capital Decision Making: Preliminary Results from Three Empirical Studies." In *Frontiers of Entrepreneurship Research*. Wellesley, MA: Babson College, 1981.

Von Weizsacker, C. C. *Barriers to Entry: A Theoretical Treatment*. Berlin: Springer-Verlag, 1980.

Waterson, M. *Economic Theory of the Industry*. Cambridge, England: Cambridge University Press, 1984.

Wells, W. A. "Venture Capital Decision Making." Unpublished doctoral dissertation, Carnegie–Mellon University, 1974.

Woo, C. Y., and A. C. Cooper. "Strategies of Effective Low Share Businesses." *Strategic Management Journal* (July–Sep. 1981): 301.

Yip, G. *Barriers to Entry: A Corporate Strategy Perspective*. Lexington, MA: Lexington Books, 1982.

Zaleznick, A. "Managers and Leaders: Are They Different?" *Harvard Business Review* (May–June 1977).

9

Analyzing Market Opportunities for New Ventures

Ernest R. Cadotte and Robert B. Woodruff

Each new business venture faces an environment that is partly friendly and partly hostile, partly known and partly unknown. Although a great idea, adequate financing, and sound management are obviously important in beginning a new venture, the external environment will also be a crucial factor in the success or failure of the undertaking. The implication is clear: new-venture decisions should be based on a careful analysis of this external environment, and this can be accomplished by conducting a market opportunity analysis (MOA).

The major elements of a market opportunity analysis are shown in Figure 9.1. With an analysis of the relevant macroenvironment, major forces (economic, social, technological, legal, and natural) are uncovered that might affect market opportunity. Second, major markets in which the product might compete are identified and segmented. Next, a wealth of information is gathered to learn about specific customers in markets, the competition, and appropriate channels of distribution. This information, in turn, both provides important guides for developing a strategy to take advantage of market opportunity and lays the foundation for forecasts of the new venture's sales. The final step in the process is an evaluation of the attractiveness of the entire market opportunity in terms of financial return, consistency with organizational objectives, and other criteria.

MACROENVIRONMENT

Every new venture seeks market opportunity in the context of a larger macroenvironment. Forces arising from this part of the external environment may affect the venture's organizational capabilities, customers, competitors, and channels of distribution. For instance, government spending priorities regarding the proposed space plane could greatly affect American Matrix Corporation's

Figure 9.1
The MOA Approach

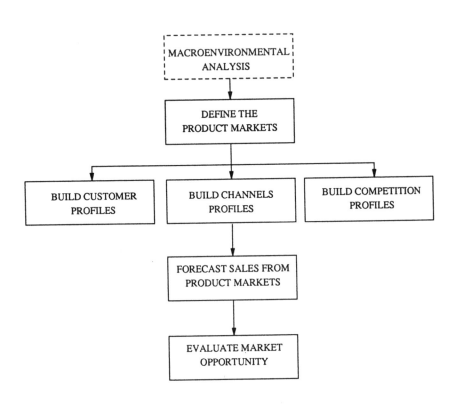

ability to sell advanced structural ceramics. Similarly, the outcome of technological advances by the Oak Ridge National Lab regarding artificial intelligence, computer imaging and manipulator arms could determine the next generation of factory robots. Or, an economic downturn cold reduce consumer spending for nonessential goods and undermine the sale of Phyton Technologies, Inc. horticultural plants, which they produce by cloning desirable characteristics.

A macroenvironmental analysis identifies important trends with regard to these forces that will affect the potential sales for the new venture. Importantly, not all aspects of the macroenvironment will be relevant for the MOA. The analyst's challenge is to selectively examine those forces operating on the determinants of market opportunity.

PRODUCT MARKETS

Markets for a new venture's product are typically not homogeneous. The idea of a market structure pinpoints this fact. Market structure is the arrangement of groups or segments of buyers comprising a total market. Notably, each segment differs from the others in the way its buyers will respond to a marketing strategy. In fact, this structure exists, for the most part, because customers in different groups have at least somewhat different market requirements. Market requirements are the benefits that buyers expect from sellers as a condition of buying. Probably the most important and difficult challenge for an MOA is to find out what the market structure is and what its customers' market requirements are.

A good starting point for describing market structure is to search for markets' competing, but existing products. Rarely does a new venture have an entire market to itself, regardless of the innovative quality of its product. Customer needs are seldom created by new products. Rather, new products provide new ways of meeting existing needs. For example, when Sony brought out the VCR, a very innovative consumer product, it was meeting the needs of customers who wished to watch programming at their convenience.

This relationship between market needs and products is the basis for the concept of product-markets structure. Markets are created by needs, buying power, and products to satisfy needs. If a need is present, the overwhelming odds are that there are already some products around to satisfy that need. Thus, such products become a source of competition. For each customer need, there are typically several products available to satisfy that need. A generic class groups all these products into one category, and each product in the generic class provides an alternative way of satisfying the need. These products are the different product types or forms. Finally, each product type has one or more similar brands (i.e., different company offerings) competing with each other. See Figure 9.2.

The restaurant business provides a familiar illustration of product-market structure. The need, or interest, is eating out, where various aspects of the meal are provided for the customer, including menu selection, food preparation, and cleanup. The generic class of products available to satisfy this need is restaurants (see Figure 9.3). In turn, the restaurant class is comprised of different subclasses of restaurants such as fast food, family, and atmosphere restaurants. Each restaurant subclass may, in turn, be further broken down into specific types of restaurants such as fast food hamburger, pizza, and chicken restaurants. Notice that each restaurant type is, in reality, a rather unique way to meet the underlying consumer need. That is, each restaurant type provides a unique and different combination of benefits and costs. Thus, customers must choose which benefit/cost combination is best for them.

Each restaurant product-type category can be further broken down into competing brands. To build an edge over competitors, each company offers a somewhat unique brand. Of course, a brand has the characteristics of one of the product types in the generic class. McDonald's, Burger King, and Wendy's represent similar brands that compete in the hamburger fast food restaurant product type.

Generic classes, product types, and brands comprise a market arena. Each company and its brand is competing for business in this arena, taking on both similar and dissimilar brands of other product types when competing for a share of sales. McDonald's is really competing with other fast food hamburger restaurants, other fast food restaurants (e.g., chicken and pizza), as well as all other types of restaurants (e.g., family-style table service, family-style self-service, ethnic, atmosphere, etc.). An MOA must develop a picture of what this larger arena is like.

The task of defining product markets is challenging, because more than one generic class and product type classification is possible. If fact, even different companies selling in the same general arena may see the product-market structure differently. Ultimately, management must decide what structure makes the most strategic sense for the company. For example, American Matrix Corporation initially positioned its ceramic reinforcing materials within the advanced structural ceramics market, but further analysis revealed that high-performance ceramics also competed with reinforced polymers and metal matrix composites in the aerospace, automobile, and sporting equipment industries. By expanding their definition of product-market structure, management was able to identify new market opportunities (substituting ceramics for plastics and metal in planes, cars, and sporting equipment). It also helped to identify entrenched competitors who would not easily yield their positions in these markets.

Figure 9.2
Product-Market Structure

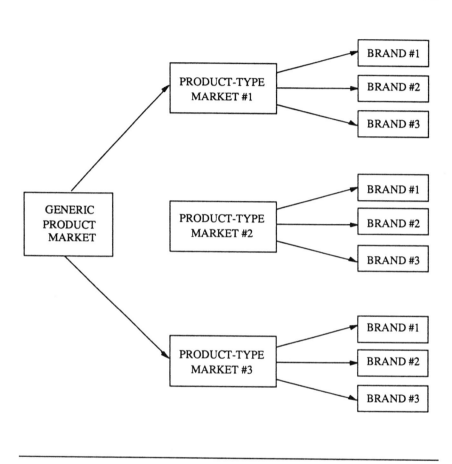

Figure 9.3
Example of Market Structure for Restaurant Industry

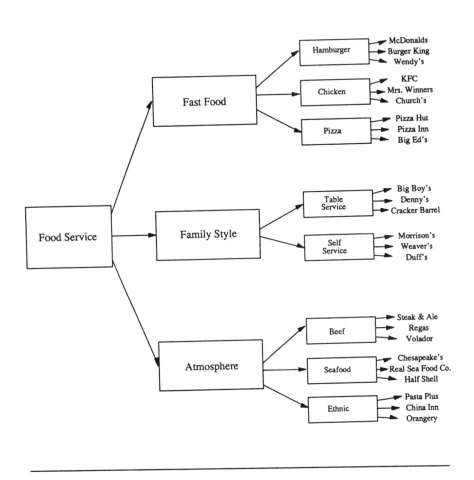

BUILDING CUSTOMER PROFILES

With product-market defined, the MOA can concentrate on describing the customers that comprise these markets. Table 9.1 provides a listing of the kinds of information needed. Essentially, management will want to know (1) what customers are like as real people; (2) how they go about deciding what to buy to satisfy the need/want; and (3) what outside, uncontrollable (by the company) influences are affecting buying decisions. Together, the information gathered forms a profile of the customers in product-markets.

Building useful customer profiles usually involves putting together a large body of information. Information about customers that may be important in planning marketing strategy can come from several sources, including suppliers and channel members, marketing research, and company personnel with market connections (e.g., salespersons). Further, building customer profiles can be complicated by the fact that separate profiles may be necessary for each market segment in the product-market structure. Therefore, it is essential to systematically gather and record information that will be integrated into the customer profile. Expert assistance may also be needed to plan marketing research if that source is to be used effectively.

BUILDING CHANNEL PROFILES

More often than not, cooperative channel partners are a key to success of a marketing strategy, particularly for a new venture. Recently, Computer Technology and Imaging (CTI) substantially expanded its prospects for PET scanners by signing an exclusive distribution contract with Siemens, Inc. CTI had previously developed the capability to produce a high-performance ECAT brain scanner at a comparatively low price. Their price advantage made it possible for many regional medical centers to purchase scanners, whereas previously only research hospitals could afford to buy them. One of their major obstacles was the channel: no one know who CTI was. CTI also encountered a very long selling cycle because ECAT scanners represented a major capital expenditure. Their salespeople were spending all their time flying around the country in order to make countless presentations to various hospital committees. CTI's distribution agreement with Siemens turned these problems around. It gave the customers a name they could trust and CTI a worldwide sales force. CTI is now free to focus on improving their production facilities and developing new products while Siemens focuses on creating sales.

In contrast to CTI, Phyton Technologies found it necessary to distribute a high-tech product (cloned horticultural plants) through low-tech channels. Its

Table 9.1
Components of a Customer Profile

What are customers like as people?

- Needs and wants
- Important use situations
- Activities and interests
- Opinions and attitudes
- Demographic characteristics
- Values

How do people decide to buy?

- Problem recognition
- Search for and use of product information
- Evaluation of alternatives
- Purchase procedures
- Satisfaction with past purchases

What outside influences are affecting buying?

- Population and social forces
- Legal forces
- Technological forces
- Economic forces
- Natural forces

cloned Boston ferns and rhododendrons could literally end up in the garden shop of K-Mart, in the local nursery, or in the florist down the street. After developing the cloning technology, Phyton's next task was to find out how shrubs and household plants are sold throughout the country. What trade shows should they attend? Who are the distributors? How far in advance could they book their orders? When do nurserymen pay their bills? These and many other questions had to be answered before the business could become viable.

In the more innovative ventures, the company may have little experience with channels for the product. However, a logical starting point is to examine the existing channels used by competing companies with products in the generic class. Special attention should be given to identifying which types of firms compose the channel (e.g., brokers, drop shippers, wholesalers, rack jobbers, etc.) and what their normal functions are. It is also important to know the protocol for conducting business within the relevant channels, including the normal terms of trade, special discounts and fees, minimum order quantities, lead time requirements, seasonal purchase patterns, promotional support requirements, and so on. Table 9.2 illustrates the kinds of information needed to develop a channel profile. This type of information can help management decide whether existing channels can be entered, whether they can and will provide the cooperation required, and whether other channel options are available. Further, the information should provide leads and contacts with specific channel firms for later use in negotiating a working arrangement for handling the product.

BUILDING COMPETITION PROFILES

Competition is comprised of all sellers who are appealing to the same product-markets. The essence is vying for sales by employing marketing strategies. An MOA tries to uncover these comparative strategies and identify their strengths and weaknesses.

The product-market arena in which a brand competes includes different forms of competition—competition from alternative product types (e.g., family self-service restaurants versus family table-service restaurants) and from similar brands of the same product type (Big Boy versus Denny's). The MOA must alert management to the nature of both of these kinds of competition. Thus, it is essential to start with a broad look at competition within a generic class of products. Then the process can be narrowed down to competition between product types and finally to similar brands of a product type.

When looking at competition broadly, a company can gather information on each and every firm with product offerings in an entire generic class. Thus, the starting point is to analyze whole industries. This can be done with an industry

Table 9.2
Components of a Channel Profile

What is the needed channel arrangement?

- Number of levels in channel
- Types and number of firms at each level
- Geographic coverage

What cooperation is needed from the channels?

- Advertising assistance
- Market coverage
- Pricing assistance
- Displays of product
- Personal selling presentations
- Inventory maintenance
- Product servicing

What incentives are required by channel?

- Price discounts
- Advertising allowances
- Ordering assistance
- Sales promotion allowances
- Delivery terms

What are the normal operating procedures of the channel?

- Terms of trade
- Functions performed at each level
- Typical order cycle and quantities
- Standard discounts

analysis. The purpose is to form a picture of the competitive practices typical of the entire industry and to uncover differences in the strategies typical of different product types. For instance, an MOA for a robotic manipulator arm might examine the robotics industry, comprised of all firms that offer industrial robots. The task would be to gather the kinds of information shown in Table 9.3.

The next step would be to do additional industry analyses, but now by narrowing the selections to just those firms handling one (or more) selected product types. Following the manipulator arm analysis, the MOA would assess major product types for the industrial robot industry. These product types are broken out by the major applications of industrial robots and include process operations (e.g., machining, painting, welding, etc.), assembly operations, materials handling, and testing and inspection. The market analyst would try to understand what makes each group of firms unique as opposed to the rest of the robotics industry. Again, the focus is on what commonly happens in the entire robotics industry as it taps market opportunity. Table 9.3 suggests that the product type industry analysis should parallel the generic class industry analysis so that comparisons can be made.

The last step in the competition analysis is to assess key competitors. These are the specific competitor companies that are going to have the greatest impact on the new venture's ability to achieve objectives in markets. By conducting the overall industry analysis first, the analyst will have a sound perspective, by this time, to identify these key competitors. For manipulator arms, the key competitors are General Motors Fanuc (GMF), Asea, Unimatton, and probably a relatively few other companies. So that comparisons can be made to see how the key competitors are positioned in their industry, the information on each key competitor should cover the items shown in Table 9.4.

FORECASTING SALES

As Figure 9.1 illustrated, forecasting sales is the last step in the MOA prior to conducting a comprehensive evaluation of market opportunity. Although it is beyond the scope of this chapter to review the many different techniques for forecasting, the nature of the task can be briefly examined. Essentially, forecasting involves anticipating how much buyers in product-markets will purchase in the future. For instance, IBM's forecasting for its PC new venture looked ahead more than a decade. Forecasting must rely on information that estimates important determinants of market opportunity. For this reason, forecasting should be attempted only after the other components of the MOA have been completed.

Table 9.3
Components of an Industry Profile

What industry is to be described?

- Name
- Geographic coverage

What is the industry's size, growth, structure?

- Number of firms
- Sales
- Market shares
- Industry structure
- Life cycle stage

What are the industry's marketing strategy and tactics?

- Market targets
- Marketing objectives
- Marketing mix

What changes in the industry's size and marketing strategy/tactics are anticipated?

- Size and strength
- Market targets
- Marketing objectives
- Marketing mix

Table 9.4
Components of a Key Competitor Profile

What are the key components?

- Companies serving the same markets
- Companies successful in meeting demand

What is the key competitor's financial size and strength?

- Sales
- Profit margins
- Total assets
- Debt
- Equity
- Various financial ratios

What are the key competitor's technical, marketing, and management capabilities?

- Mission and business objectives
- Market share position and trends
- Management capabilities and limitations
- Technical and operating capabilities
- Target market strategies
- Access to key resources

What changes are anticipated?

- Size and strength
- Market targets
- Marketing objectives
- Marketing mix

Generally, several kinds of forecasts are important. First, forecasts of sales for an entire generic class can be made. Forecasts of horticultural plants, industrial robots, or reinforcing materials fit into this category. Second, forecasts of particular product types in the class—house plants, assembly robots, or reinforced polymers—are also useful. Note that forecasts for a product type can be compared to those for the generic class to see the anticipated relative popularity of that product type against its competitors in the class. Third, sales of the company's brand are essential to the evaluation of market opportunity. Further, brand sales can be compared to product type sales (this is one way to measure predicted market share) to see how effective a company's brand strategy is expected to be.

EVALUATING MARKET OPPORTUNITY

At this point in the MOA process, all the ingredients for an evaluation of market opportunity are available. The challenge is to put them all together into an overall picture of market opportunity. There are two different aspects to the evaluation. One is the very qualitative description of the market arena in which a brand will compete for business. This description includes five major components: (1) the structure of the market, (2) the market requirements of the customers, (3) the capabilities and requirements of distributors, (4) the strengths and weaknesses of competition, and (5) the important environmental trends expected to cause change in market opportunity. Each of these factors plays an important role in planning marketing strategy for the new venture.

Market structure provides a picture of the market groups or segments that are potential target markets for the company. An entrepreneur needs this input in order to select a targeting strategy. Market requirements must be met by the company's marketing mix (product, price, promotion, distribution, and service). Management must assess the capability of the company to successfully meet the requirements of each candidate segment. This assessment is an important factor in selecting which segments eventually become targets. Further, the requirements provide important guides as to what to build into each component of the marketing mix.

Channel capabilities and requirements determine how much work the entrepreneur must do in selling to the endorser versus how much can be farmed out to distribution specialists. This is especially important if the new venture does not have the resources to contact the final customer directly. In addition, existing channels may be able to readily accommodate the new product with very little increase in selling effort. The entrepreneur must know the distribution options and be able to identify the factors necessary to attract key distributors.

Competitive strengths and weaknesses must also be considered when selecting market targets. No company wants to enter market segments that are saturated with competitors. More often than not, the success of a new venture depends on finding market segments where the company can develop a competitive edge. Further, management will need guidelines on how to compete with key competitors in each target segment. The strengths of competitors must be matched or avoided, and the weaknesses must be scrutinized for possible ways to create differential advantages. Finally, environmental trends are important for determining how stable or long-lasting the opportunity in market segments will be.

The other aspect of the evaluation of market opportunity is quantitative in nature. The forecasts of sales provide estimates of magnitude of market opportunity. These estimates, in turn, are crucial for determining financial performance of a new venture. Analyses of profits, return on investment, payback periods, cash flow, and other such performance measures all depend on having accurate estimates of sales.

Ultimately, many different factors are likely to be considered in making the go or no-go decision on a new venture. No doubt, particularly the entrepreneurial kind of manager will always rely on subjective judgment or "feel" in making the final decision. In fact, an MOA is not intended to be a substitute for judgment. An MOA simply cannot eliminate all the risks and uncertainties that accompany new venture decisions. However, an MOA can help the entrepreneur clarify and better understand the dimensions of the risk and uncertainty. That is an MOA's real contribution—to help entrepreneurs see all facets of the opportunity as well as to understand possible threats. In this way, the MOA ensures that the judgment of an entrepreneur is an informed one.

RESEARCH OPPORTUNITIES AND THE MARKETING MIX

10

Product/Service Development in New/Growing Firms

Robert D. Hisrich

Innovation is the key ingredient in new venture creation and economic development in today's hypercompetitive environment. Even though innovation is so important, the United States is becoming less innovative. For the first time ever, in 1986, more U.S. patents were granted to foreigners than U.S. citizens. One of the reasons innovation is such a key variable is the entrepreneur—the individual who is able to champion the innovation into the market place. This entrepreneur, and those that manage firms with fewer than 100 employees, create 80 percent of all new jobs and produce two and one-half times as many innovations as large firms per employee. These firms bring innovations to the market more quickly despite significant problems, particularly in finance and marketing.

IMPORTANCE OF RESEARCH INTERFACE

One of these problems, marketing, can be thought of in two ways—from a social perspective or a managerial perspective (Hunt 1986). From the managerial perspective, marketing is "the process of planning and executing the conception, pricing, promotion, and distribution of ideas, goods, and services to create exchanges that satisfy individual and organizational objectives" (Board of Directors, American Marketing Association 1985). Although taking into account the social perspective, this definition focuses more on the managerial aspect of marketing, which is the aspect more closely related to entrepreneurship.

Entrepreneurship is an even more confusing term with a multitude of definitions being advanced from an economic, psychological, and business perspective. To the economist, an entrepreneur is one who brings assets such as resources, labor, and materials into a new combination of greater value than existed before. To the psychologist, an entrepreneur is a person driven by such forces as the need to achieve, to experiment, to accomplish, to succeed, and to be in a position of authority. To the business person, an entrepreneur and his or her innovative behavior can actually be a threat, because an entrepreneur often finds better ways of utilizing resources and, in the process, creates wealth and employment opportunities.

Although each of these definitions views entrepreneurship from a different perspective, they do have some commonalities: newness, resources, organizing, creating wealth, and risk taking. Yet, in spite of these similarities, each perspective is somewhat restrictive because entrepreneurs are found in all professions—education, medicine, research, law, architecture, engineering, politics, and business. The following definition includes these various types of entrepreneurship and entrepreneurial behavior: "Entrepreneurship is the process of creating something different with value by devoting the necessary time and effort, assuming the accompanying financial, psychic, and social risks, and receiving the resulting monetary rewards and personal satisfaction" (Hisrich and Peters 1989).

RELATIONSHIP IMPORTANCE OF MARKETING/ ENTREPRENEURSHIP

Given these definitions, why is the interface between marketing and entrepreneurship important? There are several reasons. First, and perhaps most important, surveys of entrepreneurs in the United States as well as throughout the world reveal that the two biggest problem areas are marketing and finance. The problems in finance include obtaining start-up capital, financing growth, cash flow management, and financial control. Of these, it is particularly difficult for the entrepreneur to obtain the initial funding needed to build a prototype or start initial production of the product. The second problem area—marketing—is separate and yet tied to the financial problem. It is related in that the lack of a marketing plan, accurate determination of market size, and reliable sales forecasts often preclude the entrepreneur from obtaining the initial seed capital funding. Also, the slowness or even lack of sales resulting in part from the poor marketing effort or poor sales estimates frequently is the cause of the cash flow problems. Sound marketing is a necessary component for developing the new product or service for the market as well as successfully selling, nurturing, and growing the company in this market.

Contributing to the problem is the misguided belief that many entrepreneurs have that *everybody* needs their innovation. Most entrepreneurs feel their new creation is something that everyone wants and needs and have no concept of market reality. This is, of course, often the demise of the new venture (if indeed it ever gets started) because one marketing/entrepreneurial axiom is that you cannot be all things to all people. An entrepreneur needs to determine appropriate market segments and then design and implement a marketing plan to successfully market the segments identified.

One factor causing this erroneous belief is the entrepreneur's "bag mentality" —the entrepreneur is concerned that someone will steal his or her invention. This concern often causes the invention to be hidden "in a bag," without any market feedback being obtained. This can lead to the development of unmarketable products and unrealistic sales expectations.

A fourth reason for the importance of the marketing/entrepreneurship interface is that entrepreneurs have limited marketing knowledge. Marketing knowledge is particularly lacking in entrepreneurs that come from a technical (engineering) background. These entrepreneurs, having no marketing understanding, frequently believe that the only thing necessary for success is having the best possible product. Sometimes this product is so "over-engineered" that the market does not want all the options or quality offered, which is reflected in an increased price. In addition, such marketing concepts as target marketing, price thresholds, distribution margins, manufacturer representatives, and sales promotion techniques are often foreign to the entrepreneur, as are the techniques for developing and implementing a successful marketing plan, accessing published data, implementing a primary research project, and developing sales forecasting, all so important to successful marketing.

The final reason for the importance of the interface is that entrepreneurs can be poor managers. Entrepreneurs almost invariably underestimate the time and effort needed to accomplish a marketing task and overestimate the sales that will result. This can result in many problems, including the loss of the venture when the entrepreneur is tied to a specific sales performance by the funding source. General principles in the marketing/entrepreneurship interface reflecting this problem are it will take 30 percent more time, it will cost 30 percent more than has been estimated, there will be 30 percent less sales achieved than forecasted, and everything that can happen, will.

ASPECTS OF THE INTERFACE

One of the most important aspects of the marketing/entrepreneurship interface is their commonalities. Both marketing and entrepreneurship should be based on customer orientation—the customer should be the focal point. Both also have a "deal" mentality—the deal being a central factor in conceiving and developing a new venture for the entrepreneur and closing a sale for the marketing manager. Several other commonalities exist between the two: both involve the development of distinctive competence; both are driven and affected by the environmental turbulence; both have a behavioral orientation; and both are all encompassing

—marketing in terms of its models, and entrepreneurship in terms of developing an entirely new venture.

Although marketing and entrepreneurship have some similarities, operationally, conceptually they are different and may not even interface. There are several reasons for this. For entrepreneurship, the real focus is on the innovation, being innovative, and the drive for independence. Although marketing should also be innovative, this frequently is not the case. In fact, much of marketing is more duplication than innovation—with companies merely following a successful pattern established by the market leader in such areas as advertising appeal, product design, sales promotion techniques, and the distribution system. Divergence between the two also occurs in the area of internality/externality. Entrepreneurship is much more internally oriented in focus than marketing. All the aspects of the venture must come together in order for a successful launch to occur. This aspect, as well as the other commonalities and differences, is often affected when external financing is involved. The presence of external financing can significantly change the entrepreneurial process by impacting the activities of the entrepreneur and the new venture. With external financing, often an entrepreneur can no longer freely direct and guide the venture as there is now a need to satisfy another party—particularly when it is the one providing the needed capital. This can eventually lead to less innovative, creative behavior, and a more controlled entrepreneurial process similar to that which occurs in many marketing situations. The effect of third-party finance is particularly evident when an entrepreneurial firm issues an initial public offering and becomes concerned about the evaluation by the stock market of its activities as is reflected in the price of the stock.

The third aspect of the marketing/entrepreneurship interface is the role of customer interface. Interfacing with potential customers early on in the innovation process as well as the product planning and development process is a key variable for successful new venture and new product launches. Even though this interface with the customer is important, it is often not accomplished to the extent needed. This reflects the "bag mentality" of the entrepreneur and the large-versus-small-company syndrome. Many entrepreneurs are afraid to obtain market input on their innovation due to their concern that the idea will be stolen and produced by someone else. Although this is indeed possible, since it rarely occurs it is much more important to assume any risks involved and interact with consumers obtaining valuable feedback throughout the new venture creation process. Similarly, smaller companies tend to have more direct interface with their customers and potential customers than larger ones. This, in part, reflects the organizational structure and size. Small firms place more emphasis on their relationship with their customers, particularly when only a few customers account for 80 percent or more of their sales, which is frequently the case.

What conditions are necessary for this marketing/entrepreneurship interface? One of the most important conditions is the type and level of technology involved. Technology companies, particularly those with products at a very high level, tend to achieve less interface with marketing than less technologically-based companies. Similarly, industrial market companies tend to have less interface with marketing than consumer market companies. In spite of these tendencies, both high-technology and industrial companies need marketing. In fact, when marketing is not successfully interfaced with the technology or the industrial market, problems often occur. Success in all areas can only be achieved when the market is identified, listened to, and then served with the correct product offering regardless of the technology or market involved. Another condition affecting the interface is the degree of market acceptance of the product. Companies having a good market acceptance and who are, in effect, market driven rather than technology driven tend to have a better marketing/entrepreneurship interface than those that are technology driven. A third condition is the role of the business plan in the company formation and growth process. When the business plan plays an essential role in the entrepreneur starting and growing the new venture, the importance of the interface is evident and is therefore not only readily accepted but actively solicited and endorsed. Most entrepreneurs develop and use a business plan to start and grow their venture and should therefore understand the importance of a strong marketing/entrepreneurship interface.

The similarities between marketing and entrepreneurship are clearly evident in the overlap between the entrepreneurial process and the product planning and development process. Both processes involve the identification of an opportunity and the development of the business plan. The entrepreneurial process indicated in Figure 10.1 involves four stages—identify and evaluate the opportunity, develop the business plan, assess the resources required, and manage the enterprise. The product planning and development process that evolves into the product life cycle involves the idea stage, the concept stage, the product development stage, the test marketing stage, and then the five stages of the product life cycle—introduction, growth, competitive turbulence, market maturity, and decline (see Figure 10.2). Both of the processes have several common dimensions, the first of which is time. Time is a key dimension in the entrepreneurial process in many ways.

It takes more time than anticipated in starting up a business, particularly in creating the needed business plan. Also more time is required than estimated to achieve the initial forecasted sales and collect the resulting revenues. This reflects the policy of some retail stores of paying with 60 to 90 days of receipt of goods with the variance depending on the time of the month the invoice is received. Similarly, time is a factor in the product planning and development process. One return resulting from successfully integrating the process in an organization is the reduction of the time it takes to go from idea generation to

Figure 10.1
Elements of the Entrepreneurial Process

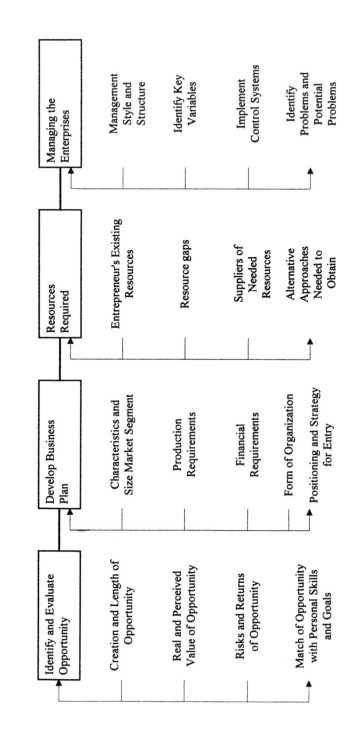

Figure 10.2
Product Planning and Development Process and Product Life Cycle

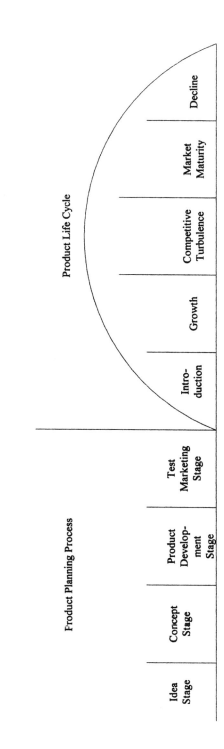

market introduction. This period has lasted as long as twenty years; when it is too long, there is a risk that the product idea will become obsolete or have its potential market captured by a competitive product.

The second dimension involves the size and structure of the organization. An entrepreneurial firm tends to have a flat management structure with multiple informal networks existing. This allows individuals to carry a task through to its completion instead of carrying it forward only up to the point of another individual's responsible domain. By allowing a task to be completed, the employee's desire for self-fulfillment and a feeling of more independence can be at least partially fulfilled within the organization's structure. Also, key non-controlled resources can be better coordinated as the overall good of the organization becomes a paramount decision factor. The size and structure of the organization is also a key dimension in the product planning and development process. This is reflected in the various new product organizational structures that have been developed to increase the effectiveness in conceptualizing and introducing new products.

Alternative organizational structures for new product development generally fall into one of the following four types: new product department, new product committee, new product manager, or venture team. The type of organization most beneficial is a function of the size of the firm, its resources, and its objectives within the context of its product and market.

Multi-divisional firms often use the new product department organization, which is also called the new product development department, product planning department, or market development department. This organizational structure separates the new product development, planning, and management tasks from the existing divisions in the organization in order to centralize the new product decision-making process and eliminate redundancy of tasks across divisions. Management of this central authority is frequently given to a new product manager or director who has a staff position and likely reports to a vice president or executive vice president of the firm. An example of how the new product department might relate to other departments within the organization is indicated in Figure 10.3. Here, the manager or director of the new product department reports to the executive vice president who, in turn, reports to the president of the firm. Although in this simplified organization chart, the new product department is a staff rather than a line function, some feel that new product development should be a line function with the accompanying authority. Whether line or staff, the functions of the new product department generally include recommending new product objectives, developing new product ideas, screening new product ideas, developing new product specifications, recommending and implementing test markets, and coordinating interdepartmental efforts during the evolution process.

Figure 10.3
Relationship of New Product Department to Other Departments

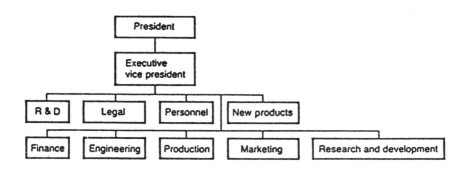

Another approach is using a new product committee. Sometimes different committees are used in the product planning and development process. One committee may exclusively serve the purpose of idea screening, whereas another may be used for business analysis, and so on. Each committee becomes a specialist in a different aspect of the development process. The major problem with the committee approach is that coordination becomes difficult, unless one individual assumes responsibility for all committee decisions.

The product manager concept, innovated by Procter & Gamble nearly 50 years ago, is the third organizational structure for product planning and development. The product manager typically has the responsibility for the planning and administration for a product or group of products. They are specialists in a particular product market, yet generalists in that they are concerned with all the variables in the marketing mix important to their product or product lines. At Procter & Gamble, the product managers are called brand managers, with each one being responsible for one brand as a part of a brand group or product line. A brand manager must work closely with other managers to function effectively (see Figure 10.4). This collaboration of effort is extremely difficult and in some firms may not provide the desired results, especially when brand managers lack the authority to effectively carry out their responsibilities.

Figure 10.4
Typical Interfacing of Brand Manager

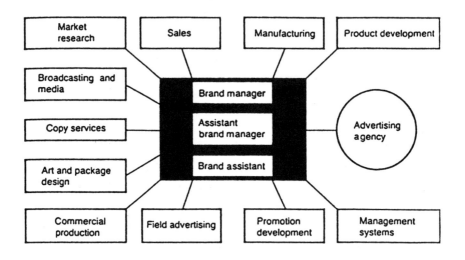

From Robert D. Hisrich and Michael P. Peters, *Marketing Decisions for New and Mature Products*, New York: Macmillan Publishing Co., 1991, p. 97.

Although a significant part of the product manager's duties center on existing product(s), the individual must also assume a role in the development of new products, particularly if the new product idea is an extension of the existing product line. The product manager often conceives of new, unique products because he or she is required to have a comprehensive knowledge of the buying process for the product or products. Although the role of the product manager varies in each firm, it typically includes all aspects of the new product evolutionary process.

The final type of organization for new product development—the venture team—is best suited to the design and development of products that do not fit into the ongoing business of the firm. A venture team is generally separate from the remainder of the organization; has members recruited from various functional areas such as engineering, production, marketing, and finance; moves across the existing lines of authority in the permanent organization; usually reports to the chief executive officer; has authority to make major decisions; remains together until the task is completed; and has freedom from the time pressures and deadlines to foster creativity and innovation.

Figure 10.5 illustrates a venture team organization. Members of the venture team are chosen from various functional areas, with one person given the title of venture team manager, reporting to the division head or some other upper-level administrator.

The third dimension common to both the entrepreneurial and product-planning and development processes is risk taking and uncertainty. The concept of risk taking is important in entrepreneurship, with almost every definition of entrepreneurs at least alluding to its importance. Risk taking by the entrepreneur involves two aspects in terms of the business venture—the perceived level of risk in starting a new venture and the perceived possibility of failure if the venture is not successful. In both instances (due in part to their belief in their ability to influence the attainment of business goals), entrepreneurs are moderate risk takers, having a low perception of the possibility of failure. Risk taking and assessment of the uncertainty are also inherent in the new product development process, as indicated in the fact that at least seven out of ten new products introduced fail within the first few years. The constant focus in the new product planning process is to develop a product and a marketing plan that decreases the possibility of failure. Without any risk taking ability few, if any, new products would ever be introduced in the market place.

The fourth dimension—change—is closely related to risk taking. Inherent in any strong entrepreneurial or product planning and development process is change and the acceptance of change. The more change is accepted and even encouraged in an organization, the more risk taking, innovative, and proactive the firm becomes. This acceptance of change radically impacts both the entrepreneurial and the product-planning and development processes as creativity abounds and newness is a thing cherished and sought after. This allows the entire organization to become more flexible, have a shorter response and decision time, and insist on the timely completion of the tasks involved. An open, supportive culture encourages innovation, moderate risk taking and faster response time while positively impacting the entrepreneurial and product-planning and development track records.

Figure 10.5
Venture Team Organization

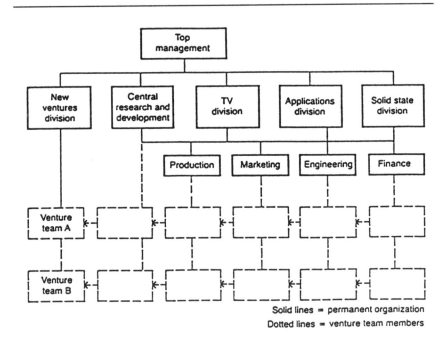

Solid lines = permanent organization
Dotted lines = venture team members

RESEARCH OPPORTUNITIES

There are a number of areas needing research. Although the following list is not exhaustive, research in these areas would greatly improve the understanding of the marketing/entrepreneurship interface:

- The availability of marketing infrastructure and company starts and growth
- The relationship between firm growth and market size limitation
- The differences in marketing strategy in new versus established firms by industry, size of firm, local market area versus regional versus national versus international, desire

for growth, elasticities of marketing activities, funding requirements, and availability
- The entrepreneurs' knowledge of marketing and marketing tools and their perceived need and use of them
- The effect of environmental change on spawning new companies and their growth
- The role of the technology structure and the level of competition on new venture formation and growth
- The nature of the target markets (broad versus narrow) and entrepreneurial success
- The level of technology and innovation in start-up versus established firms
- The relationship between technical sophistication versus marketing orientation and the success rate of firms
- The entrepreneur's marketing decision making (intuitive or scientific) and new venture success.

THE FUTURE

Given the importance of the topic and the research areas needing to be explored, there is ample research opportunity for developing and defining the marketing/entrepreneurship interface. In order for this interface to be developed in a systematic manner, several areas must be addressed. First, a framework is needed to provide the foundation for the research effort. Two possibilities discussed were the entrepreneurial process and the business continuum perspective. The entrepreneurial process framework includes four stages that a new venture goes through: (1) identify idea, (2) develop business plan, (3) identify and fill any resource gaps, and (4) manage the enterprise. The business continuum framework focuses on the product and firm life cycle. These or any other conceptual model need modification to provide a solid conceptual framework for developing the marketing/entrepreneurship interface.

The second area involves several methodological issues and research reporting requirements. The first of these is *defining terms*. In the past, entrepreneurship research has had the problem of a lack of consistency in employing an operational definition of an entrepreneur. The terms entrepreneur, marketing, the units of analysis, and all independent and dependent variables need to be defined and consistently used. Second, the *universe* from which the sample is drawn needs to be fully specified in terms of size, composition, key characteristics, and relevancy to the question at hand. Third, the *sampling frame and size* need to be indicated. Generally, past entrepreneurial research has suffered from extremely small sample sizes drawn more or less on a convenience basis. Whenever possible (except in those research issues where in-depth case studies are appropriate), statistically valid samples should be drawn using a valid technique that minimizes Type II errors. Fourth, a valid *questionnaire* that has been pretested should be employed. Whenever possible questions should be used that have been tested for reliability and/or have been used in previous entrepreneurial research. Most past researchers in entrepreneurship are willing to share their questionnaires for use in other research, which is often not the case in other academic disciplines. Fifth, the appropriate *data collection* technique needs to be employed. Whether this be the more commonly used mail survey, telephone interview, in-depth interviews, or the more infrequently used Q-sort technique, focus group, or repertory grid, the methodology employed needs to be carefully selected and used to ensure that no non-sampling errors occur. Finally, the appropriate non-parametric and parametric *data analysis technique* should be used to test the various hypotheses established and determine the nature of any relationships, particularly any casual ones.

The final area affecting the future of the marketing/entrepreneurship interface is the reporting of the results. Results need to be reported in a clear, concise manner, with studies being replicated and, whenever possible, longitudinal studies undertaken.

REFERENCES

Board of Directors, American Marketing Association. *Marketing News* 19(1) (1985).

Hisrich, R. D., and M. D. Peters. *Entrepreneurship: Test and Cases.* Plano, TX: Business Publications, Inc., 1989).

Hunt, H. K. "Marketing and Entrepreneurship." *Proceedings, American Marketing Association* (1986): 95–100.

11

Pricing for Entrepreneurial Firms

Richard D. Teach and Robert G. Schwartz

BACKGROUND

In 1964, Udell conducted a multi-industry study and found that chief executive officers (CEOs) ranked price only eighth in importance out of 12 policy areas. Although Oxenfeldt (1973) claimed that pricing decisions were highly intuitive and had historically been based on cost considerations, the importance of pricing to a firm's management had changed over time (Samiee 1987). Current literature suggests that pricing strategies are now considered to be one of the most important aspects of a firm's overall strategic business planning process (Ferrell, Lucas, and Bush 1989).

Porter (1980) postulated that there were three generic dimensions to a firm's marketing strategy. These were: cost leadership (resulting in low prices), focus (the careful selection of specific target markets), and product differentiation (having unique products). This generic view of a firm's marketing strategy leads to a diversity of strategic management choices. Rich (1983) found that smaller firms in technology-intensive industries tended to be price followers and provided profitable but higher-priced offerings. Cost leadership strategies were also deemed infeasible for small firms (Dess and Davis 1984).

ENTREPRENEURIAL FIRMS AND PRICING

Teach, Schwartz, and Tarpley (1992) researching price positioning and price leadership, reported that micro electronic companies considered price positioning and price leadership strategies as independent strategies. In contrast to Rich, they found that 37 percent of their sample of CEOs considered their firms to be "low priced" and 29 percent "high priced." In addition, 27 percent of the CEOs considered their firms as having a "price leadership" strategy, whereas only 18 percent reported a "price follower" strategy.

Although the responding firms reported strategies all along the price leadership and price positioning continuums, no single strategy emerged as "the best." However, two strategies appeared to be the "worst." Firms that reported their strategies as "neither a leader nor follower" or "middle of the road" pricing had lower earnings and less sales per employee. The implications of this research were clear for the entrepreneur: select a niche, know the customer, sell system solutions with service, thus increasing value to the customer, with resulting enhanced sales. (Note to researchers: The current importance of pricing to the CEO could be researched. The determination of pricing strategies and their relative import across industries, with the development of longitudinal data bases for future efficacious study, should be noted.)

DEFINING PRICE

Economic Theory of Pricing

From an economist's viewpoint, the price of a product should be set at the point where marginal revenue equals marginal cost. By definition, marginal revenue is the additional revenue received from selling one additional unit of production. Marginal cost is thus the cost incurred as a result of producing that unit. Profitability is also related to this definition.

Figure 11.1 shows that, if the price was set at point B, the marginal cost would be lower than the marginal revenue, thus allowing additional profit to be made from a price reduction to from B to A. If the price was set at point C, the marginal cost would be greater than the marginal revenue creating a loss for the firm on the additional units sold. This, of course, assumes the firm has the capacity to produce at any volume along the marginal cost curve.

Reality does intrude on the theoretical "economic model" of pricing. The theoretical relationships are not valid over time because certain *ceteris paribus* conditions have been assumed that are not constant. The model also assumes that true marginal costs are determinable and continuous, and that consumers respond in predictable ways. Thus, the use of the model for new products may tend to serve as a guideline, but in reality there are few guidelines that the entrepreneur can follow when setting prices for new products.

For old products, pricing decisions that would a priori appear to be made more easily, are not. Consumer responses remain unpredictable. However, although the use of trends to support marketing decisions may lead to forecasting errors, history can provide some useful guidelines.

Figure 11.1
Economic Model of Pricing

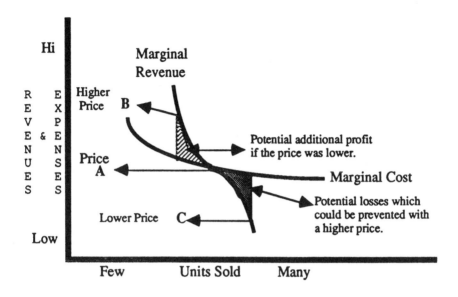

VALUE AND PRICING

Because the economic model of pricing may only serve as a guideline for entrepreneurs, perhaps price ought to be considered from other perspectives. For example, when price is quoted in monetary terms, it is the dollar amount that a willing buyer will exchange with a willing seller. Sometimes goods and/or services are swapped for desired products or services or this exchange is referred to as barter. Perhaps then price should not solely be considered as monetary in nature, but should be related to "value," as demonstrated by an exchange as in the barter situation.

Value is defined by the perceived importance (quality?) of a product or service in the eyes of the buyer. This perceived importance or desirability, that is, "value," sets the upper or highest price the purchaser would be willing to pay. If the price is exactly equal to the product's value, the buyer might be indifferent to the purchase. The greater the ratio of value to price, the greater the likelihood of the willingness to purchase. If the value is less than the price, the product or service will likely not be purchased, a conclusion that is not 100 percent valid due to the emotional, rather than logical, nature of cognitive processes. Thus, the definition of price must account for the human thought as well as the decision-making process, an extremely complex accounting problem.

Cost and Pricing

Many entrepreneurs (and non-entrepreneurs) want to base prices on their costs, thinking that costs should somehow determine the price of products, that is, price is a number times cost. Although direct costs determine minimum long-run prices (otherwise the firm is out of business), many other factors determine the actual selling price for a product or service, thus serving to determine value. (Note to researchers: Certainly, firm economic viability requires that long-run prices create revenues that are ultimately greater than total costs. But, the only up-side barrier to price is the buyer's willingness to pay [value]. Therefore, the key in determining price for a product would be the amount the buyer is prepared to pay under the specific conditions of sale. Thus, research on the sellers understanding of the buyers decision-making process and the buyers' understanding of their decision-making process would be useful.)

LEARNING CURVES AND PRICING

For entrepreneurs developing new products that have sold below cost, there is a dependency on a phenomenon known as the "learning curve" (Day and Montgomery 1983). That is, the direct cost of manufacturing will fall as a function of the log of the cumulative number of units produced. By pricing below initial costs to discourage competitors from entering the market, market share may be gained.

Subsequently, if competitors do not enter the market, they do not learn the "tricks" of manufacturing and discovering the long-run costs. If this occurs, a "low-cost low-price strategy" may work (Ghemawat 1983). However, this strategy fails when new technology is brought to bear on the manufacturing process (or the product) or if the firm overestimates the slope of the experience curve and cannot manufacture the item for the estimated long-run costs.

Economies of scale are often confused with learning curves. Economies of scale refer to spreading fixed costs over additional units of output and lowered variable costs per unit as well. Experience affects both fixed and variable costs. As more units are produced, the firm gains knowledge, is able to be more efficient, and applies its increased knowledge to reducing its costs. (Note to researchers: What is the reality of a firm's use of experience in reducing costs to manufacture?)

KNOWLEDGE AND PRICING

A purchaser's knowledge regarding a manufacturer or distributor impacts price, because knowledge adds or subtracts from perceived risk. Buyers are reluctant to add new and unknown suppliers to their buying lists. A missed delivery, a divergence in expected versus actual quality, slower response times for maintenance or repair or other intangible product attributes may "cost" the buyer more than potential savings. As a result, price alone is rarely the sole determinant in a purchase, but many decisions are made with inadequate and imperfect information.

QUALITY AND PRICING

Quality and its perception impacts perceived value and pricing decisions. It is ironic, but quality is rarely discussed in marketing textbooks; yet quality, from the purchasers perspective, should be defined by the seller in order to determine an offering price. The lack of definition may be because quality is buyer, product, and opportunity specific (Forbis and Mehta 1981) and difficult to determine unless personal selling is involved (which is when personal selling is needed or at least most effective).

The measures of quality can be quite varied. Specific or "hard" measures of quality might include:

1. The expected economic life
2. The expected time to failure
3. Mean time between failures
4. Expected cost of a failure
5. The cost of routine maintenance
6. The expected training costs
7. Operating costs over the economic life of the machine
8. Replacement costs.

There are also "soft" measures of quality. These could include:

1. The reliability of the distributor/OEM
2. The expertise of the distributor/OEM
3. The width of product lines sold or carried
4. The ability to quickly obtain spare parts
5. Previous experience with either the manufacturer or the distributor
6. The reputation of the manufacturer and/or distributor
7. The personal relationship between the buying and the selling employee (firm).

If quality is situation specific, criteria vary. However, an entrepreneur should realize that a buyer's *perception* of quality is a major arbiter of value/price. The buyer might consider a particular product as having more or less quality than a very close inspection might reveal (perception is in the eye of the beholder) or that the manufacturer intended its actual quality to be (again, relative in nature). Both the hard and soft measures of quality come into play.

However, no matter what the entrepreneur thinks, it is the perceived quality that determines the desirability of the product and it is the entrepreneur's job to understand the buyer's decision process.

PRICING IN ENTREPRENEURIAL FIRMS

Substantial marketing-related academic research has concentrated on products in the mature stage of their product life cycle (if position in the life cycle is determinable), with many of those products being produced by mature firms. For the entrepreneur, survey work is costly in terms of both time and money, and interpretations of the likely results are skewed by the entrepreneurs emotional status related to his/her new offerings. This skewing often leads to the "everyone will buy it" response that most entrepreneurs adopt, meaning that the offering is already doomed to failure.

Morris and Calantone (1990) reported that most small and entrepreneurial industrial firms tend to manage their pricing function in a reactive rather than a proactive mode. This not only disadvantages the firm, but also confounds academic researchers!

Consider the problem of Jobs and Wozniak when they first formed Apple Corporation. They faced the problem of determining the value associated with their new Apple II and the subsequent price it should be offered for. There were few microcomputer sales at the time, and those that did occur were not discussed with competitors. Generally only "innovators" purchased the product. Although the Apple II was not the first microcomputer, it was the first one designed for someone other than a hobbyist or technophile and pricing decisions were unclear as to their impact, if not import as well. Other entrepreneurs often face these challenges when innovative products are brought to market.

Fax machines, now common, were available twenty years ago, but the pricing strategies and overall marketing programs adopted by the producers limited the product's appeal. As a result, sales languished for years. Although few, if any, evolutionary technological changes occurred (after the microchip's development) in the 1980s, prices were significantly reduced and a price-based marketplace resulted, with simultaneous extensive product offerings. Thus, as prices fell and product attributes were enhanced, perceived risk was reduced and perceived value increased.

PRICE AND THE PRODUCT LIFE CYCLE

If an entrepreneurial firm competes in a market at a generally "accepted" price level, there are several traditional techniques of pricing likely utilized. One introductory price strategy would be to price products within the competitive range. Another strategy is known as penetration pricing, or pricing the product at a low price in order to gain product entry (or penetration) into the market. It is assumed that the firm will be able to capture substantial market share with this pricing strategy and ultimately both the learning curve and economies of scale phenomena will serve to earn back lost profits.

If there exists a significant learning curve effect, a market share larger than any competitor will also likely result in a lower cost of production and the long-term ability to maintain a low price strategy. (Note: this only works if there exists substantial price elasticity and if competitors do not have, or cannot obtain, a cost advantage when the product is substitutable.)

Another introductory pricing strategy is identified as a skimming strategy. To implement this strategy, the firm sets a substantially higher than perceived value price. The added gross margin makes the firm much more profitable than if the firm had charged a lower price. For this strategy to work there must be some price inelasticity and some barriers to product substitution. This barrier could be simply a lack of knowledge on the part of the customer. It could also be some inherent product advantage or a reluctance of the customer to switch suppliers (perceived risk). Unlike penetration pricing, skimming does not require a cost advantage to be successful. (Note: The product life cycle is a nice pedagogical device, but can a business really "know" what phase they are in?)

BUNDLING

Bundling is a common form of establishing a pricing strategy. In this case, several complementary products are bundled or grouped together and priced as a single unit. Thus, the individual items within the bundle are not priced and customers cannot unbundle them. Direct price comparisons cannot be made. Developers of vertical software frequently use this approach. For certain products, if the bundle is complete, this system of pricing and delivery is referred to as a turn-key operation.

"Everything" the buyer needs is included and the buyer only needs to "turn the key" to begin operations. This technique is most successful if the competitive offerings are not bundled and there is higher perceived leverage related to the purchase of the entire bundle. The primary advantage of bundling to the selling firm is that it can frequently make its normal return on the product as well as the added gross margin from the sale of the additional equipment/service. The primary advantage to the buyer is that all the equipment is designed to work together, purchased from a single source.

PRICE AND THE OTHER MARKETING MIX VARIABLES

Price cannot be singled out as the only factor, or even a unique factor, that impacts sales. There are a number of additional factors that impact sales of a firm's products or services. These are highly interrelated. Khandwalla (1973, 1981) cited advertising, promotion, technology, and price, as domains in which competitive pressure can occur. Issues such as maintenance, performance, and installed base are all important to the industrial buyer of physical products (Kelly and Coaker 1976). These factors combine with media selection, public relations, and the channel selection (Rich 1983), as well as buyer perceptions, to form a very complicated, n-dimensional (not 4 dimensional, i.e., the 4Ps) impact on sales of the marketing mix.

The problem facing the practitioner and academic alike is that the variables in this n-dimensional space are not uniquely related. The buyers' responses to any one marketing variable are highly correlated to the response to one, or many, variables. As research into the marketing-entrepreneurship interface continues, exploring these inter-relationships and their impact on start-up and emerging business strategies will be a primary challenge for academic researchers.

METHODS OF PRICING

The methods used in setting prices vary from situation to situation. Examples are given in the following.

Entrepreneurial Firms Entering Business with Products Similar to Existing Products

Many firms are established by individuals who perceive that they have a better way, or a less expensive way, to manufacture an existing product. Many times this new firm's product has been redesigned in order to incorporate useful new features, or the new design allows one to produce the product at less cost, or it has been redesigned to "invent around" an existing patent. In this situation, the new firm is entering an existing market with a new product that is a direct substitute for an existing product. Pricing, in this case, can be less complicated.

The price of the existing products or the direct substitutes becomes the base line price. The actual asking price for the new entrant may be above this base line, depending on the buyer's perception of the value of the new features. The asking price may be below the competitor's prices if the producer perceives buyer resistance to changing suppliers. Careful attention needs to be given to pricing when entering a new market, and a policy of setting prices below those currently established in the market place is not recommended.

It is far better to bring an enhanced product to market at a similar price than to gain the immediate attention of the older, existing firms, with deeper pockets and longer staying power. Many price wars have resulted, pushing the new firm out of business. Predatory pricing is the legal name for extreme responses by competitors.

Firms Entering Markets with Unique Products

Firms entering the market with a unique product face a most difficult problem in pricing goods. There are no direct comparisons to currently existing products that can be made. In this case, the producer must develop some type of a cost-benefit analysis for the potential customer. Perceptions and value play a key role and the manufacturer or seller needs to determine, as accurately as possible, the customer's rationale for the purchase.

Firms Entering Consumer Markets with a Product Similar to Existing Products

When an entrepreneur manufacturing a new consumer good enters the market, the choice of a distribution channel is paramount and likely determines the required mark ups at the various channel locations. If the manufacturer sells directly to the consumer, although risk of the unknown still exists, a consumer's normal risk is limited to the amount of the purchase price. There are exceptions, as in the case of refrigerators, freezers, and some hard goods (automobiles), but for most consumer products, the cost of product failure is limited to the cost of the product. End-user prices are determined by prices of the existing products. Even if new channels and/or different retail outlets are utilized, prices are still tied, of course, to what consumers are willing to paying for the existing products.

Firms Entering Consumer Markets with a Unique Product

When a firm introduces a unique product to the consumer market, the problem is more difficult than when the market is industrial in nature. Businesses can more easily evaluate their cost savings and/or added capabilities that the new product provides. A new product to a consumer may mean more pleasure (as in stereophonic recordings), less time required in garden care (as in tillers), more freedom in telecommunications (as in cellular phones), or better TV picture quality (as in HDTV). The pricing problem exists in attempting to determine how much a person would be willing to pay for a device with which they have no experience. After the fact, value differences between cellular and conventional phones can be determined. But before the fact, when entrepreneurs need to know, perception and the buyer's decision processes are of paramount importance—and not easy to determine validly (leading to many new product failures).

SPECIFIC PRICING EXAMPLES

Software Pricing

Early in the sales of microcomputers, an entrepreneurial firm was formed to develop and market MSDOS-based accounting software. The firm licensed the source code from an individual software developer for a per-copy royalty, produced the manuals, and sold the program through the traditional channels of distributor to retail computer store to all users, business and final consumer alike.

In order to cover the costs of distribution and support, the retail price was set at about $300 per module and three modules were required to operate a basic system, with a total of seven available. As it was very early in the microelectronics market (1981), the product was a quality product, there were few competitors and extensive effective promotion was undertaken, the firm became well known and the industry leader in its niche.

In the mid-1980s, strong competition developed and prices fell, but the costs of licensing and support increased in the channel, which did not allow for price cuts. Sales fell and the firm became unprofitable. After extensive reflection, the new ownership (1989) undertook a radical marketing step, changed to direct sales, renegotiated its license and slashed its prices from over $2,000 to $199 for the complete package. Support was unbundled from the software package and put on a pay-as-you-go basis. Sales skyrocketed, literally overnight (after the first *Wall Street Journal* ad). The elasticity of demand created by the price decrease once again produced a profitable, rapidly growing firm, now with over $10,000,000 in sales.

Shareware

Free is not a price, and no value might be associated with such a price, but in the software business it is called shareware and it has worked quite well for some firms. Shareware allows users to use the product before paying for it. Shareware programs are copied freely, from one electronic bulletin board or end-user to another. Word-of-mouth is about the only form of promotion utilized. A user reads about a program on the bulletin board and copies it to his/her computer via modem.

The name and address of the selling firm is included in the software along with a suggested price to be paid, if the computer operator utilizes and registers the program. Support is provided to registered users only, along with a charge for the service. Because there are little or no distribution or promotion costs, prices are low, but no mechanism exists to require users to pay for the program, except their desire to have a printed instruction manual and later upgrades.

The authors are friends with one such entrepreneur, who started his company in his college dorm room. The company now has revenues in excess of several million dollars a year and employs a large staff to provide support for the program users as well as the other more traditional products which the firm offers. Although this strategy has worked for this entrepreneur, has it worked for the myriad others?

Specialty Dolls

This doll company is a small, start-up firm manufacturing a line of specialty dolls. The dolls were designed to be educational in order for parents and others to explain many medical details of sickness, accidents, and child birth to children. The dolls and accompanying illustrated books allowed children to "act out" what may be happening to themselves, a sibling, or a friend. The firm faced the problem of establishing a suggested retail price and a channel discount structure before any units were produced. The products were unique and no substitutes existed for them, thus not allowing for price (value) to be initially determined.

Although initially the firm did not want to utilize the normal channels of distribution of manufacturer to toy distributor to retailer, it needed to be sure its prices and gross margin were adequate to eventually support the traditional channel.

One of the firm's officers first contacted a few toy distributors and determined the usual mark-ups for both distributors and retailers. Then, he visited several specialty shops that sold high-end children's dolls. He also interviewed gift shop clerks on price resistance, and spoke with several pediatricians about children's medical concerns and their parent's reaction to these concerns. Based on these discussions, an expected retail price was established. The channel and volume discounts were applied to determine the expected per-doll revenue to the firm. Then the firm set about completing the designs in order to be able to produce the doll at a long-run cost that would be less than the expected revenues. (Design to cost, rather than performance.)

SOME CONCLUDING THOUGHTS ON OTHER PRICING ISSUES

There are two almost universal problems facing entrepreneurial endeavors: the inadequacy of time and the inadequacy of money. Prices need to be estimated and established before products are produced. During the business-planning stages of the start-up, estimates of revenues must be made before the pro-forma statements required by venture capitalists and banks can be developed (for successful start-ups receiving funds from their own and relatives' accounts, the same is true) and before initial funding can begin.

Because the prime ingredients of revenue flows are price and volume, establishing a price schedule is one of the first problems a budding entrepreneur faces. Yet a new firm expends most of its energies on getting their new concept designed and produced. The mundane marketing problems of what price to charge is left until all the costs are known, but all the costs are not known until the product is completed (and price is not a number times cost anyway), when revenues are needed and products must be sold. No one then has the time to establish a well-thought-out pricing policy. Besides, doing customer research requires executive commitment, money, and time, all of which are scarce in entrepreneurial firms! Without it firms are doomed to failure.

One of the major problems in pricing by large firms is product-line pricing. That is, how to equitably price several products that may either directly compete with one another or compliment one another. In the competing case, overpricing one product in a line may cause shifts in demand large enough to alter the costs of all products (cannibalism). Price, in this case, may be used to balance the production process and to efficiently utilize the machines and storage space in a factory.

In complimentary situations, pricing can be used to ensure that the full line is sold. In some cases, a few products may be sold at a loss in order to sell other products that are highly profitable. These problems seldom exist in entrepreneurial or small firms, simply because they seldom have wide product lines. Many entrepreneurial firms are, at least initially, single-product companies.

Derived Demand

In many cases, especially in business-to-business marketing, the amount of product or service demanded is almost independent of the price. The demand for carburetors from the manufacturer of automobiles, say Ford Taurus, is generally fixed at the number of that particular model produced. If the supplier of carburetors increased or decreased the price, the number purchased would remain the same, in the short run. The price of a carburetor is very small in relation to the overall cost of the automobile. In other words, the demand for the carburetor is derived from the sale of automobiles and the price of the carburetor is not a significant factor in the cost of producing that automobile, or in the resulting demand for the car. In the long run, however, a price increase could cause the auto manufacturer to search for a new supplier of carburetors (a shift to elastic demand). This is not a happy situation, or a situation that is likely to be recoverable.

Relationship Marketing

Obviously, it is essential that the entrepreneur attempt to determine what the customer is willing to pay for a product. Prices need to be determined by the customers' perception of the value received. Pricing the product too low reduces the profit potential, but pricing the product too high ensures its failure.

An entrepreneur must by now realize that products are rarely, if ever, purchased exclusively on a price basis. This is true even when the products are direct substitutes for one another and may be technically, or even physically, identical. Issues such as delivery time, terms of trade, historical relationships, and the like, will affect the marketability of a new product when it competes directly with an existing product.

When a firm or an individual purchases a product, a bundle of services is purchased that the product carries along with it. That may be clean clothing, as in washing machines; prestige, as in some automobiles or other high-visibility goods; or "freedom from worry," as provided by warranties and guarantees. Expected on-time delivery and freedom from product failure may be a major reason to purchase from a particular manufacturer or distributor. Purchasers may also be buying certain financial arrangements such as delayed payments, extra discounts for cash, or product tie-ins with other goods or services. The reasons for any particular purchase are many.

Herein lies the difficulty for the entrepreneur. If the entrepreneur has few or no friends in the new marketplace, how does he or she make friends? The technology-based entrepreneur typically believes that the nature of the product is what sells. Pricing is frequently based on the "hard" measures of cost and quality, not the "soft" measures of value. How then, is one to convince entrepreneurs to change their ways?

Many years ago, one of us worked as a supervisor in the new product development laboratory for a Fortune 500 chemical firm. His manager, the lab director, had been the head of commercial development for a $700 million division of the firm. The manager's only marketing advice was "make friends with every potential customer."

Another example of relationship-marketing was shown by a salesperson with limited experience. Her experience was limited to selling commodity-like, electronic distribution products for about one year. Yet, in a recessionary year, in a tough market with severe price erosion, she managed to build her monthly sales from zero to over $100,000. She states that the reason for her success is, "I am very nice to my customers. Even if I miss the sale this time around, they will come back to me because I treat them right." To a competitor, she is a tough salesperson, but her concern for the customer comes through. It's her nurturing of customers that makes her a top salesperson.

For the entrepreneur, having the "right attitude," is paramount and today, "politically correct." Although putting the consumer first, or customer satisfaction, has always been one of the primary marketing edicts, it has now become an accepted pronouncement of the more precocious businesses, thanks to the Total Quality Management movement. It all comes down to treating your customers as clients and "friends." The "golden rule," "the customer is king" or any of a number of other trite-but-true phrases apply. Although a customer orientation may not be sufficient to guarantee success, it is necessary to succeed.

REFERENCES

Abbratt, R., and L. F. Pitt. "Pricing Practices in Two Industries." *Industrial Marketing Management* 14 (Winter 1985): 301–6.

Calantone, R. J., and C. A. di Benedetto. "Defensive Industrial Marketing Strategies." *Industrial Marketing Management* 19 (Summer 1990): 267–8.

Chaganti, R., R. Chaganti, and V. Mahajan. "Profitable Small Business Strategies Under Different Types of Competition." *Entrepreneurship: Theory and Practice* (Spring 1989): 21–35.

Corey, R. J., and D. T. Wilson. "Negotiating Price for Long-Term Relationships. *Journal of Pricing Management* 1 (Fall 1990): 11–18.

Cressman, G. E. "Successful Business Strategy Needs a Consistent Pricing Policy." *Journal of Pricing Management* 2 (Spring 1991): 11–15.

Day, G. S., and D. B. Montgomery. "Diagnosing the Experience Curve." *Journal of Marketing* 47 (Summer 1983): 44–58.

Dunn, D. T., Jr., J. H. Friar, and C. A. Thomas. "An Approach to Selling High-Tech Solutions." *Industrial Marketing Management* 20 (Spring 1991): 149–59.

Ferrell, O. C., G. H. Lucas, Jr., and A. J. Bush. "Distinguishing Market Segments From Added Price Responsiveness." *Journal of the Academy of Marketing Science* 17 (Winter 1989): 325–31.

Forbis, J. L., and N. T. Mehta. "Value-Based Strategies for Industrial Products." *Business Horizons* 24 (Summer 1981): 32–47.

Ghemawat, P. "Building Strategy on the Experience Curve." *Harvard Business Review* 63 (Sep.–Oct. 1985): 143–49.

Grunenwald, J. P., and T. T. Vernon. "Pricing Decision Making for High-Technology Products and Services." *The Journal of Business and Industrial Marketing* 1 (Winter 1988): 61–70.

Holt, D. H. *Entrepreneurship: New Venture Creation.* Englewood Cliffs, NJ: Prentice-Hall, 1992.

Ishikawa, K. *Introduction to Quality Control* Tokyo, 3A Corporation, 1990.

Jain, S. C., and M. V. Laric. "A Framework for Strategic Industrial Pricing." *Industrial Marketing Management* 8 (Summer 1979): 75–80.

Kelly, J. P., and J. W. Coaker. "The Importance of Price as a Choice Criterion for Industrial Purchasing Decisions." *Industrial Marketing Management* 5 (Fall 1976): 281–93.

Khandwalla, P. N. "Viable and Effective Organizational Design of Firms." *Academy of Management Journal* 2 (Spring 1973): 481–95.

Khandwalla, P. N. "The Properties of Competing Organizations." In *Handbook of Organizational Design*, edited by P. C. Nystrom and W. H. Starbuck, 121–34. New York: Oxford University Press, 1981.

McDougall, P., and R. B. Robinson, Jr. "New Venture Strategies: An Empirical Identification of Eight Archetypes of Competitive Strategies for Entry." *Strategic Management Journal* 11 (Nov.–Dec. 1990): 447–67.

Monroe, K. B. *Pricing: Making Profitable Decisions,* 2nd ed. New York: McGraw Hill, Inc., 1990.

Morris, M. H., and D. Fuller. "Pricing an Individual Service." *Industrial Marketing Management* 18 (Winter 1989): 139–46.

Morris, M. H., and R. J. Calantone. "Four Components of Effective Pricing." *Industrial Marketing Management* 19 (Fall 1990): 321–29.

Nagle, T. "Pricing as Creative Marketing." *Business Horizons* (July–Aug. 1983): 14–19.

Oxenfeldt, A. R. "A Decision-Making Structure for Price Decisions" *Journal of Marketing* 37 (Jan. 1973): 48–53.

Patton, W. E., III, Christopher P. Puto, and Ronald H. King. "Which Buying Decisions Are Made by Individuals and Not by Groups?" *Industrial Marketing Management* 15 (Fall 1986): 129–38.

Perdue, B. C., R. L. Day, and R. E. Michaels. "Negotiation Styles of Industrial Buyers." *Industrial Marketing Management* 15 (Spring 1986): 171–76.

Porter, M. E. *Competitive Strategy.* New York: Free Press, 1980.

Prybeck, F., F. Alvarez, and S. Gifford. "How to Price for Successful Bundling." *Journal of Pricing Management* Part 1 in Vol. 1 (Fall 1990): 5–10; Part 2 in Vol. 2 (Winter 1991): 16–20.

Raju, J. S., V. S., and R. Lal. "The Effects of Brand Loyalty on Competitive Price Promotional Strategies." *Management Science* 36 (Summer 1990): 276–304.

Reid, D. A., and R. E. Plank. "A Guide to Pricing in Business Markets." *Journal of Pricing Management* 1, (Fall 1990): 19–25.

Rich, S. U. "Price Leadership in the Paper Industry." *Industrial Marketing Management* 12 (Summer 1983): 101–4.

Samiee, S. "Pricing in Marketing Strategies of U.S. and Foreign-Based Companies." *Journal of Business Research* 15 (Summer 1987): 17–30.

Shapiro, B. P., and B. B. Jackson. "Industrial Pricing to Meet Customer Needs." *Harvard Business Review* 56 (Nov.–Dec. 1978): 119–27.

Shilpey, D., and E. Bourdon. "Distribution Pricing in Very Competitive Markets." *Industrial Marketing Management* 19 (Spring 1990): 215–24.

Stanley, L. R., and C. Nemeth-Johannes. "How Software Publishers Make Pricing Decisions." *Journal of Pricing Management* 2 (Spring 1991): 5–10.

Teach, R. D., R. G. Schwartz, and Fred A. Tarpley, Jr. "Pricing Strategies And Performance In Entrepreneurial MicroElectronics Firms." In *Frontiers of Entrepreneurship Research 1992*. Wellesley, MA: Babson College, 1992.

Tellis, G. J. "Beyond the Many Faces of Price: An Integration of Pricing Strategies." *Journal of Marketing* 50 (Summer 1986): 146–60.

Tellis, G. J. "The Price Elasticity of Selective Demand: A Meta-Analysis of Econometric Models of Sales." *Journal of Marketing Research* 25 (Nov.1988): 331–41.

Udell, J. G. "How Important is Pricing in Competitive Strategy." *Journal of Marketing* 24 (Jan. 1964): 44–48.

Wagner, W. B. "Changing Industrial Buyer-Seller Pricing Concerns." *Industrial Marketing Management* 10 (1987): 109–17.

Yoon, E. "Pricing Imitative New Products." *Industrial Marketing Management* 20 (1991): 115–25.

12

Distribution in New/Growing Firms

Charles H. Davis
and Mohammed Y. A. Rawwas

Distribution channels are primarily set up to perform a set of essential economic functions in society, bridging the gap between production and consumption (Stern and Reve 1980). To manage distribution within a new venture is to manage those activities that bring the marketing function full circle. The core component of the distribution system is customer service. Service to the customer facilitates the ability of the marketing mix ingredients to satisfy consumer wants and needs. Therefore, to be successful, distribution must be an integral part of the management of the marketing function.

However, of all the areas in marketing, distribution management in new and growing ventures provides one of the biggest dilemmas for the entrepreneur. It is a dilemma because the management of distribution activities is an area in which entrepreneurs typically have the least amount of knowledge and experience. Further, they have little leverage in controlling the costs associated with distribution. Thus, it is one area of business that has great potential for causing frustration, impacting cash flow, and ultimately threatening the survival of the venture. (For example, Ballou [1992] estimates logistics costs of 10 to 15 percent for manufacturing firms, and approximately 25 percent for merchandising firms.)

One of the reasons entrepreneurs have found it difficult to acquire the requisite knowledge and experience in distribution management is because the study of the area has been split between two or more disciplines. For so long, the critical and often overlapping components of "marketing channels" and "physical distribution" have been taught and researched from different perspectives, and each has had its own orientation generated from separate disciplines.

Traditionally, marketing has focused on the relationship between the institutions involved in establishing a "channel of distribution" while overlooking the study of the physical movement of products through those institutions. It has investigated the power that exists in channel relationships, including all the cognizant and related component issues, between manufacturer, wholesaler, and retailer. But it has failed to adequately link these behavioral dimensions with the management of the physical flow. Logistics, on the other hand, has focused on how to smoothly manage the physical flow of the product through the channels, and has set out models for the handling of activities such as transportation, inventory, and storage. It has studied the institutions involved with each of these aspects. The transportation discipline, itself a significant economic component of distribution management, has its own discipline, which studies the geographical movement of people and goods by various modes.

Therefore, distribution management has truly been studied and researched in a multi-faceted approach. Yet, this approach by different disciplines has made it a difficult concept for entrepreneurs to grasp and even more difficult to manage. Wagenheim, addressing the National Council of Physical Distribution Management, suggested that if firms are to be successful, distribution must become an integral part of their marketing strategy (Maher 1981).

CONCEPTUAL FOUNDATIONS

Because of the separation of the conceptual approaches, it has been difficult for any one person to develop the level of understanding that is necessary for the efficient management of distribution in most new ventures. This difficulty is readily apparent in entrepreneurs who frequently have problems meeting delivery schedules, bargaining with customers and suppliers, and purchasing proper inventory levels. Each problem can lead to poor cash management and ultimately a venture's failure. The leading cause of business failure is continually listed as poor management. Poor marketing is poor management and causes poor cash flow. Given the size and significance of costs associated with distribution activities, their impact on cash flow is paramount. (See Ballou [1987, 13-16] for cost estimates associated with various distribution activities.) As Timmons (1990) points out at least three times in his Seven Secrets to Success for entrepreneurs: "Happiness is a positive cash flow."

Figure 12.1 describes the way in which this chapter will deal with the topic of distribution management. It conceptualizes the fact that distribution strategies grow out of an understanding of both physical movement and channel behavior. Further, it assumes that the prevailing strategies of management are the result of (1) identifying the relevant management issues in each area to be resolved, (2) the institutions involved, and (3) the prevailing environmental factors likely to influence the institutions and management issues.

For example, an explanation of the physical movement of goods through a distribution network would be as follows: Supplier availability, their geographic

Figure 12.1
Distribution Management Relationships

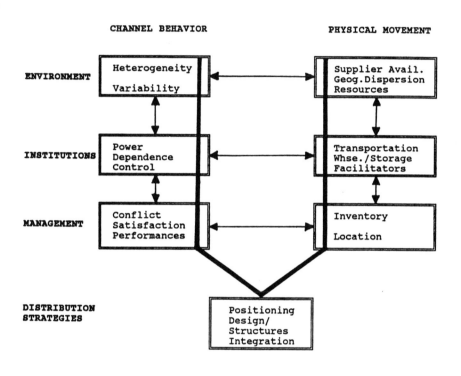

dispersion, and the firm's own resources, create an environment that affects the methods of transportation, warehouses selected, and the likelihood of using third-party facilitators (institutions). Additionally, transportation and warehousing affect the levels of inventory carried and/or the location of physical facilities (management issues). A similar flow explanation is possible for the channel behavior side of any distribution network.

One environment also affects the other. Supplier availability, and their geographic dispersion, play a significant role in determining how heterogeneous the environment is perceived by the entrepreneur. This perception guides management decisions of how the firm will behave in relation to other channel members as it attempts to control the channel. Power, in terms of channel leadership, and the corresponding degree of control, enables the channel leader to achieve economic advantages by influencing how goods are physically transported and stored. Therefore, comprehensive distribution strategies of channel design, integration, and firm positioning all hinge on the ability of the entrepreneur to either manage the system to their advantage, choose to fit within a prevailing system, or design their own separate system.

RESEARCH TO DATE

Research on the topic of distribution management in new and growing ventures is limited. Much of today's research deals instead with large corporate entities. On occasion, research findings are analyzed on the basis of company size—that is, small business. But, rarely does current research focus solely on firm longevity or growth as research variables. Therefore, this chapter will attempt to shed some light on the topics in Figure 12.1 by reviewing research, empirical or conceptual, from which implications about new and growing ventures can be made. Such research may be entrepreneurial, small business, or corporate-based. Where possible within each area, relevant propositions will be presented. Propositions also will be put forth when sufficient information exists to demonstrate the interaction between the various component stages of Figure 12.1. Each proposition is designed to capitalize on the existing research or concept and provide a direction for potential future research.

CHANNEL BEHAVIOR

Much more empirical and conceptual research has been performed in the marketing discipline related to channel behavior rather than to physical movement. To understand the behavior of channel members, it is necessary to explore the impact of the environment on marketing channels, examine the behavioral processes (power, sources of power, manipulative power, counter-vailing power, and conflict) of institutions within marketing channels, and study the effective procedures for managing conflict, satisfaction, and the performance of channel members.

Environment Issues

Marketing channels do not exist in a vacuum. They develop and function in a complex and continuously changing environment. Environmental changes and their underlying forces interact with marketing channels and can have serious influences on the behavior and performance of channel members (Dwyer and Welsh 1985).

Achrol, Reve, and Stern (1983) have applied Zald's (1970) political economy approach to marketing channels. In general, the political economy framework observes the environment in terms of opportunities and constraints. Channel members focus on the environment as a source of information to reduce uncertainty, and to adjust their resources so as to become less dependent on others in the channel (Aldrich and Mindlin 1978).

Heterogeneity

Uncertainty causes a channel member to collect and forecast environmental changes in order to plan marketing channel strategies. These activities include assessing the complexity of environmental conditions and their rate of change (Aldag and Storey 1973). Heterogeneity is the number of environmental entities and their dissimilarity. Heterogeneous environments epitomize greater uncertainty for channel members as a result of the greater difficulty in obtaining and integrating information into their decision-making processes. Empirical research has found that heterogeneous channel environments are associated with more retailer control over marketing decisions within the channel than manufacturers (Dwyer and Welsh 1985). This reasoning leads to the following proposition.

> Proposition 1: The greater the heterogeneity in the environ-ment, the more new retail ventures can control channel marketing decisions, and the less new manufacturing and wholesale ventures can control channel marketing decisions.

Variability

Variability arises from intense interchannel competition, resource scarcity, and instability of demand. It creates a high degree of dependence on suppliers to smooth the demand fluctuations in the environment. Dwyer and Welsh (1985) also found that channels facing variability in the output sector are related with less retailer control over marketing decisions. In line with this concept, the following proposition is posed.

> Proposition 2: The greater the variability in the environment, the less new retail ventures can control channel marketing decisions, and the more new manufacturing and wholesale ventures can control channel marketing decisions.

Institution Issues

Power

Dahl (1957) defines power as the ability of one individual or group to get another unit to do something that it otherwise would not have done. Applied to marketing channels, El-Ansary and Stern (1972) define power as the ability of a channel member to control decision variables in the marketing strategy of another member in the channel. The key to determining which channel members are likely to have the most power in any given situation lies in an understanding of the sources or bases of power.

The sources of power are identified as referent, legitimate, expert, reward, and coercive. Referent power stems from the extent one firm identifies in terms of belief, attitude, or behavior, with another (French and Raven 1959). Congruent goals can be the basis for referent power. As such, the following proposition is possible:

> Proposition 3: Only when other firms in a channel perceive their interests to be closely allied with those of a new or growing venture, is the new venture likely to exert referent power.

Legitimate power of one firm over another is based on their respective roles or positions within the channel (French and Raven 1959). Legitimate power is by no means a pervasive or well-accepted phenomenon in conventional, loosely aligned channels of independent business firms, because there is no definite superior-subordinate relationship. It does, however, exist in more formal, contractually-linked channel systems.

> Proposition 4: New and growing ventures are most likely to be able to exercise legitimate power when they are the

franchisor and can rely on the contract agreement with franchisees.

Expert power exists when one firm possesses superior knowledge or ability within some specific domain (French and Raven 1959). Expert power is quite common in the marketing channel. Manufacturers and wholesalers supply retailers with management assistance. Retailers use their consumer knowledge to influence wholesalers and manufacturers (Mallen 1963).

> Proposition 5: New and growing ventures initially will be subject to expert power unless they develop a technological expertise relevant to other channel members.

Reward power is the ability of one firm to reward conformity to its policies and operations (French and Raven 1959). Rewards are usually financial in nature. Channel members, whether manufacturers, wholesalers, or retailers, will leave a channel if they cannot realize financial benefits from their membership.

> Proposition 6: Because of financial considerations, new and growing ventures are more likely to be the recipients of reward power than the dispensers of such power.

Coercive power is essentially the opposite of reward power. It is the ability of one firm to punish another if it does not comply (French and Raven 1959). Coercive power occurs frequently in marketing channel relationships with powerful channel members dominating weaker channel members, including using threats and coercion.

> Proposition 7: New ventures are likely to be the recipients of coercive power, while rapidly growing ventures may be able to exert limited coercive power, using their growth as a base for punishing others.

Beier and Stern (1969) considered power as a function of the perception of power sources. El-Ansary and Stern (1972) indicated that the power of any given channel member is a function of the sources of power available to them. Hunt and Nevin (1974) developed an interactive model of channel member power. The type and degree of interaction has been the basis for many research investigations. Some found positive interactions between sources of power and power (Hunt and Nevin 1974; Etgar 1976b, 1978b; Wilkinson 1981; Lusch and Brown 1982; Kale 1986), whereas others have found negative or inverse relationships (Brown and Frazier 1978; Schul and Babakus 1988).

Research has also tended to focus on the ability of one channel member to inhibit another channel member from influencing their decision variables (Gaski 1984). This concept is countervailing power, and it comes from the same sources as the original power. Therefore the following proposition is possible.

> Proposition 8: A new venture's countervailing power is not
> likely to exceed its channel power.

Empirical research has documented the inverse power relationship between power and countervailing power (Etgar 1976b; Phillips 1981; Butaney and Wortzel 1988). Two studies (Wilkinson and Kipnis 1978; Frazier and Summers 1986) have found a positive link between countervailing power and other power sources.

Dependence

Emerson (1962) pointed out that social relations commonly entail ties of mutual dependence between the parties. By virtue of mutual dependency, each party is able to control or influence the other's conduct over the things the other party values.

> Proposition 9: A growing venture is more likely to experience
> mutual dependency with another channel member than is a
> new venture.

Based on Emerson's (1962) work, Frazier (1983a) determined a target firm's dependence in a channel relationship with a source firm was a function of the target firm's need to maintain the channel relationship. El-Ansary and Stern (1972) developed the sales and profit approach that noted that the greater the percentage of sales and profit contributed by the source firm to the target firm, the greater the target's dependence on the source. The costs of switching to another alternative source firm also influence dependency (Cadotte and Stern 1979). Translating these concepts to new and growing ventures, yields:

> Proposition 10: A new venture is likely to be the target for a
> dependent relationship with a source firm.

Empirical studies have found a positive relationship between dependence and power (Etgar 1976b; Phillips 1981; Brown Lusch, and Muehling, 1983; Skinner and Guiltinan, 1985; Kale, 1986; Anderson and Narus 1990); a positive relationship between dependence and coercive power strategies (Brown, Lusch, and Muehling 1983; Frazier and Summers 1986; Kale 1986; and Frazier, Gill, and Kale 1989); and an inverse relationship between dependence and countervailing power (Phillips 1981; Anderson and Narus 1980). Thus, the following proposition deals with dependence and power.

> Proposition 11: Within a marketing channel, the dependence of new ventures on a dominant channel member will produce a stronger positive impact on its power and coercive power, but a negative impact on its ability to develop countervailing power.

Control

Both academics and practitioners agree on the importance of channel control and its effect on the overall performance of the marketing channel. Manufacturers strive to control distribution channels for better execution of their marketing strategies. Wholesalers want control of the channel to avoid being bound by manufacturer-determined strategies. Likewise, retailers try to create dependence of other channel members by controlling certain markets or accounts that make them susceptible to influence by the other parties (Beier and Stern 1969). Tedeschi and Bonoma (1972, 15) related control to manipulative power by defining manipulative power as the ability of one firm to control or modify critical aspects of another firm's environment. Therefore, a control proposition for new ventures is as follows:

> Proposition 12: Within a distribution channel, the channel leader will manipulate the sources of power (coercion, reward, legitimate, referent, and expert) over new ventures to gain control.

Management Issues

Conflict

Channel control is accomplished by the exercise of power that may cause a tension among channel members. According to Rosenberg and Stern (1971), conflict in distribution channels is pervasive and stems from the natural interdependency inherent in interfirm exchange relationships. Raven and Kruglanski (1970) define conflict as tension between two or more social entities, which arises from the incompatibility of actual or desired responses. Thus, conflict in the channel stems from an incompatibility of goals. Competition for scarce resources, status, power, or any of a number of other objectives may serve as a basis for conflict, provided that sharing is not seen as possible.

Proposition 13: The more new and growing ventures are seen
to compete with larger, existing ventures, the more likely they
will experience conflict with other channel members.

However, conflict itself is not evil (Thomas, 1976). More and more social
scientists are discrediting the belief that conflict is only destructive. A more
general recognition is that interpersonal and intergroup conflict can serve useful
functions (Blake and Mouton 1964; Boulding 1964; Coser 1956; Deutsch 1971;
Hoffman, Harburg, and Maier 1962; Litterer 1966; Pondy 1967; Schmidt and
Tannenbaum 1969; Thompson 1960; Van Doorn 1966). Likewise, others have
viewed intrachannel conflict as a critical outcome of channel-member interaction,
affecting all aspects of the interfirm exchange relationship, including individual
role satisfaction and functional performance (Alderson 1965; Frazier 1983b;
Robicheaux and El-Ansary 1975; Rosenberg and Stern 1971; Rosenbloom 1973).

Dahl (1957) suggests that conflict is inevitable when firms are functionally
interdependent. In addition, conflict may be influenced by the rewards (i.e.,
reward power) and deprivations (i.e., coercive power). Lusch (1976a) proposed
that the use of noncoercive power sources (reward) is negatively associated with
intrachannel conflict and positively associated with coercive power sources. This
concept and finding has its empirical support (Brown and Frazier 1978;
Wilkinson 1981; Gaski and Nevin 1985; Schul and Babakus 1988; Frazier, Gill,
and Kale 1989), however, it is not without challenge (Etgar 1978a; Frazier and
Summers 1984). Walker (1972) found powerful bargainers are capable of
securing agreements unfavorable to less powerful bargainers, which is compatible
with the hypothesis that the existence of power produces dyadic conflict. This
result was confirmed later by Wilkinson (1981) and Anderson and Narus (1990).
Because of the low amount of channel power attributed to new ventures, the
following proposition is possible.

Proposition 14: New ventures will experience conflict initiated
by larger, more powerful channel members.

Satisfaction

Satisfaction is defined as a channel member's overall approval of the channel
relationship (Gaski and Nevin 1985). Therefore as one would surmise,
satisfaction is strongly correlated with the perception of a channel partner's
cooperativeness (Dwyer 1980; Wilkinson 1981). Conflict would be viewed as
a major source of dissatisfaction in the channel's dyadic relationship (Rosenberg
and Stern 1971). Empirical studies have shown a negative causal relationship
between conflict and satisfaction (Kale 1986; Anderson and Narus 1990).
Therefore, conflict affects the new venture's satisfaction as follows:

Proposition 15: Within a marketing channel, the intergroup conflict between channel leader and new ventures is inversely related to the satisfaction of channel entity.

Satisfaction appears to increase when noncoercive sources of power are used (Hunt and Nevin 1974; Lusch 1977; Michie 1978; Dwyer 1980; Wilkinson 1981). Other empirical studies show that coercion is negatively related to channel member satisfaction (Brown and Frazier 1978; Frazier and Summers 1986).

Proposition 16: Within a marketing channel, the exercise of coercive sources of power by the dominant channel member will be inversely related to the satisfaction of new ventures.

Performance

Performance is defined as the channel member's perceived assessment of its suppliers' services (Foster and Shuptrine 1973). An administratively coordinated channel, produces superior operational efficiency to an uncoordinated system (Etgar 1976a). Therefore, power properly applied should boost channel performance.

Proposition 17: Within a marketing channel, the more power the channel leader exercises over new ventures, the better performance of these members.

Conflict, on the other hand, tends to reduce performance. Lusch (1976b) produced evidence that, in some cases, channel conflict tends to reduce a dealer's operating performance, measured as a return on assets and asset turnover. The findings are important because, as previously noted, channel members, whether manufacturers, wholesalers, or retailers, will leave a channel if they cannot realize financial benefits from their membership. Therefore, the following proposition is put forth.

Proposition 18: Within the channel, the intergroup conflict between the channel leader and new ventures is inversely related to thc satisfaction of the channel.

PHYSICAL MOVEMENT

Environment Issues

Supplier availability

One of the critical environmental issues for any firm is locating and selecting the proper vendor. The new venture may be a small manufacturer whose growth demands new types or better quality raw materials, or they may be a merchandiser seeking new product lines. However, it is more likely that a new venture will be a supplier to a larger manufacturer or merchandiser. Although research has yet to focus specifically on new ventures, there has been significant research regarding the criteria used by purchasing department personnel and marketing managers in vendor selection. Bellizzi (1981) noted that the size of a firm affects purchasing operations. But, the effect of firm size and/or longevity as a vendor selection criteria is undetermined as yet. Jackson (1986) reviewed previous research and concluded the most critical selection criteria to be price, delivery, reputation, reliability, and overall service, in that order. It can be surmised that new ventures will find it difficult to compete on the basis of reputation and reliability, therefore the following proposition may be formed:

> Proposition 19: To compete with the price and reputation of mature vendors, new ventures must have superior delivery and overall service.

Geographic dispersion

The prime area of research into the geographic spread of the distribution network has led to the study of the role of new and small ventures in the international arena. For example, international shippers account for 28 percent of small shippers tonnage. (Murphy, Daley, and Dalenberg 1991) Entrepreneurial new ventures (start-ups) that are international in focus are known to use more aggressive entry into their markets and to develop and control more than a single distribution channel (McDougall 1989). Further, Lucash, Geisman, and Contente (1991) developed ground rules for choosing an international distributor. They included evaluating organizational and technical abilities, knowing their management abilities, studying the cultural differences, and understanding the native or local laws. From this information, one might surmise the following proposition about the physical distribution environment.

Proposition 20: International new ventures tend to make use of international facilitators in their quest to develop and manage distribution across national boundaries.

On a more domestic front, Mix, Massey, and Dunipace (1992) determined that the distance between small suppliers and their larger manufacturing customers has hindered the implementation of "just-in-time" (JIT) inventory methods even though they may be a supplier to the manufacturer's JIT system. This condition suggests:

Proposition 21: Distance is a key factor in the ability of new and/or small ventures to implement key cost saving logistical procedures as part of a larger distribution network.

Resources

Davis, Hills, and LaForge (1985) proposed that smaller firms were more likely to be successful if the entrepreneur understood logistical trade-offs. Lin (1980) and Staples and Swerdlow (1980) pointed out that successful entrepreneurs are those that have been able to find efficiencies in such trade-offs at lower volumes. Dillard, Madison, and Bates (1985) argued that all firms would be best served and find the most efficiency by a simple organizational structure to handle logistical activities—located primarily in one office. Murphy, Daley, and Dalenberg (1991) found in a survey of small firms engaged in international trade, that 75 percent had a logistics or distribution department. The research detailed here focuses on small, not necessarily new, businesses, but consistently suggests:

Proposition 22: To better understand the logistical trade-offs available, the entrepreneur in a new venture, or a single person or department in a growing firm, should be the center of all logistical activity.

Institution Issues

Transportation

Dependability, timely service, and the quality of freight handling are the most important attributes sought by shippers (Jensen, Rottmeyer, and Walker 1985). However, firms with low channel power have less control over the selection of the transportation mode or carrier when dealing with larger, more powerful channel partners (Little 1970). Small retailers send smaller shipments and are forced to pay higher rates (Wood and Johnson 1983). Therefore, it would be prudent to assume that:

> Proposition 23: New ventures have little control over selection of the transportation mode or carrier, and as a result suffer higher costs. To grow, a venture will have to adapt other operations to compensate for this lack of control in order to be perceived as dependable and offering timely service and quality.

This proposition is supported by the finding that small retailers, like their larger counterparts, perceived their transportation charges as too high and that their current level of service as unrelated to those charges (Davis 1986).

Warehouse/storage

Warehousing and storage issues have been studied significantly less than transportation issues. Traditional issues have surrounded determining the number of storage facilities and their location. Economic models as well as new computerized approaches have been developed to assist firms in their pursuit of finding the lowest cost number and locations for storage facilities. Obviously, for many new ventures, these decisions are moot issues.

However, for a growing venture, these issues may be central to growth. With this growth, the issues of ownership of facilities and the diversity of their function also arise. Cost projections and cash flow implications, considering lease versus own versus public storage, play a major role in determining which alternatives are best for the growing venture. The proposition that follows is built on the implications of these needs and the existing models as applied to growing ventures. (See Johnson and Wood [1986, 305–11] and Ballou [1992, 236–49] for a more detailed description of decision models.)

> Proposition 24: As a firm grows, it typically will expand distribution using public warehousing located close to the geographic center of their markets.

Facilitators

Third-party facilitators are those individuals that McCammon (1963) classically referred to as complementors and transients. Complementors neither are nor seek channel membership. Transients are actually in another channel or industry, but move in and out of the channel on the basis of short-run opportunities. Brown (1990) however, has discovered that entrepreneurial opportunities that exist both for facilitators and their use by new and growing ventures. He investigated the new classification of broker—general commodity brokers—and found them to be new small firms created to fill the gap left by larger freight forwarders. They serve small manufacturing firms by consolidating shipments and use contract carriage rather than common carriers to reduce empty mileage for the carrier and lower transportation costs for the small manufacturer.

> Proposition 25: As ventures grow, they will typically become heavy users of facilitating agents to reduce transportation and other logistics costs.

Management Issues

Inventory

The management of inventory is a critical issue for all businesses, and especially so for new ventures. Products that sit and do not sell build substantial costs. Although inventory carrying costs vary from product to product and business to business, the old adage is that on average they run 25 percent per year of the products value. At such high rates, inventory carrying costs can play havoc with the secret to success—cash flow. *Inc.* magazine recently reported that growing companies tied up cash unnecessarily in inventories (Fraser 1991).

Managing inventory also impacts customer service. On the one hand, excess inventory builds costs unnecessarily, but too low inventory reduces a firm's ability to service customer orders in a timely fashion. For these reasons, Economic Order Quantity (EOQ), JIT, Kanban, and a host of other models have been developed to assist in the management of inventories. Sounderpandian (1989) reported and evaluated "do-it-yourself" materials requirement planning (MRP) software programs that are available for smaller firms. However, Mix, Massey, and Dunipace (1992) have determined that small and rural suppliers do not receive all the cost benefits of JIT because of their position in the channel, their resource base, and their geographic location. Fraser (1991) suggests moving to continual or more frequent inventory updates rather than lengthy time periods between inventory reconciliations and assessments will provide greater efficiency. For these reasons, the following proposition was created.

> Proposition 26: In order to grow, new ventures need to pay close attention to inventory levels and costs, constantly evaluating the impact of their policies on the trade-off between cash flow and customer service.

Location

Linking new venture location and the inventory issues just discussed, Mix, Massey, and Dunipace (1992) discovered that small suppliers in rural communities were at an economic disadvantage in applying JIT if they were greater that sixty miles from their customers. Such findings have grave implications for the rural economic development efforts of many communities in the country. In addition to such items as lifestyle in rural communities, economic developers tout low costs associated with such items as low employee turnover and high productivity (based on work ethic), low property taxes, low utility costs, and the like. Thus, the following proposition is possible about new venture location.

> Proposition 27: Operational cost savings must be sufficient to
> offset the economic disincentives in channel logistics in order
> for rural entrepreneurship to be viable.

DISTRIBUTION STRATEGIES

Positioning

As previously noted, new and growing ventures must find unique bases on which to build a base of power if they hope to exercise control over other members of the channel and influence the physical flow of goods through those members. The position of channel leader will rarely be yielded to a new venture unless they become "outside innovators" and develop their own distribution system (McCammon 1963). It appears that new ventures that focus on the international marketplace from start up are doing just that. They have positioned themselves aggressively to develop and control more distribution channels that their counterparts focusing solely on the domestic markets (McDougall 1989). Therefore, the following proposition is possible:

> Proposition 28: New ventures that desire channel leadership
> and power must aggressively focus on developing their own
> distribution systems from start-up.

Design/Structure

Arguing whether distribution strategy influences channel design and structure more than a channel's design influences channel member's strategies is a "chicken and egg" argument. Instead, Peterson (1991) suggests that creatively based strategies that focus on flexibility, speed, and surprise allow small firms to compete on a more equal footing with large firms. Hutto (1992) did not study small firms per se, but did find that "channel design innovations" such as new, non-traditional methods of distribution gave new products a competitive edge in terms of niche marketing, influencing image, spurring impulse purchases, and reducing or containing distribution costs. A survey of *Inc.* 500 companies determined that channel efficiency and product service affect sales volume (Andrus, Norvell, and McIntyre 1986). All of these findings tend to demonstrate why there has been success in the direct marketing and/or more direct distribution of products.

> Proposition 29: New and growing firms must be creative when designing distribution strategies that focus on product service and innovative in their application.

> Proposition 30: New firms can retain channel power and control by developing more direct marketing methods of reaching their consumer targets at start-up.

Integration

Nwachukwu and Tsalikis (1990–91) determined that structural integration had a positive impact on channel members when the channel environment was heterogeneous in nature. However, they noted that more homogeneous conditions hold less potential for negative effects on channel members, and therefore informal collaboration would suffice for coordinating the channel operations and physical movement. This finding is important for new and smaller ventures, because distribution channel alliances, rather than structured integration, will allow the entrepreneur greater independence and control. (Independence and control are two personality features important to every entrepreneur.) Forrest (1990) determined that such alliances help technology-based companies maintain their technological power and competitiveness in the channel. Gales and Blackburn (1990) found that detailed planning between smaller channel entities in cooperation with wholesalers, can reduce uncertainty in the environment and essentially match the achievements of the more structured links of larger, competitive distribution systems. In essence, structural integration is not the only alternative for new and growing businesses.

> Proposition 31: New and growing businesses are able to maintain their independent status and improve their service to a competitive level by better planning and the formation of alliances with other members of the distribution system.

To facilitate the development of these strategic alliances in distribution, it is important that the focus of such plans be on distribution continuity, continual training, and mutual support among all entities (Drozdow 1992). In other words, service, the core concept of distribution, needs to be kept at the forefront of all strategic alliances. Therefore, the following proposition is recommended:

> Proposition 32: In the formation of distribution alliances, power and control are likely to be shared among a greater number of organizations; however all firms, including new and growing ventures, must seek out other distribution partners who have the same commitment to service.

To execute this proposition there must be a greater spread of power. However, it also notes that in order to achieve success, service must be the key focal point.

SUMMARY AND CONCLUSIONS

The preceding discussion of the interface between entrepreneurship and distribution management intended to allow the drawing of several conclusions. First, an effective and efficient distribution system is an important marketing tool for a new venture. If one believes that the objective of marketing is to satisfy consumer wants and needs, then distribution plays an integral part in servicing those needs. New ventures, quite frequently, succeed or fail on the basis of whether or not they provide a desired level of service to their target consumers. Therefore, the management of the distribution system by the entrepreneur to achieve the desired service level will contribute to a new venture's success.

Second, it appears difficult for entrepreneurs to manage the distribution system. Except under rare circumstances, a new venture is not likely to be championed channel leader. Therefore, power and control of the channel may be beyond the grasp of the entrepreneur. And although this conclusion may be modified for growing firms who may attain greater power with their growth, there exists a behavioral question: Given the personality inclinations of entrepreneurs, will they be able to accept and function effectively in a situation where others control so much of their destiny?

The third conclusion is related to, but different from the second conclusion. Substantial costs are associated with the channel operations. New or growing ventures have little power within the channel, and without some creative positioning, have little opportunity to influence channel strategy. Therefore, entrepreneurial ventures are more likely than other ventures to be placed in a cash flow/financial bind. Again, this situation will be somewhat moderated as firms grow. However, can entrepreneurs, who have their personal wealth and professional reputations invested in the business, deal within such structures?

Finally, it should be patently clear to the reader that distribution management is one area that has not been historically treated as a single set of functional activities. For the entrepreneur, it is essential that information and knowledge about managing operations within a channel be complete and coherent. Research needs to be overlapping between environmental issues, institutions, and management decisions. It also should be overlapping between the behavior of channel members and how the physical movement of goods occurs. Further, for the new and growing venture, it is time that research stop looking only at corporate channels or even large versus small firms operating within the channel. Longevity, stage of the firm life cycle, and growth rates need to be variables included in the analyses. Research may even choose to focus on entrepreneurial behavior and its impact on the management of the venture's distribution operations.

It is critical in this day, when every net new job to be created will come from new and smaller ventures, to start analyzing their impact on distribution. It is equally important to assess the opportunities and roadblocks for entrepreneurs created by current distribution systems.

REFERENCES

Achrol, R. S., T. Reve, and L. W. Stern. "The Environment of Marketing Channel Dyads: A Framework for Comparative Analysis." *Journal of Marketing* 47 (Fall 1983): 55–67.

Alderson, W. *Dynamic Marketing Behavior.* Homewood, IL: Richard D. Irwin, 1965.

Aldrich, H. E., and S. Mindlin, "Uncertainty and Dependence: Two perspectives on Environment." In *Organization and Environment,* edited by Lucien Karpik. Beverly Hills, CA: Sage Publications, Inc., 1978.

Anderson, J. C., and J. A. Narus. "A Model of Distributor Firm and Manufacturer Firm Working Partnerships." *Journal of Marketing* 54 (Jan 1990): 42–58.

Andrus, D., W. Norvell, and P. McIntyre. "Marketing Strategy Elements and Business Performance: Inc. 500 CEO's Views." In *Proceedings,* edited by Thomas D. Jensen, 120–23. Southwestern Marketing Association, 1986.

Ballou, R. H. *Business Logistics Management,* 3rd ed. Englewood Cliffs, NJ: Prentice Hall, 1992.

Ballou, R. H. *Basic Business Logistics,* 2nd ed. Englewood Cliffs, NJ: Prentice Hall, 1987.

Beier, F. J., and L. W. Stern. "Power in the Channel of Distribution." *Distribution Channels: Behavioral Dimensions,* edited by Louis W. Stern, 92–116. Boston: Houghton Mifflin, 1969.

Bellizzi, J. A. "Organizational Size and Buying Influences." *Industrial Marketing Management* 10 (Feb. 1981), 17–21.

Blake, R. R., and J. S. Mouton. *The Material Grid.* Houston: Gulf Publishing, 1964.

Boulding, K. E. "Two principles of Conflict." In *Power and Conflict in Organizations,* edited by K. L. Kahn and E. Boulding. New York: Basic Books, 1964.

Brown, J. R., and G. L. Frazier. "The Application of Channel Power: Its Effects and Connotations." In *Research Frontiers in Marketing: Dialogues and Directions,* edited by Subhash C. Jain, 266–70. Chicago: American Marketing Association, 1978.

Brown, J. R., R. F. Lusch, and D. D. Muehling. "Conflict and Power-Dependence Relations in Retailer-Supplier Channels." *Journal of Retailing* 59 (Winter 1983): 53–80.

Brown, T. A. "Size and Operating Characteristics of Property Brokers." *Transportation Journal* 29 (Summer 1990): 52–57.

Butaney, G., and L. H. Wortzel. "Distributor Power Versus Manufacturer Power: The Customer Role." *Journal of Marketing,* 52 (Jan. 1988): 52–63.

Cadotte, E., and L. Stern. "A Process Model of Interorganizational Relations in Marketing Channels." In *Research in Marketing, Vol. 2,* edited by Jagdish Sheth. Greenwich, CT: JAI Press, Inc., 1979.

Coser, L. *The Functions of Social Conflict.* New York: The Free Press, 1956.

Dahl, R. A. "The Concept of Power." *Behavioral Science* 2 (July 1957): 201–18.

Davis, C. H. "Small Versus Large Retailer Costs and Perceptions of Transportation Rates and Services." *Proceedings,* edited by Thomas D. Jensen, 296–98. Southwestern Marketing Association, 1986.

Davis, C. H., G. E. Hills, and R. W. LaForge. "The Marketing/Small Enterprise Paradox: A Research Agenda." *International Small Business Journal* 3 (Spring 1985): 31–42.

Deutsch, M. "Toward an Understanding of Conflict." *International Journal of Group Tensions* 10 (Jan.-Mar. 1971): 42–54.

Dillard, J. E. Jr., D. L. Madison, and D. L. Bates. "A Case For A Simple Logistic Organization Structure." *Proceedings,* edited by J. C. Crawford and Barbara C. Garland, 204–7. Southwestern Marketing Association, 1985.

Drozdow, N. "Wisdom from Wharton: The Distribution Decade." *Chief Executive* (Mar. 1992): 62–64.

Dwyer, R. F. "Channel-Member Satisfaction: Laboratory Insights." *Journal of Retailing* 56 (Summer 1980): 45–65.

Dwyer, R. F., and N. A. Welsh. "Environmental Relationships of the Internal Political Economy of Marketing Channels." *Journal of Marketing Research* (Nov 1985): 397–414.

El-Ansary, A. I., and L. W. Stern. "Power Measurement in the Distribution Channel." *Journal of Marketing Research* 9 (Feb 1972): 47–52.

Emerson, R. M. "Power-Dependence Relations," *American Sociological Review* 27 (Feb 1962): 31–41.

Etgar, M. "Intrachannel Conflict and Use of Power." *Journal of Marketing Research* 15 (May 1978a): 273–74.

Etgar, M. "Selection of an Effective Channel Control Mix." *Journal of Marketing* 42 (July 1978b): 53–58.

Etgar, M. "Effects of Administrative Control on Efficiency of Vertical Marketing Systems." *Journal of Marketing Research,* 13 (Feb. 1976a): 12–24.

Etgar, M. "Channel Domination and Countervailing Power in Distributive Channels." *Journal of Marketing Research* 13 (Aug. 1976b): 254–62.

Forrest, J. E. "Strategic Alliances and the Small Technology Based Firm." *Journal of Small Business Management* 28 (July 1990): 37–45.

Foster, J. R., and F. K. Shuptrine. "Using Retailers' Perceptions of Channel Performance to Detect Potential Conflict." In *Increasing Marketing Productivity and Conceptual and Methodological Foundations of Marketing,* edited by Thomas V. Greer. Chicago: American Marketing Association, 1973.

Fraser, J. A. "Hidden Cash." *Inc.* 13 (Feb. 1991): 81–82.

Frazier, G. L. "Interorganizational Exchange Behavior in Marketing Channels: A Broadened Perspective." *Journal of Marketing* 47 (Fall 1983a): 68–78.

Frazier, G. L. "On the Measurement of Interfirm Power in Channels of Distribution." *Journal of Marketing Research* 20 (May 1983b): 158–66.

Frazier, G. L., J. D. Gill, and S. H. Kale. "Dealer Dependence Levels and Reciprocal Actions in a Channel of Distribution in a Developing Country." *Journal of Marketing* 53 (Jan. 1989): 50–69.

Frazier, G. L., and J. O. Summers. "Interfirm Influence Strategies and Their Application within Distribution Channels." *Journal of Marketing 48* (Summer 1984): 43–55.

Frazier, G. L., and J. O. Summers. "Perceptions of Interfirm Power and its Use Within a Franchise Channel of Distribution." *Journal of Marketing Research* 23 (May 1986): 169–76.

French, J. R. P., and B. Raven. "The Bases of Social Power." In *Studies in Social Power*, edited by Dorwin Cartwright. Ann Arbor, MI: University of Michigan Press, 1959.

Gales, L. M., and R. S. Blackburn. "An Analysis of the Impact of Supplier Strategies and Relationships on Small Retailer Actions, Perceptions, and Performance." *Entrepreneurship: Theory and Practice* 15 (Fall 1990): 7–21.

Gaski, J. F. "The Theory of Power and Conflict in Channels of Distribution." *Journal of Marketing* 48 (Summer 1984): 9–29.

Gaski, J. F., and J. R. Nevin. "The Differential Effects of Exercised and Unexercised Power Sources in a Marketing Channel." *Journal of Marketing Research* 22 (May 1985): 130–42.

Hoffman, L. R., E. Harburg, and N. R. F. Maier. "Differences and Disagreement as factors in creative Group Problem Solving." *Journal of Abnormal and Social Psychology* (Mar. 1962): 64, 206–14.

Hunt, S. D., and J. R. Nevin. "Power in a Channel of Distribution: Sources and Consequences." *Journal of Marketing Research* 11 (May 1974): 186–93.

Hunt, S. D., N. M. Ray, and V. R. Wood. "Behavioral Dimensions of Channels of Distribution: Review and Synthesis." *Journal of the Academy of Marketing Science* (Summer 1985): 1–24.

Hutto, A. "Exploring Why Manufacturers Implement Channel Design Innovations." *Proceedings*, edited by Robert L. King. Southern Marketing Association, (1992): 337–40.

Jackson, R. W. "Vendor Selection Criteria: Which are the Most Important." In *Proceedings*, edited by Thomas D. Jensen. Southwestern Marketing Association (1986): 235–37.

Jensen, T. D., L. W. Rottmeyer, and T. Walker. "Empirically Derived Attributes Utilized by Shippers for the Selection of a Motor Carrier." In *Proceedings*, edited by John C. Crawford and Barbara C. Garland. Southwestern Marketing Association (1985): 208–11.

Johnson, J. C., and D. F. Wood. *Contemporary Physical Distribution and Logistics*. New York: MacMillan Publishing Co., 1986.

Kale, S. H. "Dealer Perceptions of Manufacturer Power and Influence Strategies in a Developing Country." *Journal of Marketing Research* 23 (Nov. 1986): 387–93.

Lin, E. "Inventory Control System for Small Business." *American Journal of Small Business* (Spring 1980) 11–19.

Litterer, J. A. "Conflict in Organizations: A Reexamination." *Academy of Management Journal* 9 (Sep. 1966): 178–86.

Little, R. W. "The Marketing Channel: Who Should Lead This Extra-Corporate Organization?" *Journal of Marketing* (Jan. 1970): 31–38.

Lucash, R. M., J. Geisman, and W. Contente. "Choosing an Overseas Distributor." *Small Business Reports* 16 (Aug. 1991): 68–71.

Lusch, R. F. "Franchisee Satisfaction: Causes and Consequences." *International Journal of Physical Distribution* 7 (Feb. 1977): 128–40.

Lusch, R. F. "Sources of Power: Their Impact on Intrachannel Conflict." *Journal of Marketing Research* 13 (Nov 1976a): 382–90.

Lusch, R. F. "Channel Conflict: Its Impact on Retailer Operating Performance." *Journal of Retailing* 52 (Summer 1976b): 3–12, 89–90.

Lusch, R. F., and J. R. Brown. "A Modified Model of Power in the Marketing Channel." *Journal of Marketing Research* 19 (Aug. 1982): 312–23.

Maher, P. "Distribution Key to Strategy." *Industrial Marketing,* 66 (Dec. 1981): 29–30.

Mallen, B. "A Theory of Retailer-Supplier Conflict, Control, and Cooperation." *Journal of Retailing* (Summer 1963): 31.

McCammon, B. C., Jr. "Alternative Explanations of Institutional Change and Channel Evolution." In *Toward Scientific Marketing*, edited by Stephen A. Greyser. Chicago: American Marketing Association, 1963.

McDougall, P. P. "International Versus Domestic Entrepreneurship: New Venture Strategic Behavior and Industry Structure." *Journal of Business Venturing* 4 (Nov. 1989): 387–400.

Michie, D. "Managerial Tactics: An Alternative Explanation of Warranty Satisfaction in a Channel of Distribution." *In Research Frontiers in Marketing: Dialogue and Directions*, Subhash Jain, 260–65. Chicago: American Marketing, 1978.

Mix, R. A., T. K. Massey, and R. A. Dunipace. "Proposed Diseconomic Consequences of Adopting Just-In-Time in the Channel: Are Suppliers Selling Goods or Are They Being Sold JIT?" *Proceedings,* edited by Robert L. King. Southern Marketing Association (1992): 346–50.

Murphy, P., J. Daley, and D. Dalenberg. "Smaller Shippers Play Important Global Role." *Transportation and Distribution* 32 (Dec. 1991): 41–43.

Nwachukwu, O. C., and J. Tsalikis. "Environmental Heterogeneity, Strategy-Making, Structure and Small Business Performance: A Path Analytic Model." *Journal of Applied Business Research* 7 (Spring 1990–91): 38–44.

Peterson, R. T. "Small Firms Use Creativity to Compete with the Big Guys." *Marketing News* 25 (Apr. 15, 1991): 7.

Phillips, L. W. "Assessing Measurement Error in Key Informant Reports: A Methodological Note on Organizational Analysis in Marketing." *Journal of Marketing Research* 18 (Nov. 1981): 395–415.

Pondy, L. R. "Organizational Conflict: Concepts and Models." *Administrative Science Quarterly* 12 (Sep. 1967): 296–320.

Raven, B. H., and A. W. Kruglanski. "Conflict and Power." In *The Structure of Conflict*, edited by Paul Swingle, 69–109. New York: Academic Press, Inc., 1970.

Robicheaux, R., and A. El-Ansary. "A General Model for Understanding Channel Member Behavior." *Journal of Retailing* 52 (Winter 1975): 13–30, 90–94.

Rosenberg, L. J., and L. W. Stern. "Conflict Measurement in the Distribution Channel." *Journal of Marketing Research* 8 (Nov. 1971): 437–42.

Rosenbloom, B. "Conflict and Channel Efficiency: Some Conceptual Models for the Decision-Maker." *Journal of Marketing* 37 (July 1973): 26–30.

Schmidt, W. H., and R. Tannenbaum. "The Management of Differences." *Harvard Business Review* (Nov.–Dec. 1969): 38, 107–15.

Schul P. L., and E. Babakus. "An Examination of the Interfirm Power-Conflict Relationship: The Intervening Role of the Channel Decision Structure." *Journal of Retailing* 64 (Winter 1988): 381–404.

Skinner, S., and J. Guiltinan. Perceptions of Channel Control." *Journal of Retailing* 61 (Winter 1985): 65–88.

Sounderpandian, J. "MRP on Spreadsheets: A Do-It-Yourself Alternative for Small Firms." *Production and Inventory Management* 30 (Second Quarter 1989): 6–11.

Staples, W. A., and R. Swerdlow. "Planning and Budgeting for Effective Retail Merchandise Management" (Oct. 1980): 1–6.

Stern, L. W., and T. Reve. "Distribution Channels as political Economies: A Framework for Comparative Analysis" (Summer 1980): 52–64.

Tedeschi, J. T., and T. V. Bonoma. "Power and Influence: An Introduction." In *The Social Influence Process*, edited James T. Tedeschi, 1–49. Chicago: Aldine-Atherton, Inc., 1972.

Thomas, K. "Conflict and Conflict Management." In *Handbook of Industrial and Organizational Psychology*, edited by Marvin D. Dunnette, 889–935. Chicago: Rand McNally, 1976.

Thompson, J. D. "Organizational Management of Conflict." *Administrative Science Quarterly* 4 (Mar 1960): 389–409.

Timmons, J. A. *New Venture Creation*. Homewood, IL: Richard D. Irwin, 1990.

Tosi, H., R. Aldag, and R. Storey. "On the Measurement of the Environment: An Assessment of the Lawrence and Lorsch Environmental Uncertainty Scale." *Administrative Science Quarterly* 18 (1973): 27–36.

Van Doorn, J. A. A. "Conflict in Formal Organizations." In *Conflict in Society*, edited by A. de Reuck and J. Knight, 111–33. Boston: Little, Brown, 1966.

Walker, O. C., Jr. "The Effects of Learning on Bargaining Behavior." In *1972 Combined Proceedings,* edited by F. C. Allvine, 194–99. Chicago: American Marketing Association, 1972.

Wilkinson, I. F. "Power, Conflict, and Satisfaction in Distribution Channels— An Empirical Study." *International Journal of Physical Distribution and Materials Management* 11(7), (1981): 20–30.

Wilkinson, I. F., and D. Kipnis. "Interfirm Use of Power." *Journal of Applied Psychology* (1978): 15–20.

Wood, D. F., and J. C. Johnson. *Contemporary Transportation.* Tulsa, OK: Penn Well Co., 1983.

Zald, M. N. *Organizational Change: The Political Economy of the YMCA.* Chicago: University of Chicago Press, 1970.

13

Entrepreneurship and the Sales Function

*Michael H. Morris, Raymond W. LaForge,
and Thomas N. Ingram*

INTRODUCTION

A discussion of entrepreneurship and the sales function requires definitions of important terms. Consistent with the other chapters in this book, we define entrepreneurship as the process of creating something different, with value, by devoting the necessary time and effort; assuming the accompanying financial, psychic, and social risks; and receiving the resulting rewards of monetary and personal satisfaction.

The sales function consists of two major elements: personal selling and sales management. Personal selling includes the personal communication aspects of a firm's promotional mix. The other promotional tools, such as advertising and sales promotion, are differentiated from personal selling by being the non-personal, mass communication portions of a promotional mix. Sales management is simply the management of a firm's personal selling function (Ingram and LaForge 1992).

Sales researchers have largely ignored the entrepreneurship area. We are unaware of any studies that have examined personal selling or sales management for new ventures. Occasionally, researchers have presented some analyses that compare the sales management activities of smaller versus larger firms. Although personal selling and sales management may be important in new, entrepreneurial ventures, the reverse is also true. There is a role for entrepreneurship within the sales function itself, not only in start-up firms but in companies of all sizes and types. In fact, the sales function has the potential of being one of the most entrepreneurial areas within a company.

A considerable amount has been written about the need for companies to integrate entrepreneurship into their daily operations (e.g., Brandt 1986; Morris and Trotter 1990; Pinchot 1985). Rapid and threatening changes in the external environments of firms are creating a need for greater organizational flexibility, higher rates of new product and process development, and a more rapid ability to respond to marketplace demands. Companies are flattening their structures, eliminating middle management, streamlining policies and procedures, broadening job responsibilities, loosening control systems, and experimenting with new types of group and individual rewards (Cornwall and Perlman 1990; Peters 1988; Waterman 1987).

The ability of managers to get their firms to become more entrepreneurial ultimately depends on finding ways to integrate the attitudes and behaviors of the entrepreneur into traditional corporate functions (Brandt 1986; Kanter 1983; Morris, Avila, and Teeple 1990; Pinchot 1985). This means developing entrepreneurial approaches to marketing, finance, production, research and development (R & D), and other functional areas and fostering entrepreneurial thinking in these areas on an ongoing basis.

The need for entrepreneurship is especially critical in the sales function. Sales is a boundary function and, arguably, the single greatest source of ongoing interaction between a firm and its external environment. Turbulence in the external environment creates both opportunities and threats for the firm. The sales function is, accordingly, in a unique position to recognize opportunities, especially those involving customers, their needs, and their buying processes (Khandwalla 1977; Murray 1981).

The purpose of this chapter is to examine relationships between entrepreneurship and the sales function. Because of the lack of research investigating the sales function for new ventures, our focus is on examining the potential role of entrepreneurship in the sales function for both new ventures and established firms. Our premise is that entrepreneurship has much in common with the sales function and that promoting entrepreneurial behavior within the sales function is important for many types of firms, especially those operating in complex and dynamic selling environments. We begin by defining entrepreneurial selling and sales management. Then, important relationships between entrepreneurship and personal selling and entrepreneurship and sales management are discussed. Obstacles to achieving entrepreneurship within the sales function and limits to entrepreneurship in the sales function are then examined. We conclude by presenting several propositions to guide future research in this area.

ENTREPRENEURIAL SELLING AND SALES MANAGEMENT

Consistent with our earlier definition of entrepreneurship, entrepreneurial selling and sales management can be defined as the creation of value by combining unique combinations of resources so as to exploit sales-related opportunities. Thus, when salespeople uncover a new segment of users for a product by proposing a simple product modification, or when they design a novel approach for qualifying leads that improves their close rate by 20 percent, they are being entrepreneurial. Similarly, a sales manager who champions a unique approach to designing sales teams to better address customer needs is demonstrating an entrepreneurial orientation. Entrepreneurial selling and sales management are of potential importance to new and existing as well as large and small firms.

Entrepreneurial attitudes and behavior have been conceptualized as consisting of three underlying dimensions: innovation, risk-taking, and proactiveness (Covin and Slevin 1989; Miller and Friesen 1983; Morris and Paul 1987). Because different amounts of innovation, risk, and proactive behavior are involved in a given entrepreneurial event, varying degrees of entrepreneurship become possible. This suggests that some of the activities of salespeople and sales managers might be highly entrepreneurial, whereas others are only modestly so. The entrepreneurial sales organization produces a continual flow of activities representing numerous points along the entrepreneurial continuum.

For the sales professional, entrepreneurship involves both a way of thinking and a type of behavior. Attitudinally, those in sales should think of themselves as entrepreneurs, which implies a willingness to be creative, to take calculated risks, and to be action oriented. Behaviorally, entrepreneurship involves a process (Stevenson et al. 1989). Within sales, it is the process of identifying opportunities, developing innovative business solutions, assessing and acquiring the necessary resources, and then following through with implementation.

ENTREPRENEURSHIP AND PERSONAL SELLING

There are many parallels between entrepreneurship and personal selling. We discuss similarities between the characteristics of entrepreneurs and salespeople, the processes of entrepreneurship and personal selling, and the development and management of new ventures and sales territories.

Characteristics of Entrepreneurs and Salespeople

Attempting to identify the characteristics of successful entrepreneurs was a favored research topic in the early 1980s. Although the volume of work on the subject is impressive, a decade later there remains much controversy and little consensus. Researchers have attempted to develop a profile of the "typical" entrepreneur, and to distinguish him/her from corporate managers (or society at large) on the basis of psychological traits and personal descriptors (e.g.,

Brockhaus 1982; Brockhaus and Horwitz 1986). The findings have failed to produce a single profile, instead suggesting a number of different entrepreneurial "types" may exist. However, it does appear that entrepreneurs do share certain traits, and that these traits differentiate them as a group from managers.

A similar research tradition has evolved in the personal selling literature, also producing mixed and controversial results. Again, although no one stereotype of the successful salesperson has been identified, certain personal characteristics and traits appear to distinguish high-performing from low-performing salespeople (Churchill et al. 1985; Ford et al. 1988). Many of the characteristics identified account for fairly small percentages of the variance in sales performance, but their impact is statistically significant. There is also evidence that the relative importance of a given characteristic varies as a function of the type of sales position being examined (e.g., new account selling versus trade selling).

Table 13.1 presents summary lists of traits and characteristics that have been associated with entrepreneurs and successful salespeople. The traits themselves are listed in no particular order, but an attempt has been made to demonstrate parallels between the two sets. These parallels are striking and, in fact, most of the traits are identical. Although it might be argued that some of the traits are critical for any number of occupational pursuits, the degree of similarity is so extensive as to suggest that entrepreneurs and salespeople are the same type of people.

One implication of these similarities is that efforts to foster entrepreneurial thinking among salespeople makes sense, and salespeople might naturally be expected to demonstrate entrepreneurial behaviors. Traits and characteristics such as those identified in Table 13.1 are probably not genetically endowed, but are learned over a period of time. The challenge to sales organizations is to create work environments that both permit and foster the development and manifestation of such traits.

The Entrepreneurship and Personal Selling Processes

Entrepreneurship involves people such as those just described, but it also involves a process. In fact, the prevailing conceptualization of entrepreneurship in the past decade has been as a process that can be managed and that has applicability in organizations both large and small (Stevenson et al. 1989). Once again, a parallel can be drawn with personal selling, which has also been conceptualized as a process (Weitz, Castleberry, and Tanner 1992).

The process of entrepreneurship begins with opportunity identification and assessment, as does the personal selling process. When prospecting for customers, the salesperson is attempting to uncover opportunity in terms of new

Table 13.1
Common Characteristics of Entrepreneurs and Salespeople

- Achievement oriented
- Persistent
- Persuasive
- Assertive
- Take initiative
- Versatile
- Perceptive
- Energetic
- Self confident
- Internal locus of control
- Independent
- Calculated risk taker
- Creative
- Resourceful
- Opportunity seeker
- Comfortable with ambiguity
- Hard worker
- Well organized

---

accounts or existing accounts with untapped needs. Assessing the nature and potential of an opportunity is similar to evaluating and qualifying prospects. The salesperson must determine the willingness and ability of prospects to buy, and establish their long-term potential. Priorities must be established in terms of which business to pursue.

Next, the entrepreneur develops a business concept, which is analogous to the salesperson developing and delivering a unique selling proposition. Both the concept and the proposition must be designed around the principle of value creation for a customer. Much information may be gathered regarding the needs, requirements, and buying behaviors of prospects, especially in planning how to approach an account. The delivery of the selling proposition can also involve considerable creativity in getting to the right person(s), obtaining sufficient time with the prospect, and even arranging to meet with prospects at neutral locations.

The entrepreneur then assesses and acquires the resources necessary to implement the business concept. The salesperson is also making resource decisions, including how to allocate his/her time and sales budget. In addition, salespeople sometimes must go back to their own firms and argue for special price deals, different delivery arrangements, additional after-the-sale servicing, and even product modifications, all to satisfy a customer. The ability to obtain such resources can require ingenuity and persistence on the part of the salesperson.

The final step in the entrepreneurial process involves managing and harvesting the venture. This step is not unlike the post-sale activities of a salesperson. The challenge is not simply to ensure the customer is satisfied with a transaction but to build a long-term relationship, which entails ongoing investments of differing types and amounts over time.

Despite these similarities between the two processes, many sales transactions are fairly non-entrepreneurial, and many sales activities are repetitive and routine. However, it should be remembered that entrepreneurship occurs in varying degrees and amounts. A given venture may be highly entrepreneurial or only nominally so. A given entrepreneur may continually innovate and take risks, or do so rarely. The implication is that salespeople should recognize the entrepreneurial potential of the sales process and introduce varying degrees and amounts of entrepreneurial behavior, depending on the sales opportunities available at a given point in time. Moreover, opportunity can present itself to the proactive salesperson at any one of the stages in a given process.

Entrepreneurial Ventures and Sales Territories

Perhaps the most important aspect of the analogy between entrepreneurship and personal selling lies in the nature of the tasks that comprise each of these occupational pursuits (see Table 13.2). Entrepreneurship offers certain advantages to the individual, especially when compared to traditional corporate management.

These advantages include independence, personal freedom, ownership of one's accomplishments, variety and challenge in one's daily work, and the potential for significant financial gain, among others. There are, of course, concomitant disadvantages, such as the personal financial risk and work-related stress the individual typically endures.

An examination of the job of a salesperson as he/she manages a sales territory produces the same set of advantages, and some of the same disadvantages. Salespeople exercise significant freedom of action, spending most of their time in the field without direct supervision. They organize their own time and do

Table 13.2
Common Activities of Entrepreneurs and Salespeople

- Deal with a variety of both routine and nonroutine tasks on a daily basis
- Work independently with a great degree of personal freedom
- Perform challenging work due to high level of business uncertainty
- Operate in ambiguous situations
- Develop creative solutions to business problems
- Driven by opportunities rather than resources
- Work under significant pressure and stress
- Receive fairly immediate feedback from job performance
- Define success largely in measurable, financial terms
- Derive much of income from financial performance
- Organize time and work schedule
- Responsible for accomplishments

the job in their own way, so long as they produce satisfactory results (Churchill, Ford, and Walker 1990). Their performance is largely based on their own efforts, and they typically receive personal recognition for that performance. The fact that each customer has different needs, problems, and buying behaviors indicates the sales job has considerable variety and challenge. Also, salespeople commonly earn part or all of their income through some type of incentive compensation. As such, some sales professionals earn six-figure annual incomes, amounts that exceed the compensation of their managers. The point is not simply that there is great income potential, but that their own efforts determine how much of that potential is reached, which introduces both variability and uncertainty into the sales job.

A sales person managing his/her territory deals with a fair amount of ambiguity, much like the entrepreneur. Sales may or may not happen, whereas customer requirements and buying behaviors can not only be difficult to decipher but are continually changing. A potential deal might fall apart after months of effort, whereas another may close with only a modicum of work. Many leads prove to be dead ends, just as the entrepreneur may experiment with a variety of approaches to a problem without success. Being well organized in terms of time management, account prioritization, call planning, and follow-up activity is a key to sales success, much as organization appears to distinguish successful from unsuccessful entrepreneurs (Brandt 1982). Moreover, the salesperson is continually jumping from activity to activity, such that a given day might include some prospecting, first-time calls, paperwork, a follow-up call on an unclosed account, a service call to a current customer, direct mail correspondence, complaint handling, and so forth. In the same vein, the entrepreneur may jump from overseeing production to dealing with payroll, handling customer calls, addressing an employee problem, and fixing a piece of equipment in a given day. And, it is not unusual for the salesperson and the entrepreneur to share a mutual disdain for the extensive paperwork with which each must deal.

Ultimately, the end result in both sales and entrepreneurship is a function of the personal drive, initiative, discipline, and talents of one person. Certainly the successful salesperson and entrepreneur have strong teams of employees behind them, but both pursuits are highly individualistic. Both have significant latitude to fail and carry the burden of having to succeed in measurable financial terms.

ENTREPRENEURSHIP AND SALES MANAGEMENT

Management of the sales function has the potential to be an entrepreneurial pursuit as well. Most of the activities that comprise the sales manager's job demand a high degree of innovativeness, calculated risk-taking, and proactiveness. To demonstrate how entrepreneurship can be applied, let us briefly examine each of the major components of the sales management process.

Designing the Sales Organization

When making decisions regarding the structure, size, and deployment of the sales force, the sales manager should emphasize flexibility, minimal hierarchy, empowerment, and open communication. The guiding principle in deciding how to organize the sales force should be value creation for customers, whereas experimentation should be the byword. Novel structures and sales force sizes should be developed and subsequently modified based on marketplace conditions and opportunities. This is especially the case as markets become more segmented, fragmented, and niched. Territories should be designed as if they were of entrepreneurial ventures to be developed by the assigned sales personnel. Sales managers should have fairly broad spans of control. An entrepreneurial perspective might also find managers looking for innovative ways to tie in telemarketing and newer computer and telecommunications technologies with the sales force, as well as creatively mixing independent contractors with company reps when designing and organizing the sales force.

Developing the Sales Force

Recruitment and selection of salespeople should be based on an analysis of the specific selling tasks to be performed, as well as insights regarding the traits that differentiate people who have performed well versus poorly at those tasks. Yet, there continues to be disagreement regarding which traits correlate with which tasks, as well as the best ways to properly assess those traits (e.g., Ford et al. 1988). Alternatively, it may be useful for sales managers to emphasize traits associated with successful entrepreneurship when recruiting and selecting salespeople. Also, the operative question might not simply be what tasks are required of the salesperson, but instead, how much entrepreneurship is desirable in performing each of those tasks.

Entrepreneurship also has implications for sales force training. Studies have suggested that training programs tend to emphasize selling skills and product knowledge, whereas attitudinal factors receive little attention (Kerr and Burzynski 1988). This occurs despite the fact that attitudinal factors are viewed as a more significant factor than skills or knowledge in explaining success in sales. There is a need not only to further develop the attitudinal component of training programs, but to concentrate on developing entrepreneurial attitudes. Although it may not be possible to "teach" someone to be an entrepreneur, training that reinforces achievement motivation, tolerance for ambiguity, non-conformity, acceptance of change, assumption of risk, and creativity may help individuals develop more of their own entrepreneurial potential. Such reinforcement can be accomplished in part by identifying sales behaviors that reflect such attitudes and incorporating them into behavioral modeling training programs (e.g., Shaw 1981).

Directing the Sales Force

Once salespeople are in place, ongoing efforts are needed to motivate, compensate, and supervise them toward entrepreneurial behaviors. Motivating salespeople to be innovative, take risks, and engage in proactive behaviors requires that they perceive a linkage between such behaviors and the criteria on which they are evaluated by management, as well as between those criteria and the rewards they receive. Rewards themselves should be tailored to the individual, and probably should include a structure that is heavily commission and incentive based. Because entrepreneurs tend to be reward conscious, continuous reinforcement may be required, such as with "Entrepreneur of the Quarter" awards or bonuses for successful sales "innovations."

Sales force direction should be centered around the concept of "directed autonomy" (Waterman 1987). This concept involves management defining boundaries for the sales force, providing overall direction, and being a source of ample sales support resources. At the same time, managers empower salespeople to make many decisions for themselves. Such a broadening of salesperson responsibility might include decisions regarding which products to push and when, individual pricing decisions, and decisions regarding expenditures for sales support activities (e.g., telemarketing, direct mail) in a particular territory. Salespeople might be empowered to "purchase" resources from the firm. As explained by Waterman (1987), directed autonomy finds the sales manager "giving up control to gain control."

Determining Sales Force Effectiveness and Performance

When evaluating salespeople, managers tend to stress output measures of performance that are quantifiable, such as sales in dollars or new account sales (Morris et al. 1991). Accordingly, performance is generally viewed by sales managers as being relatively easy to assess, especially when compared to other occupations. However, the ability of managers to realize the entrepreneurial potential of the sales force probably entails the use of more complex performance measures.

On one hand, traditional measures of sales performance are likely to appeal to the entrepreneurial personality because of their simplicity and the immediacy of the feedback they provide. Moreover, they are designed to reflect individual performance. On the other hand, entrepreneurship involves activities that may take time, involve considerable experimentation, and entail high risk. Encouraging a salesperson to look beyond this week's selling and servicing schedule and to develop innovative sales solutions may require that traditional measures be supplemented. Measures might also be employed that focus on inputs and are qualitative in nature. For instance, salespeople might be subjectively evaluated on how innovative or creative they have been over the past twelve months, or on the number of new selling-related approaches they have developed.

It is also important that sales managers evaluate how much of the potential of a given sales territory is being realized. More specifically, territories should be assessed as if they were entrepreneurial ventures, or mini-enterprises unto themselves. Similarly, the salesperson's evaluation should become more than a question of reaching or exceeding quota, but instead, a question of how well they capitalized on available opportunities.

RESISTANCE TO ENTREPRENEURSHIP IN THE SALES FUNCTION

Although we have attempted to demonstrate the nature and importance of entrepreneurial approaches to personal selling and sales management, organizations and many of the people inside them can be expected to resist entrepreneurship (Morris, Avila, and Teeple 1990). Entrepreneurship represents continuous change in an organization, and many people are threatened by change. In sales, entrepreneurial change means ongoing pressure to develop new ways to find customers and make sales happen, and new approaches to all of the tasks of sales management. The key is to help employees recognize that change represents not threat but opportunity, and to give them a stake in identifying and implementing change.

Entrepreneurship is also likely to be resisted because of a fear of failure. Sales is a very success-driven field, and, as stated earlier, success in sales can be fairly easy to measure. Moreover, if salespeople aren't making sales, both the individual and the company are affected. Salespeople encounter "small failures" all the time, in the sense that they fail to close a sale or lose a current account. However, entrepreneurship means pursuing aggressive, risk-oriented behaviors that have a greater likelihood of failure. The challenge is to change attitudes on the part of both sales managers and salespeople regarding failure, helping them to recognize that failure is a positive source of learning and an investment in the future.

Finally, entrepreneurship is likely to be limited unless those in sales perceive a need to be entrepreneurial. Entrepreneurship in established sales organizations is a two-way relationship. Salespeople will see more reason to be entrepreneurial if sales managers are demonstrating entrepreneurial behavior. Further, sales managers will look "up the organization" for a commitment to the entrepreneurial concept. They will look for role models at the top, for a resource commitment, and for the same types of decentralized structures and empowerment discussed earlier. Thus, entrepreneurship cannot be applied to sales in isolation, but should transcend the entire organization.

LIMITS TO ENTREPRENEURSHIP IN THE SALES FUNCTION

To suggest sales should provide a home for entrepreneurship in organizations does not mean there should be no limits on the entrepreneurial efforts of employees. Both the frequency and degree of entrepreneurship must be managed to avoid its potential dysfunctional aspects. Five key problem areas include strategy inconsistencies, unfocused efforts, unrealistic customer expectations, alienation of co-workers, and the cost of failure.

Salespeople can create significant problems when they pursue innovative opportunities that conflict with the strategic direction of the firm, such as going after accounts that do not fit with the firms distribution channels or the image it wishes to project. Also, entrepreneurship entails innovation, but it must be directed innovation. That is, salespeople who attempt a wide array of innovative behaviors, but do not focus on each of them in sufficient detail to ensure successful implementation, can be a major source of frustration to the company and irritation to customers and middlemen. Additionally, in the name of entrepreneurship, salespeople may make promises or suggestions to customers, such as for a possible price deal or product modification, that prove to be unfeasible when presented to the salesperson's superiors. The customer's expectations are raised unrealistically, and they may subsequently become alienated or over-demanding. Entrepreneurship also relies on a degree of teamwork, as meaningful change typically requires help and support from a number of others. Free-spirited entrepreneurs in the sales organization must remember they are part of an organization, and if they attempt to expedite implementation of their innovative ideas by ignoring, exploiting, or mistreating co-workers and superiors, the result can be dysfunctional for the entire firm. Lastly, riskier entrepreneurial pursuits can also prove to be more costly if they fail. There certainly can be levels of potential costs that are deemed too high, and degrees of risk that those in sales are precluded from pursuing.

The issue of excessive entrepreneurship involves a balancing act between the need for control and the desire not to overly constrain or discourage the entrepreneurial instinct. This brings us back to the concept of boundaries. Sales managers must define the operating boundaries for their salespeople based on an understanding of the need for, the sources of resistance to, and the cost of overly excessive amounts of entrepreneurship in sales. In this manner, entrepreneurship becomes a viable concept in even the largest of corporate sales forces.

RESEARCH DIRECTIONS

Research addressing entrepreneurship and sales is extremely limited. Most of the ideas discussed in this chapter are based on a synthesis of the entrepreneurship and sales literatures. The Morris, Avila, and Teeple (1990) study is the only one known that has been directed specifically at some of the entrepreneurship and sales issues. Clearly, research in this important area is needed.

To motivate researchers and provide direction for entrepreneurship and sales research, we have developed a number of propositions. The propositions, although general in nature, translate some of our ideas into researchable form.

We have developed separate propositions for the personal selling and sales management areas.

Entrepreneurship and Personal Selling Propositions

The propositions pertaining to entrepreneurship and personal selling are presented in Table 13.3. As discussed previously in the chapter, salespeople can exhibit varying amounts of entrepreneurship and the desired level of entrepreneurship is likely to be dependent on the characteristics of the selling environment. The entrepreneurship literature suggests the need for more entrepreneurial behavior the more complex and dynamic the environment. Therefore, as suggested in proposition 1, our judgment is that the more complex and dynamic the selling environment, the more the need for an entrepreneurial sales function.

The remaining propositions assume the need for entrepreneurial salespeople. The propositions suggest that in these types of environments, salespeople are likely to be more successful the more they possess entrepreneurial characteristics (proposition 2), perform the sales process as an entrepreneurial process (proposition 3), and manage their sales territory as an entrepreneurial venture (proposition 4). These propositions offer a starting point for testing some of the major ideas discussed in this chapter.

Entrepreneurship and Sales Management Propositions

The entrepreneurship and sales management propositions are presented in Table 13.4. Because the role of sales management is to manage the personal selling function, the propositions are written from the perspective of sales managers developing entrepreneurial salespeople. Performing these types of activities would also require entrepreneurial behavior on the part of sales managers.

The propositions address the major areas of the sales management process (Ingram and LaForge 1992). Sales management activities related to designing the sales organization (proposition 1), developing the sales force (proposition 2), directing the sales force (propositions 3 and 4), and determining sales force effectiveness and performance (proposition 5) are suggested.

Our hope is that this chapter and these propositions will be instrumental in generating entrepreneurship and sales research. The entrepreneurship and sales areas have much in common. Research that integrates an entrepreneurship perspective into the sales area has the potential to make important contributions to theory development and practice in both the sales and entrepreneurship areas.

Table 13.3
Entrepreneurship and Personal Selling Propositions

Proposition 1
  The more complex and dynamic the selling environment, the more the need for an entrepreneurial sales function.

Proposition 2
  In complex and dynamic selling environments, the more a salesperson possesses entrepreneurial characteristics, the more successful the salesperson will be.

Proposition 3
  In complex and dynamic selling environments, the more a salesperson performs the sales process as an entrepreneurial process, the more successful the salesperson will be.

Proposition 4
  In complex and dynamic selling environments, the more a salesperson manages his/her sales territory as an entrepreneurial venture, the more successful the salesperson will be.

Table 13.4
Entrepreneurship and Sales Management Propositions

Proposition 1

> The more that sales managers design their sales organizations to encourage entrepreneurial activity, the more entrepreneurial their salespeople will be.

Proposition 2

> The more that sales managers develop recruiting, selecting, and training programs to hire and develop salespeople with entrepreneurial characteristics, the more entrepreneurial their salespeople will be.

Proposition 3

> The more autonomy that sales managers give to salespeople, the more entrepreneurial the salespeople will be.

Proposition 4

> The more sales managers employ incentive compensation programs, the more entrepreneurial salespeople will be.

Proposition 5

> The more that sales managers evaluate the entrepreneurial activity and financial performance of salespeople, the more entrepreneurial their salespeople will be.

REFERENCES

Brandt, S. C. *Entrepreneuring: The Ten Commandments for Building a Growth Company.* Reading, MA: Addison-Wesley Publishing Co., 1982.

Brandt, S. C. *Entrepreneuring in Established Companies.* Homewood, IL: Dow Jones-Irwin, 1986.

Brockhaus, R. H. "The Psychology of the Entrepreneur." In *Encyclopedia of Entrepreneurship*, edited by C. Kent et. al. Englewood Cliffs, NJ: Prentice Hall, 1982.

Brockhaus, R. H., Sr., and P. S. Horwitz. "The Psychology of the Entrepreneur." In *The Art and Science of Entrepreneurship*, edited by D. Sexton and R. Smilor, 25–48. Cambridge, MA: Ballinger Publishing Co., 1986.

Churchill, G. A., Jr., N. M. Ford, S. W. Hartley, and O. C. Walker, Jr. "The Determinants of Salesperson Performance: A Meta-Analysis." *Journal of Marketing Research* 22 (May 1985): 103–18.

Churchill, G. A., Jr., N. M. Ford, and O. C. Walker, Jr. *Sales Force Management.* Homewood, IL: Richard D. Irwin, 1990.

Cornwall, J. R., and B. Perlman. *Organizational Entrepreneurship.* Homewood, IL: Richard D. Irwin, 1990.

Covin, J. G., and D. P. Slevin. "Strategic Management of Small Firms in Hostile and Benign Environments." *Strategic Management Journal* 10 (Jan. 1989).

Ford, N. M., O. C. Walker, Jr., G. A. Churchill, Jr., and S. W. Hartley. "Selecting Successful Salespeople: A Meta Analysis of Biographical and Psychological Criteria." In *Review of Marketing,* edited by Michael J. Houston, 90–131. Chicago, IL: American Marketing Association, 1988.

Ingram, T. N., and R. W. LaForge. *Sales Management: Analysis and Decision Making.* Fort Worth, TX: Dryden HBJ, 1992.

Kanter, R.M. *The Change Masters.* New York: Simon and Schuster, 1983.

Khandwalla, P. *The Design of Organizations.* New York: Harcourt, Brace, and Jovanovich, 1977.

Kerr, M. and B. Burzynski. "Missing the Target: Sales Training in America." *Training and Development Journal* (July 1988): 68–70.

Miller, D., and P. H. Frieson. "Innovation in Conservative and Entrepreneurial Firms: Two Models of Strategic Momentum." *Strategic Management Journal* 3 (1983): 1–25.

Morris, M. H., and G. W. Paul. "The Relationship Between Entrepreneurship and Marketing in Established Firms." *Journal of Business Venturing* 2 (1987): 247–59.

Morris, M. H., and J. D. Trotter. "Institutionalizing Entrepreneurship in a Large Company: A Case Study at AT&T." *Industrial Marketing Management* 19 (May 1990): 131–39.

Morris, M. H., R. Avila, and E. Teeple. "Sales Management As an Entrepreneurial Activity." *Journal of Personal Selling and Sales Management* 10 (Spring 1990): 1–15.

Morris, M. H., D. L. Davis, J. W. Allen, R. A. Avila, and J. Chapman. "Assessing the Relationships Among Performance Measures, Managerial Practices, and Satisfaction when Evaluating the Salesforce: A Replication and Extension." *Journal of Personal Selling and Sales Management* 11 (Summer 1991): 1–11.

Murray, J. A. "Marketing in the Home for the Entrepreneurial Process." *Industrial Marketing Management* 10 (1981): 93–100.

Peters, T. *Thriving on Chaos.* New York: Alfred A. Knopf, 1988.

Pinchot, G., III. *Intrapreneuring.* New York: Harper and Row, 1985.

Shaw, M. E. "Sales Training in Transition." *Training and Development Journal* (Feb. 1981): 74–83.

Stevenson, H. H., M. J. Roberts, and H. I. Grousbeck. *New Business Ventures and the Entrepreneur.* Homewood, IL: Richard D.Irwin, 1989.

Waterman, R. H. *The Renewal Factor: How the Best Get and Keep the Competitive Edge.* New York: Bantam Books, 1987.

Weitz, B. A., S. B. Castleberry, and J. F. Tanner. *Selling: Building Partnerships.* Homewood, IL: Richard D. Irwin, 1992.

14

Research on Marketing Communication at the Marketing/Entrepreneurship Interface

Rae K. Eighmey, John B. Eighmey, and H. Keith Hunt

INTRODUCTION

Marketing communication refers to all selling and promotion efforts other than personal selling and the management of the sales force. Marketing communication is often divided into two major categories: advertising and public relations. Advertising typically refers to those marketing communication tactics that involve the use of purchased media such as radio and television commercials, newspaper ads, and billboards. The advertising message is designed and written by the company or its agencies and placed according to a specific schedule. Public relations involves the implementation of non-paid media such as the placement of press releases as well as those activities where the company interacts directly with one or more audiences, such as shareholders, customers, suppliers or media, to inform or generate goodwill. In general, public relations activities provide less control over the specific information shared and the goal accomplished than do advertising messages.

Direct marketing is often a mix of personal selling and marketing communication. For example, information is directed to a customer or potential customer through media advertising or materials mailed to the target audience with follow-up direct sales calls either coming from the company to the customer or incoming from the customer to the company sometimes via an 800 number.

RESEARCH FINDINGS ON THE PERCEIVED IMPORTANCE BY ENTREPRENEURS OF MARKETING COMMUNICATION

Although few studies have been done linking marketing communications and entrepreneurs or their ventures, five studies have addressed this topic.

Gartner (1984) identified marketing/selling as one of six functional areas of the start-up process. For the 106 entrepreneurs participating in this study, the two primary problem areas were financial management and marketing/selling. Technical experts said marketing/selling was their only problem area. Professionals (CPAs, consultants) reported marketing/selling as one of their primary problem areas. To solve this deficiency, experts tended to associate with a partner who had marketing/selling skills, whereas professionals tended to learn marketing/selling skills themselves.

Fischer, Dyke, Reuber, and Tank (1990) found that experienced entrepreneurs perceived some marketing activities as critical to success but regarded other activities as relatively unimportant. Communication and promotion was mentioned as being important one and a half times as often as was expected. They also found that as a firm moved from initial start-up into later stages of survival and success, marketing and promotion was mentioned nine of 11 times for the later stages and only twice in the initial stage, indicating that marketing and promotion is perceived to be more important as the firm matures.

Boag and Munro (1986) have noted that among all marketing activities, promotion comes next to new product development in importance in their sample of high-technology firm marketing managers. Ram and Forbes (1990) found that in an array of marketing activities ranging in rated difficulty from 15 to 80, the three marketing communication items were very close to average difficulty. Allocating the advertising budget was rated 50, developing an ad campaign was rated 47, and developing a promotions campaign was rated 42. Creating awareness for the product/service was considered the third most difficult general category of activities. When the respondents were asked to state how much improvement they felt was necessary in the various aspects of their marketing strategy the maximum improvement required was in advertising and promotion strategy.

Teach, Schwartz, and Tarpley (1990) found that as firms mature from entrepreneurial endeavors to mature organizations, the importance of marketing becomes more apparent. The four marketing communications items in a 24 item questionnaire, when ratings were compared between now and when the firm was new, showed all four saying marketing communication had become significantly more difficult, significant at the .000 level. Getting the buyer's attention is a more difficult task than was initially imagined. The other three items showed a heavier reliance on advertising, heavier promotion to the channel, and the recognition that advertising positions products, all significant at the .000 level. However, in a factor analysis of the data, they found the four advertising items loading on four different factors, suggesting that advertising was not a cohesive concern in and of itself.

MARKETING SCHOLARS COMMENTARY ON THE IMPORTANCE OF MARKETING COMMUNICATIONS AT THE MARKETING/ENTREPRENEURSHIP INTERFACE

In addition to the specific research findings, other authors have indicated why they think the intersection of marketing communication and entrepreneurship is important to study.

Davis, Hills, and LaForge (1985) suggest three reasons for expecting differences in marketing strategies between large and small firms. They suggest that "Small firms typically must develop and implement marketing strategies within severe resource constraints. Thus, smaller firms are likely to have fewer viable strategic alternatives than larger firms." They also observe that "Small firms typically lack specialized marketing expertise and often have difficulty in trying to purchase this expertise." They also note that "Small firms often have different objectives than larger firms (e.g., satisficing vs. optimizing). Different strategies are often required to achieve different objectives." We must note here that there are opposite opinions of which size firm does the satisficing and which does the optimizing.

During the research symposium on marketing and entrepreneurship sponsored by The University of Illinois at Chicago and the American Marketing Association in 1989, a group of leading scholars active in consulting with new and growing businesses met in a discussion session titled "Promotion in New and Growing Enterprises." Promotion was used to mean any and all marketing communications, advertising, and public relations activities. The group suggested the following as typical marketing communication activities and needs of such companies:

1. Entrepreneurial firms are likely to have either a very strong or very weak emphasis on promotion. Promotion will typically be either an extremely important element of their overall marketing strategy or of very minor importance.

2. Entrepreneurial firms are likely to have a hierarchy of promotion objectives. The emphasis on specific objectives within this hierarchy is likely to change as firms grow and is likely to be different for entrepreneurial firms in different stages of development.

3. Promotion expenditures for entrepreneurial firms are likely to increase when financial resources become available and when expertise in promotion is developed or acquired by an entrepreneurial firm.

4. Entrepreneurial firms are likely to use objective and task methods for establishing promotion budgets. With few, if any, competitors offering the same products and with little sales history, competitive parity and percentage-of-sales methods are not appropriate for entrepreneurial firms.

5. The lack of expertise and specialization in promotion suggests the need to purchase professional marketing communications services externally, but the unique nature of the entrepreneurial firm suggests the need to perform certain promotion activities internally.

6. Entrepreneurial firms are likely to emphasize personal communication and networking as important elements of their promotion strategy.

7. Entrepreneurial firms are likely to exemplify different promotion strategies than are nonentrepreneurial firms. These differences are most likely in the types of promotion tools used, the relative emphasis on various promotion tools, and the way that the promotion tools are blended into an effective promotion mix.

8. Entrepreneurial firms are more likely to employ push strategies than pull strategies. The lack of resources and specialized promotion functions and the important role of personal communication by the entrepreneur suggest that promotion to channel members and other stakeholders is typically more cost effective than promotion to product users.

9. Entrepreneurial firms are more likely to focus on the implementation of promotion strategies than the planning of promotion strategies.

10. The planning horizon of entrepreneurial firms is normally short. Short-term promotion plans are typically developed, implemented, and then new promotion plans developed. (Hunt and LaForge 1990).

NEEDED RESEARCH ON MARKETING COMMUNICATIONS AT THE MARKETING/ ENTREPRENEURSHIP INTERFACE

There are two possible directions for research on marketing communication at the marketing/entrepreneurship interface. The first is to study only those aspects of the marketing/entrepreneurship interface that are different than they are for other interfaces with marketing. The second is to emphasize research on the marketing/entrepreneurship interface even though there is no evidence that this interface is any different in the entrepreneurship interface than in any other marketing interfaces. In the last half of this chapter we outline what we think are the primary marketing communication topics and indicate what research is needed.

There is always an opportunity for a study to find out if different individuals in different firms think a particular topic is important. We suggest, however, that all the following items are important and that any findings from such general research would add little beyond. So we do not suggest that studies be conducted to determine whether entrepreneurs and nonentrepreneurs differ in the degree to which they consider an item important. Other research is suggested that will make a greater contribution to knowledge.

Research into the Need for Marketing Communication

In its simplest and most obvious sense, the role of marketing communication is to make things happen faster in the marketplace. For an entrepreneur, that objective is paramount. An entrepreneurial business needs to establish a revenue stream quickly, and cash flow is often critical to success. In some cases, the goal may be to establish a repeat purchase relationship with a loyal base of customers. In other cases, the goal may be to establish the company and its reputation for a specialized, technical product before larger, well-financed companies can move in on its market.

Whatever the goal of the entrepreneurial company, we suspect the need for marketing communication in the entrepreneurial firm is not fundamentally different from any other firm. General research on the need for marketing communication is, therefore, applicable to the needs of entrepreneurial companies and small businesses. Although future research may be better conceptualized, operationalized, and executed than the studies currently in the literature, we expect the results will support the findings described earlier in this chapter—that entrepreneurs think marketing communication is very important and that it is recognized as being even more important as the firm matures. Although replications and additional research questions will bring additional understanding, we do not see this as a high-priority research area.

Research into the Special Marketing Communication Challenges Facing Entrepreneurial Companies

The marketing communications efforts of entrepreneurial companies and small businesses are frequently hampered by limited funds; by limited staff to perform marketing, advertising, and public relations activities; and by the tendency to assign marketing functions to a staff that does not have professional marketing communications skills and expertise. Although these constraints are primarily due to the company's size and limited resources rather than its entrepreneurial corporate culture, they do highlight the special challenges that face entrepreneurial companies as they enter and seek to survive in their chosen marketplace.

Product differentiation

Success in marketing communications depends on being able to differentiate the company's product or service from that of the competition. The smaller the company, the more important this differentiation becomes. It is critical for entrepreneurial firms to understand the unique selling proposition for their product or service. Without it, the company has no reason for being and may find itself in a long, uphill struggle to attract and keep a large and enthusiastic customer base.

Future research needs to investigate entrepreneurs' understanding and application of product differentiation, the Unique Selling Proposition, and general marketing positioning strategy. Also, what evidence is there that a correct understanding and application of these concepts results in greater market success?

Target marketing

Every advertising and public relations decision an entrepreneurial company makes must be made on the basis of knowledge about the target market and how their product uniquely fits the need of that market. Companies need to know who their customers are and how to communicate with them efficiently. Although this should not be unique to entrepreneurial companies, the efficiencies of accurate target marketing can enable a smaller company to leverage its limited budget.

Future research could shed considerable light on the importance of targeted marketing by using firms as subjects or obtaining interviews from marketing decision makers with firms of the same size but differing degrees of entrepreneurship. Some of the questions that seem worthy of further exploration include: Does it really make a difference if a firm correctly understands niche marketing? Do entrepreneurial firms differ from other firms in understanding their potential customers? What are the differences among entrepreneurial companies that do highly targeted marketing?

Marketing communications strategy

Limited financial and personnel resources mean that entrepreneurial companies' selections both of media and of the composition of advertising messages need to be carefully deliberated before they are made, and then analyzed after each campaign or project is completed. A fully-developed marketing communications strategy can help entrepreneurial companies make the most of their limited resources by providing a structure against which all specific project and media decisions can be evaluated.

Research evaluating the basic truisms of structured marketing efforts might provide some interesting insights. Are firms really better off having a marketing strategy? Do firms that progress in an orderly manner in their understanding and application of marketing communications do any better than those that dash in disarray from one application to another? It may prove challenging, however, to find even a few firms that have and are progressing in an orderly fashion in improving and expanding their marketing communications efforts.

Marketing communications budgets

Entrepreneurial companies are frequently constricted in their marketing efforts by serious budget limitations. Should the company spend only what it thinks it can afford? Or, should it find a way to fulfill certain communications objectives? An important function of developing a marketing communications strategy is the framework it provides for accurate budgeting.

Evaluation of marketing communication budgeting issues for entrepreneurial firms may also prove challenging. Are there enough firms that make marketing considerations a regular part of a formal budgeting process to even do such studies? How do we find such firms? It would also be valuable to determine what budget methods different types of firms use.

Using professionals

Advertising agencies, graphic designers, and public relations consultants can provide valuable support to entrepreneurial and small companies as they plan, prepare, and implement their marketing communications strategies. This outside experience and expertise can help companies avoid common mistakes and complete the tasks at hand more efficiently. Professionals have extensive contacts with the various media and can provide insights as well as important connections between the firm and the media.

Advertising and public relations have importantly different functions in the marketing communication objectives of a company. The basic trade-off between paid and non-paid (advertising versus public relations) is the need for absolute control of the message content and the costs related to that control. In the start-up phase, many entrepreneurial companies may be confined to public relations activities partially due to budget restrictions and partially related to the status of the product preparation for market. Furthermore, each of the variety of paid media has its own strengths and weaknesses. It is critical that a company with a limited budget understand these differences and apply them to their product and target market.

Further study can help us learn about the process by which entrepreneurial and other firms obtain professional help with marketing communications. This could be part of a larger study of how entrepreneurial and other firms obtain all types of expert help. At what stage does the firm first recognize its need for help? Is it recognized internally or introduced by an external agent? What is the decision process a firm goes through as it considers using outside experts and selects the agency or free-lance help it needs? What evidence can we find that firms who learn to effectively manage the media are more successful than those firms that have no interaction with the media? Can we find evidence that for entrepreneurial firms there is a direct relationship between the depth and correctness of the understanding of the media and of the firm's success? Effective research in this area might begin with anecdotal data describing firms' relationships with the media and their specifics.

The need for creativity

Having a unique product is not enough. An entrepreneur can build a better mousetrap, but unless the product is presented in a clear, compelling way, the satisfied customers of the competition have no reason to change their purchasing behavior. An advertisement needs to present the company's product in a human and dramatic way. Flat-footed descriptions of products and services or loose artsy image-driven advertising is not going to make an impact in a world in which the consumer has the potential to see hundreds of individual pieces of advertising in a day. For an entrepreneurial company to stand out, to be one of those handful of pieces of advertising that a consumer remembers and acts on, the work must be creative. It must appear original and highly relevant to the consumer's concerns and needs, and it must make the product the hero.

Is there any evidence that those firms that understand creativity and use professionals to produce creative marketing communications for them are any more successful than those who totally ignore creativity? Do sales build faster for the more creative firms?

CONCLUSION

It is clear from the findings on the perceived importance by entrepreneurs of marketing communications, by the comments from marketing scholars on the importance of marketing communications at the marketing/entrepreneurship interface, and by the research needs discussed in this chapter that marketing communications at the marketing/entrepreneurship interface has great potential as a research topic. It provides a seemingly endless steam of research questions worthy of academic research. Answers to those research questions have substantial potential for improving business practice.

REFERENCES

Boag, D. and H. Munro. "Analysis of Marketing Activities in High-Technology Manufacturing Companies." *Journal of Small Business and Entrepreneurship* 4(2), (1986): 48–56.

Davis, C. H., G. E. Hills, and R. W. LaForge. "The Marketing/Small Enterprise Paradox: A Research Agenda." *International Small Business Journal* (Spring 1985): 31–42.

Fischer, E. M., L. S. Dyke, A. R. Reuber, and Y. Tank. "The Critical Incident Approach to Investigating the Tacit Marketing Knowledge of Entrepreneurial Manufacturers." In *Research at the Marketing/Entrepreneurship Interface*, edited by G. E. Hills, R. W. LaForge, and H. P. Welsch, 43–54. Chicago, IL: University of Illinois at Chicago, 1990.

Gartner, W. B. "Problems in Business Startup: The Relationships among Entrepreneurial Skills and Problem Identification for Different Types of New Ventures." In *Frontiers of Entrepreneurship Research,* edited by J. A. Hornaday, F. Tarpley, Jr., J. A. Timmons, and K. H. Vesper, 496–512. Wellesley, MA: Babson College, 1984.

Hills, G. E., and A. Star. "Marketing Strategy Elements for New Venture/Early Stage Firms as Perceived by Venture Capitalists." In *Frontiers of Entrepreneurship Research*, edited by J. Hornaday, F. Tarpley, J. Timmons and K. Vesper, 211–20. Wellesley, MA: Babson College, 1985.

Hunt, H. K., and R. W. LaForge. "Promotion in New/Growing Enterprises: A Discussion Summary." In *Research at the Marketing/Entrepreneurship Interface,* edited by G. E. Hills, R. W. LaForge, and H. P. Welsch, 346–50. Chicago, IL: University of Illinois at Chicago, 1990.

LaForge, R. W., and S. J. Miller. "The Moderating Effects of Company Size on Business Level Marketing Strategies." In *Research at the Marketing/ Entrepreneurship Interface,* edited by G. E. Hills. Chicago, IL: University of Illinois at Chicago, 1987.

Ram, S., and S. J. Forbes. "Marketing Variables that Affect Entrepreneurial Success: An Empirical Investigation." In *Research at the Marketing/ Entrepreneurship Interface*, edited by G. E. Hills, R. W. LaForge, and H. P. Welsch, 99–102. Chicago, IL: University of Illinois at Chicago, 1990.

Teach, R. D., R. G. Schwartz, and F. A. Tarpley, Jr. "Firm Maturation and Marketing Changes in the Computer Software Industry." In *Research at the Marketing/Entrepreneurship Interface*, edited by G. E. Hills, R. W. LaForge, and H. P. Welsch, 17–31. Chicago, IL: University of Illinois at Chicago, 1990.

15

Market Entry Strategies for New Corporate Ventures

Zenas Block and Ian C. MacMillan

INTRODUCTION

Choosing the best, or even a satisfactory approach for launching a new product or the product of a new venture from an existing corporate base is not a simple task. Should the market entry attempt to rapidly seize significant market position or seek stealthy penetration? There certainly is no single strategy that fits all firms, products and markets. The competitive strategy for an established firm to start a new venture and launch a new product must be shaped by the characteristics of the firm, the market, and other environmental factors.

In this chapter, we discuss a number of variables that should affect the choice of a market entry strategy used to launch a new product or venture. These variables are then linked to entry strategy options. Our particular emphasis is on two that have not received very much attention, that is, strategic aggressiveness and focus, and how these options are related to market hostility and market munificence.

Aspects of Strategy

A universal component of marketing strategy is its content: details such as pricing, marketing mix, distribution channels, packaging, and target markets, which are affected by the characteristics of the product, costs, the competitive situation, market size and growth rate, industry characteristics and perhaps most important of all, the strategic marketing objectives that are sought.

Another is form, the mechanism used for execution. This mechanism might be a project team, a joint venture, a new business unit, or any other mechanism designed or selected to deliver the content of strategy. The ideal form is one that puts together the resources, skills, and attitudes required for success. From their study of a number of high-tech ventures, Roberts and Berry (1985) offer a nine-cell (3×3) matrix designed around the relative familiarity of the firm with the chosen markets and technology. Familiarity is divided into three levels: basic, new familiar, and new unfamiliar. Forms (referred to by the authors as entry strategies) considered include internal venture, joint venture, and venture capital investment or licensing. To these we would add project team, a separate business unit, a strategic alliance where the principal objective to match up the needs of the proposed venture, and the skills and resources required for success.

A third aspect that emerges from the culture of the firm is strategic posture (Miller 1983; Covin and Slevin 1989). This refers to the entrepreneurial-conservatism orientation of the firm: top management's willingness to take risks, to favor innovation and change for competitive advantage, and to compete aggressively.

There are two additional features of entry strategy that we wish to highlight in this chapter:

     a.   The aggressiveness of entry. This refers to the force applied—the power, strength and velocity of effort and amount of resources committed.

     b.   The focus of the entry effort—the extent to which the effort is sharply focused or on a broad front.

Why are aggressiveness and focus important? The fact is that highly aggressive, broad-front strategies employ the greatest amount of resources compared to other alternatives. They are enormously costly, and entail the greatest risk of money and reputation. Costly and risky as they may be, aggressive entry strategies may be warranted by competitive necessity or the promise of high return, or may be chosen because of the accepted wisdom or folklore that getting there first with the most ensures the greatest chance of success. Biggadyke (1979), in his study of new ventures by Fortune 200 companies, reports greater profitability after seven years for ventures that reach for market share rather than early profitability, implying an aggressive strategy. Tsai, MacMillan, and Low (1991), using the Profit Impact of Market Strategies (PIMS) Start-Up data base, limited to industrial markets, find a high correlation between venture performance and aggressiveness of entry (here performance was measured by market share achieved).

The evidence is quite strong that new product and new venture performance on a firm-wide basis is greatly affected and perhaps fundamentally determined not by the percentage of successful entries but rather by the losses of expensive failures, which dilute and dissipate the gains of successes. This indicates a need for effective damage control of potential failures, so they do not cripple the chances for success. Thus, the choice of entry strategy becomes particularly significant not only for the success of the new product but for the performance of the total new business internal development effort in the firm (Block 1989). Some of the big losers that highlight this problem are:

New Coke
Premier Smokeless Cigarettes
RCA's Selectavision—a $400 million loss
Federal Express Zapmail—a cumulative $600 million loss
Kodak's Disk Camera
Polaroid's Instant Motion Picture Camera
IBM's PC Jr.

The problem with such entries is the magnitude of the consequences when something is "wrong," that is, different from forecast, planned, or hoped for—which is most of the time (Block and MacMillan 1986). According to SAMI, of 6,960 new brands introduced in 1988 and 1989, 240 have reached the $1 million/year sales level. Small wonder that J. Tait Elder, former president of the New Ventures Group at Allied Corp. and, previous to that, manager of the new business group at 3M says: "I like to be dumb on a small scale."

On the other side, however, some highly aggressive and broad-front entries have resulted in major successes—such as the IBM PC, Diet Coke, and from a marketing point of view at least, *USA Today*, although this newspaper is still teetering on the edge of profitability in 1992. It is difficult to see how these entries could have been as successful except through the highly aggressive, broad-front entry.

Some new ventures simply cannot be executed at all in any other way. On March 16, 1992, the *New York Times* reported Motorola's plan to build a global cellular telephone network, requiring 77 satellites supported by at least 20 ground stations. Its purpose is to permit anyone on earth with a pocket phone to receive or make calls to anyone else anywhere on earth. The projected cost is $3.1 billion. It is difficult to imagine an entry any more aggressive or broader in scope.

Aggressiveness can be applied not only in the sales and marketing effort through expenditure on advertising and promotion, the size of the sales and marketing organization, pricing practices, discounting, deals, and publicity, but also through investment in production facilities, inventories, training of personnel in advance of entry, and number and dispersion of plant and office locations. An often disastrous aggressive entry is marked by the employment and training of sales and marketing personnel before product is available, that is, the timing of activity is based on projected, rather than actual event completion. This often leads to high cash burn rates while one part of the new organization is waiting for another part to fulfill its commitments—late (Block and MacMillan 1986). For complex major new businesses or projects, the timing strategy chosen (i.e., whether timing is based on critical path milestones or planned projections) may have more impact on potential gains and losses than any other factor.

Given the potential for big wins and for equally big losses associated with massive-scale market entry we have described, it is clear that management faces some real dilemmas in deciding whether to be aggressive and/or focused in the entry strategy. All the combinations of force and focus have their advantages and disadvantages, but we suggest that some clues as to what is the most appropriate entry strategy can be derived from looking at the nature of the market environment that the firm wishes to enter. In this chapter we propose that the market be assessed in terms of two dimensions: munificence and hostility. In the following discussion, we attempt to show how these dimensions of the market suggest the appropriate aggressiveness and scope of the initial entry.

Market factors that shape entry strategy

There are two market variables that have a tremendous impact on the strategy chosen for entry of a new product (Tsai, MacMillan, and Low 1991)—the market can either be munificent or sparse, hostile, or benign.

MUNIFICENCE

Munificence describes the structure, size, and nature of the market being entered, whereas hostility captures the structure and nature of the firms competing for that market. A market can be either potentially munificent, as for example in the case of the personal computer market before Apple and IBM entered, or actually munificent after their entry. Before entry, the market was not hostile, hostility increased with their entry and has become very intense with the entry of clone makers.

Evaluating Munificence/Sparsity

Clearly, the degree of munificence of a market is closely related to market size, but judging the market size for a new venture can be confusing. It is one thing to examine an existing market, for example, for detergents, to identify the players, determine their share, review the rate of growth of the market, determine the cost of achieving and holding share, and make some reasonable assumptions based on competitive and marketing history as a basis for entry planning.

It is quite another to examine an unfulfilled market need, to calculate a potential if the need is met with the proposed new product entry, and then to estimate what the rate of market development will be, and in addition, what competitors will do and when they will do it. Traditional market research is not very useful for this purpose. The more innovative a product is, the more difficult it is to estimate the rate of market development. This is a special problem for corporate ventures because of the widespread practice among corporations for hard market data and return projections that support the request for funds. Although there may be no question about ultimate munificence, there will be plenty about when it will occur.

Under these circumstances, feel, intuition, and direct personal contact with prospective customers and the market by the new venture champion may be more revealing that existing data about a nonexistent market. This is one area where the individual entrepreneur with a vision has an advantage over the objective market researchers of the corporation, who may only measure whether there is a market, and if so, how large. The entrepreneur adds the dimension of a vision of a future market and through personal immersion seeks a way to alter, modify, and adapt in order to fill the need that has been perceived. The fundamental difference, however, between the market analyst and the entrepreneur lies in the ability of the entrepreneur to see what is possible rather than current reality alone—to see future relationships between factors that add value, opportunities, the essence of the entrepreneurial act. An important part of the entrepreneur's view of the market in relationship to the business concept is the continuous adaptation and modification of the concept to attempt to fit concept or product to what is being learned from immersion in and contact with the market.

Ideal, of course, is a combination of whatever facts can be gleaned with the feel of the market as a result of immersion as a basis for deciding entry and entry strategy. This was the case with Conagra's creation of the Healthy Choice product line, a direct outcome of the CEO's heart attack and resulting commitment to producing foods that are good tasting as well as dietetically suitable.

For making the munificence judgment, three important characteristics besides existing size and growth rate must be examined in addition to market size: customer risk, technology turbulence, and category life cycle. For example, a market that is simply very large, but static, is not as munificent as one that is very large and growing rapidly, or a market that may not be as large but that is growing rapidly with great future market potential. An unoccupied market niche, although relatively small, can be munificent because of the potential for overwhelmingly dominant share.

Customer risk

A critical factor in assessing the market is the level of consumer risk attached to purchasing the new product. For example, efforts were made to market a new synthetic filter cloth to a vegetable oil refinery that had traditionally used canvas cloths. The cloths were such a minor item in cost, yet could produce major losses if they failed, that the refineries had no incentive to switch. It was not until the marketer of the new cloths agreed to absorb any losses due to switching that it was possible to make progress in the business. Another example is the development of the mail order computer business. Only by offering service contracts and telephone support, which reduced risk to customers, was it possible to unleash the rapid development of this market.

Sufficient understanding of the market to thoroughly anticipate and overcome customer risks is essential to market feel and resulting guesses about the rate of development of the market.

Turbulence of technology

Rapid change of technology can reconfigure the market. The creation of the word processor, for example, irrevocably altered the market for electric typewriters. In assessing the market and its munificence, it is important to consider not only the current market but the potential for that market to change. Thus, a critical question about munificence is How long will the munificence last? The market for 5 1/4" floppy disks was very munificent, and turned very sparse with the development of the hard disk and the 3 1/2" "stiffy."

Level of market development

Potential munificence is further affected by the stage of market development for the product category. For example, consider the relative munificence of the cellular telephone market compared to the market for traditional household telephones. Clearly the opportunities for success are higher quality for first movers with products in the early stages of their life cycle because of potential munificence and lack of hostility, but this is complicated by the lack of data, and thus for potential misjudgment of the market.

HOSTILITY

Competition is the principal key to determining the hostility of the market. If the market is crowded with competitors and the business is crucial to their success, the market will be very hostile. If there are no competitors, or the competition is highly fragmented and no clear market leadership is present, the market may be effectively benign.

The combined market share of the three or four principal players is a strong indicator of the extent to which they are entrenched and provides an indication of how much of the market may be left over for a new entrant.

In addition to market share, the salience of the product to each competitor will determine the strength of competitive response. If the competitor is highly dependent on the product for the firm's success, then an aggressive fight can be expected against a new entrant. That fight may not be limited to a marketplace battle, visible in promotion, aggressive pricing, incentives, deals, and guarantees, but can also include patent challenges, efforts to develop an end run around technology introduced by the new entrant, litigation, and every other weapon that can be used by a competitor.

Market hostility is also affected by industry capacity compared with market size. When capacity is greater than the market size, competitive action will be more intense, and may indeed suggest that the entry strategy to be followed is not to enter at all (Sahlman and Stevenson 1988) or to enter through acquisition of existing capacity at low cost.

Another influence is government regulation. For example, growing green concerns and increasing environmental protection regulation produces a hostile environment for products that cannot be recycled, are not biodegradable, or waste natural resources. For example, the growing compact disk market for recorded music is munificent, but the environment is hostile to waste in packaging. This has led to voluntary industry action to drastically change the size and constituents of compact disk packaging. Conversely, this element of the environment is extremely benign for packaging that is "green." Market hostility is otherwise produced through domination of the market by a small number of powerful competitors.

MAKING THE ENTRY STRATEGY DECISION

The Aggressiveness/Focus Matrix

Although the degrees of aggressiveness and focus are a continuum, for purposes of clarity and simplicity we choose two levels for each: relatively aggressive and non-aggressive and relatively focused and broad-front (Table 15.1).

Obviously, this classification is oversimplified. Aggressiveness and focus are not either present or absent, but are matters of degree. Table 15.1, therefore, should be considered an expression of relative aggressiveness and focus.

Table 15.1
Entry Strategy

	Blitzkrieg	Cavalry Charge	Strike Force	Guerrilla Tactics
FACTOR				
Market conditions				
Hostile	(+)	(-)	(+)	(+)
Benign	(+)	(+)	(-)	(-)
Munificent	(+)	(+)	(-)	(+)
Sparse	(-)	(-)	(+)	(-)
Firm condition *Resources*				
Ample	(+)	(+)	(-)	(-)
Restricted	(-)	(+)	(+)	(+)
Critical mass needed to start	(+)	(+)	(-)	(-)
Diversity				
Great (poor fit)	(-)	(-)	(+)	N
Small (good fit)	(+)	(+)	(-)	N
Corporate culture				
Risk averse, non-experimental	(-)	(-)	(+)	(+)
Supports experimentation	(+)	(+)	(+)	(+)

Table 15.1, Continued

	Blietzkrieg	Cavalry Charge	Strike Force	Guerrilla Tactics
Market life cycle stage				
Early	(-)	(-)	(+)	(+)
Developed	(+)	(+)	N	N
Mature	(-)	(-)	(+)	(+)
Salience to entry firm				
High	(+)	(+)	N	N
Low	(-)	(-)	(+)	(+)
Threat to existing customers				
Low	(+)	(+)	N	N
High	(-)	(-)	(+)	(-)
Proprietary protection				
Strong	(+)	(+)	(+)	(+)
Weak*	(-)	(-)	(-)	(-)

* Salience and resource availability will override this negative if the market is munificent.
(-) means that the strategy is less appropriate, or not necessary.
(+) means that the strategy is appropriate or necessary.
N means that the variable does not have any major effect on the appropriateness of the strategy.

Kotler and Singh (1980) used a military analogy for classifying marketing warfare strategies, focusing on existing markets and existing consumer products. The objective of those strategies is to win a battle against competitors to increase or to protect market share. The objective we are concerned with, on the other hand, is successful entry and survival during the earliest phase in the marketing life of a new venture or product.

The activities to which varying force or aggressiveness can be applied are amount and type of advertising and sales promotion, size of the sales and marketing organization, pricing, investment in production facilities, amount of service supplied to customers, level of discounting, introductory deals, inventory levels held for minimum delivery time, and, not the least, publicity. Increased aggressiveness may be reflected in the timing of these activities as well as in the amount of money spent. For example, the opening of regional sales offices and employment and training of sales and marketing people can be initiated and timed for operation to coincide with the anticipated availability of product from a plant that is in the process of being built, rather than waiting for assurance of availability of product.

The degree of focus is reflected by the number of market segments initially addressed, the extent of geographical dispersion, and the size and variety of the product or service line offered.

The Blitzkrieg

This is a highly aggressive, broad-front strategy using all forces over a wide scope of geography and market segments for the purpose of establishing a strong, widespread market position as early as possible. Examples of such entries are Nutrasweet, Pampers, and Merrill Lynch's cash management account (CMA). Each of these were major efforts, mainstream for the firm, that involved producing significant replacement of existing products by virtue of their innovative nature. The market for artificial sweeteners was then relatively small, the diaper business was cloth and geographically highly fragmented, and no brokerage firm was offering the type of service offered by the cash management account, which was actually patented by Merrill Lynch. The blitzkrieg is a no-holds-barred assault on a wide market. It is an aggressive strategy moving in full force and very quickly. Because this strategy requires rapid market penetration, it probably would not be appropriate in a situation where there is not a munificent market—existing or clearly potential. This approach might, however, be taken even in a hostile market, provided internal commitment and resources are great enough to overcome competition over an unpredictable but necessary time.

The Cavalry Charge

This strategy is highly aggressive and focused. All the elements that can be aggressive might be used, that is, advertising, public relations, sales force intensity, and aggressive pricing, and they are concentrated on a market segment and/or a limited geographical area. This strategy is not uncommon for new consumer products. In building a new business around a technology, a cavalry charge would select one application, rather than many, focusing all effort in a concentrated fashion to achieve early success. The growth of General Electric Financial Services is an excellent example of such a strategy. Starting with investigating and providing credit for the purchase of home appliances, GE moved step by step to providing financing services for larger and larger equipment and by 1992, GE leased airplanes, oil well drilling rigs, and ships and financed leveraged buyouts. The cavalry charge requires a market that is munificent but not so hostile that the market segments into which entry is deferred are lost to competition.

The Strike Force Approach

This strategy is non-aggressive and focused. It is a low-key, calculated entry into a narrowly defined market. It uses relatively fewer resources than other approaches and demands less of a commitment from the firm. An example is Motorola's entry into portable phones, starting with very small entry in portable radio communications for police cars and growing into cellular phones over a 20 year period so that it is now a world leader in this business. This was not because of lack of commitment but because commitment and effort was tied to the changing state of the market and technology.

This non-aggressive and focused strategy might be appropriate for a market that is hostile and sparse. The venture can quietly enter the market and establish itself, laying the groundwork for further expansion. In a particularly hostile market, this back door entry can give the firm a foothold without alarming competitors.

Guerrilla Tactics

A guerrilla approach calls for a non-aggressive but wider scope of entry characterized by the use of relatively low resources used to strike where they can be most effective in establishing a position in a market. The development of the IBM clone business by firms such as Gateway Technology and Dell is a fine example of effective guerrilla tactics.

A guerrilla approach is appropriate in a market that is munificent but hostile. The breadth of market will support a broad entry, but the presence of major competitors calls for a less aggressive approach. It is also appropriate for exploration to determine the markets to focus on later without generating strong competitive interest or counteraction.

INTEGRATING FIRM AND MARKET VARIABLES IN STRATEGY SELECTION

We have examined a few of the characteristics of the firm and the market that can affect the success of the new venture and the mode of market entry. But how do these variables affect the entry strategy decision?

The following case is an illustration of the interaction of variables in the market and the firm to arrive at an entry strategy. A mid-size firm with fairly limited resources developed a process for producing onion rings from chopped rather than whole onions, thus cutting the cost of producing onion rings in half due to the reduction of labor and packaging costs and increased yield. The challenge was to decide the best way to capitalize on this innovation. How should they bring this product to market? The firm was primarily a manufacturer and supplier of intermediate products to the food industry and was unfamiliar with consumer product marketing. Among its existing customers for food coatings, which included breading, were companies that produced traditional frozen onion rings.

The firm considered four options. It could produce and market onion rings for the consumer and food service market, form an alliance or joint venture with another firm to spread risk and supplement know-how, become a private label producer for other marketers, or license others under its patents to produce and market the product.

The onion ring market size at the time was only 25 million pounds per year, but it appeared that there might be a potential market of 300 million pounds with the company's higher-quality, lower-cost product. There was little competition. The market was benign and potentially munificent. Using market criteria only, an aggressive, broad-front entry as a manufacturer and marketer of onion rings seemed justified.

But the resources of the firm were not great enough to support it, and its internal culture was strongly adverse to taking what seemed to be a large risk of capital for investment and marketing. There was also the possibility of loss of existing business because of direct competition with existing customers. In addition, the company needed additional profit fast, that is, the promise of the potential in this new product was highly salient. Because of these factors, the firm decided to license the process non-exclusively to accelerate development of the business with minimum risk, coopting a number of its existing customers, and developed a highly profitable and successful licensing business. In doing so, the company forfeited the long-term profitability on a continuing manufacturing business long after the patents expired. If the firm had greater resources, more experience in consumer marketing, and a strategy and culture that made the risks acceptable, it might have chosen another strategy that would produce profits after patent expiration.

This case illustrates what the reality is: the final choice of actual entry strategy ultimately boils down to a trade-off between what may be considered ideal and what the firm thinks it is able to do. This gives rise to the last part of the chapter: a discussion of the factors that may moderate the selection of the ideal entry strategy based only on consideration of market munificence and hostility.

MODERATING INFLUENCES

Although we suggest that the preceding dimensions of the market are useful indicators of what the general strategy for entry should be, factors other than hostility and munificence can play a crucial moderating role in the final determination of entry strategy.

Salience to the Venturing Firm

Salience to the venturing firm will affect the extent to which the entry will be supported and the firm's interest in the venture. This determines the resources it will put into development and marketing of the product and thus plays a crucial role in the choice of entry strategy. The significance is based on how the project is perceived to fit into the short-and long-term objectives and needs of the company. Firms vary widely in their criteria for significance. General Electric, for example, will consider whether or not the new venture will be big enough to affect the entire firm, not just succeed on its own. 3M, on the other hand, encourages the launch of as many ventures as might be successful in their own right, with the understanding that a few of the ones that were judged to be relatively unimportant could turn out to be major successes.

Salience is also affected by how desperately the firm may need a new venture or product because of decline of its existing business, or because of decline in profit or it stock price due to new competitive products. Consider the salience of major new products to IBM or Digital in the increasingly competitively hostile market. At the opposite end of a "do-or-die" venture is the low-salience venture of a small start-up by a large firm in a non-critical market. In this case, its success or failure will not shake the organization to its roots but "would be nice to have." Highly salient ventures will tend to produce aggressive entry, with greater resource commitment.

Finally, initial salience does not remain constant. In a firm where a new venture or product may not initially show great potential, or a market is not at all measurable, entry may begin unaggressively, with little importance attached to the project. As promise develops and the rewards become clearer, its salience to the firm may become much greater.

The blitzkrieg, because of the intensity and vigor of the commitment demands a strong salience, whereas for the cavalry charge, the salience to the firm does not have to be as great, because of the limited approach to the market.

The strike force approach is useful for a firm in which the venture has little salience.

Corporate Fit

Fit and salience are closely linked. Ventures or products that are perceived not to fit are not likely to be perceived as salient. But venture ideas, products, and technologies that are not related to existing businesses do frequently emerge within a firm. This is particularly true with technologies that have application outside of a firm's business and markets, that are not related to the strategic objectives of the firm, and where the firm does not have the marketing expertise and knowledge required for success.

Here the choices boil down to developing competence slowly during unaggressive, quiet entry or making alliances similar to those used for obtaining increased resources. Clearly there is a high need for corporate fit if a blitzkrieg strategy is to be pursued, whereas a strike force approach is more appropriate when corporate fit is low.

Resource Availability

No matter what the salience of the venture is, or the characteristics of the external environment, available resources will have a most important impact on strategic choice. The market may call for an aggressive, broad-front strategy, but if the company does not have the resources to pursue that strategy, it must pursue a less aggressive path or make arrangements that provide resources not otherwise available. These arrangements may run the gamut from raising outside capital to forming joint ventures, making strategic alliances, or even to selling assets in order to finance a new, highly salient, high-potential venture.

Corporate Culture

Regardless of all external factors, this factor may be the principal determinant of entry strategy. In one firm, only projects that promise major returns fast ever have a chance of support. This has led to exaggerated projections and aggressive entry for all projects, regardless of the market, and large losses for most. Firms that are highly innovative and successful tend to start small and to increase aggressiveness with increased knowledge of the market. The ideal culture for new ventures is one in which venturing is considered a necessity for achieving the goals of the firm and is understood to be fundamentally experimental in nature, with a great deal of unknowns, and with a high percentage of failures.

Type of Market

Another factor to consider is whether the market is industrial, commercial, or consumer. More aggressive strategic options are possible for firms with limited resources in industrial markets, rather than in consumer markets, simply due to the marketing costs required.

Existing Customers

If the new venture will result in direct competition with existing customers, a strategy must be chosen that minimizes the loss of business.

Critical Mass Requirement

The size required in order for a new venture to operate at all can strongly affect strategic choice, as illustrated in the Motorola case cited earlier. It also would have been very difficult to start Federal Express, for example, on a small basis. It required a very aggressive and broad-based entry in order to achieve an adequate operating base.

Proprietary Position

The proprietary position of the product under consideration influences the options for entry that are acceptable. A very strong patent position reduces the urgency for aggressive, broad-front entry if resources are severely limited or if the market is in its early development stages. By maintaining proprietary advantages, the firm can enter markets slowly and in a small way, as Motorola did over a period of years before becoming the major factor in the cellular telephone business.

From the point of view of strategic force and focus, we suggest that it is useful to identify first what is ideal based on market hostility and munificence. Then, seek methods for achieving this that take into account the other factors that must be considered, choosing a strategic form that makes the risks affordable and the know-how needed available. Referring once again to the Motorola Iridium project, Motorola announced that it intended to invest only $150 million, with the balance of the $3.1 billion coming from other investors, thus permitting the necessary and desirable aggressive broad-front entry, but with reduced risk to the lead venturer.

Table 15.1 shows the influence of these moderating factors on the choice of entry strategy. The table may be used to scan munificence and hostility to identify an "ideal" entry strategy, and then see if any firm conditions mitigate against the ideal strategy—in which case the ideal approach should be moderated.

It is important to note that Table 15.1 consists of a mixture of hypotheses, logic, propositions, and opinions based on some experience, not on research, which we hope might be stimulated by this material.

Challenges for Research

A major challenge facing firms launching new ventures and innovative products is prediction of the rate of development and size of emerging markets, and the strategies that are most effective in such markets. This is a particularly significant problem to medium-sized and smaller firms with limited resources and major innovations—firms that simply cannot afford highly aggressive strategies. Each firm has unique characteristics and no single firm is likely to have enough new ventures going to comprise a sample that will behave like the PIMS data base samples. More study is needed of the extremes of performance of individual firms, which may provide better guidance to formulating entry strategy than the statistical results of many firms based on central tendencies.

CONCLUSIONS

In addition to the usual components of strategy, the elements of strategic aggressiveness and focus must be added in light of their significance to the outcome of new product and new venture entries. The range of choices available are described and the variables to be considered in making the choice are discussed. The primary consideration is the character of the market, specifically its munificence and hostility dimensions, but the ability and willingness of the firm to execute any chosen strategy is a result of its risk attitudes, resources, culture, and know-how.

REFERENCES

Biggadyke, R. "The Risky Business of Corporate Diversification." *Harvard Business Review* (May–June 1979): 103–11.

Block, Z. "Damage Control for New Corporate Ventures." *Journal of Business Strategy* (Mar.–Apr. 1989): 22–28.

Block, Z., and I. C. MacMillan. "Milestones for Successful Venture Planning." *Harvard Business Review* (Sep.–Oct. 1986).

Covin, J. G., and D. P. Slavin. "Strategic Management of Small Firms in Hostile and Benign Environments." *Strategic Management Journal* 10(1), (1989): 75–87.

Kotler, P., and R. Singh. "Marketing Warfare in the 1980s." *Journal of Business Strategy* (Fall 1980).

MacMillan, I. C., and D. L. Day. "Corporate Ventures into Industrial Markets: Dynamics of Aggressive Entry." *Journal of Business Venturing* 2(1), (1987).

Miller, D. "The Correlates of Entrepreneurship in Three Types of Firms." *Management Science* 29 (1983): 770–91.

Roberts, E. B., and C. A. Berry. "Entering New Businesses: Selecting Strategies for Success." *Sloan Management Review* 26(3): 3–17.

Sahlman, W. A., and H. H. Stevenson. "Capital Markets Myopia." Harvard Case 9-288-005 (1988).

Tsai, W. M.-H., I. C. MacMillan, and M. B. Low. "Effect of Strategy and Environment on Corporate Venture Success in Industrial Markets." *Journal of Business Venturing* 6(1), (1991): 9–28.

16

An Agenda for Integrating Entrepreneurship and Marketing Strategy Research

David W. Cravens, Dale A. Lunsford,
Gerald E. Hills, and
Raymond W. LaForge

Entrepreneurship has received a tremendous amount of research attention in the last decade. The premise of this chapter is that this research can be integrated into strategic marketing research programs to enrich our understanding of marketing strategy from both a theoretical and practical perspective. Entrepreneurship research suggests the need for marketing scholars to adopt a broader research paradigm for their investigation of marketing strategy. A broader paradigm would incorporate the influence of organizational characteristics on firm marketing strategy performance. Entrepreneurship research, however, often has a myopic orientation in that much of the work neglects the influence of market and competitive forces on the strategy process. Thus, a combined perspective can contribute important research and managerial insights to both areas.

Our purpose is to illustrate how an agenda for future marketing strategy research can be derived from the current work in entrepreneurship. We examine the research foundations followed by a discussion of a marketing strategy research contingency perspective.

THE INTERFACE OF MARKETING STRATEGY AND ENTREPRENEURSHIP RESEARCH

Research on marketing strategy has accumulated independently of research on entrepreneurship. This has occurred despite the obvious overlap between the study of marketing and the study of starting, developing, and managing new enterprises (Hisrich and Peters 1989). The areas of market opportunity analysis, new product development, the diffusion of innovation, and marketing strategy development for entry and growth are vital to the new enterprise and historically a research focus of marketing scholars (Hills 1987; Hills and LaForge 1992).

MARKETING STRATEGY RESEARCH

A history of marketing research would be forced to conclude that much of what we currently know about marketing strategy is derived from the experience of relatively few, atypical, U.S. corporations. Beginning with research into business portfolio matrices (e.g., Day 1977; Wensley 1981), and continuing with the Profit Impact of Market Strategies (PIMS) analysis of pooled business experience, for example, the conceptual focus and empirical examination of marketing strategy has centered on the problems and experiences of very large, high profile, Fortune 500-type firms.

A case in point is the importance of PIMS research to our understanding of strategic marketing. The PIMS data base consists of market, strategic, and performance information for 3,000 Small Business Units (SBUs) of 450 firms. The contribution of research into the marketing strategies of these firms has been and continues to be core to our understanding of the topic (Buzzell and Gale 1987). Yet, the characteristics of these firms are not typical of most business enterprises and they are representative of a much different stage of the organizational life cycle than new ventures and small, growth-oriented firms.

Recent conceptual work offers a promising framework for marketing strategy analysis and choice by examining evolutionary processes in competitive markets (Lambkin and Day 1989). Several important strategic issues impacting emerging firms are discussed. Embryonic, developing, and maturing markets are evaluated in terms of population density, size and rate of environmental change, predominant organizational form, other competitors, and the best performers.

Integrating entrepreneurship research into the study of marketing strategy can broaden our focus from an exclusive analysis of only the very largest firms. A review of research on entrepreneurial strategy illustrates the major role of markcting strategy variables in explaining the creation and emergence of new firms (see Table 16.1). The valuable contribution to the marketing strategy literature is that these variables have been studied within organizational contexts rarely examined in the marketing literature.

Considering the importance of marketing strategy in launching and sustaining a new enterprise and deficiencies in the marketing expertise of many entrepreneurs (Stasch and Ward 1987), research at the interface of marketing strategy and entrepreneurship can greatly improve our understanding of entrepreneurship. In addition, integration of entrepreneurship and marketing strategy research can greatly improve our understanding of marketing strategy in all firms, not just the very largest.

Table 16.1
Selected Empirical Entrepreneurial Strategy Studies

Author(s)	Variables Examined	Results
Alpander, Carter, and Forsgren (1990)	Owner characteristics Business problems	Marketing is one of the most commonly reported problems in first three years of firm existence. Finding new customers and market expansion were cited.
Drazin and Kazajian (1990); Miller and Friesen (1984)	Strategy Situation Structure Decision-making style	Strategy differs across firm life cycle stages. Product innovation, backward vertical integration, niche strategy, and market segmentation use varied across life phases.
Feeser and Willard (1990)	Sales growth Founder's previous business Size of founding team Initial product/market choice Timing of entry Geographic scope Growth method	Firms with high growth rates reported fewer changes to their initial product/market choices. High-growth firms also reported greater emphasis on foreign markets. Use of acquisitions was unrelated to sales growth.

Table 16.1, Continued

Author(s)	Variables Examined	Results
Shan (1990)	Cooperation Strategy Competitive position Firm size Product diversity National target market	The further behind the firm is in competition with its rivals the more likely a new biotechnology product will be launched using a cooperative arrangement. Small firm size and foreign target markets are positively correlated with use of strategic alliances.
Tucker, Singh, and Meinahard (1990)	Organization form Number of foundings Number of disbandings Population density Institutional change	Founding of specialist service organizations (few product offerings) differs from the founding of generalists (broad offerings).
Chaganti, Chaganti, and Mahajan (1989)	Type of competition Strategy Profitability	The effectiveness of various strategies varied across four competitive environments. Even for small firms, a broad product scope was associated with high profitability.
Miller, Gartner, and Wilson (1989)	Market entry order Market share Differentiation	Examination of new corporate ventures in PIMS data base found significant advantages for market pioneers.

Table 16.1, Continued

Author(s)	Variables Examined	Results
Covin and Slevin (1988)	Industry life cycle Strategy Performance	New firms in emerging industries reported the poorest performance. Pricing, advertising, and product line strategies varied across industry life cycle stages.
Bruno and Leidecker (1988)	Product/market Financial management	The majority of major reasons reported for new venture failure were product/market related.
Kazanjian (1988)	Firm size Firm age Rate of sales growth Dominant management problems	The self-reported dominance of sales/marketing problems were related to the firm's stage of growth. Marketing problems were most dominant in the growth stage.
McDougall and Robinson (1988)	New venture strategy Industry structure Performance	An important predictor of new venture performance was industry/strategy interaction. New venture strategy must be matched to industry structure.

Table 16.1, Continued

Author(s)	Variables Examined	Results
Miller (1988)	Entry order Differentiation Relative cost, price	Significant competitive advantages accrue to market pioneers. Pioneers were able to better differentiate their products. Followers were not able to exploit lower cost advantages.
Boag (1987)	Marketing control Firm age, size Performance	Evidence supporting a model of the metamorphosis of marketing control systems among new firms was found. Increasing control was positively related to performance.
Chaganti (1987)	Strategy Industry life cycle ROA	In contrast to research on large firms, different growth environment required different strategies among small firms.
MacMillan and Day (1987)	Market share ROI Market conditions Marketing strategy	Firms that invest aggressively in marketing soon after new venture launch achieve superior market share and ROI.

Table 16.1, Continued

Author(s)	Variables Examined	Results
McDougall and Robinson (1987)	Firm age Strategy	Factor analysis identifies eight strategic orientations taken by 269 new ventures. Number of channels, product diversity, number of customers, and promotion expense were among marketing variables describing types of new ventures.
Davig (1986)	Profit growth Sales growth Strategy type	In mature, fragmented industries, small manufacturers emphasizing product quality or product uniqueness reported greater profit growth.
O'Neill and Duker (1986)	Strategy Initial firm performance	In agreement with PIMS findings, product quality was found to be positively related to firm survival.
Sandberg (1986)	Industry structure Strategy Entrepreneur characteristics	Industry structure and strategy impacted new venture performance. Ventures employing a product differentiation strategy in an industry characterized by heterogenous products performed best.

MARKETING STRATEGY RESEARCH—A CONTINGENCY PERSPECTIVE

Integration of entrepreneurship and marketing strategy research calls for a contingency perspective in studying marketing strategy. Conceptual work by Cravens (1991) and Cravens et al. (1989) provides the framework for integrating entrepreneurship research into the study of marketing strategy (see Table 16.1). The core concepts that guide the development of the research agenda are (1) strategy choice is influenced by situational contingencies and (2) strategy performance is determined by the strategy that is selected and the effectiveness of implementation.

A RESEARCH AGENDA

Fruitful areas for research can be identified. The major components of a research agenda include the strategic situation of the organization, the strategy choice process, implementation of the strategy, and strategy performance (see Figure 16.1). These areas are discussed and propositions for research are derived.

Strategic Situation

The attractiveness of a product-market, the differences in the needs of buyers, the structure and intensity of competition, the organization's skills and resources, and other situational factors influence the choice of a marketing strategy (Cravens 1991). Entrepreneurship research suggests the importance of organizational contingencies in defining the strategic situation of new enterprises.

Product-market structure

There is a tendency in entrepreneurship research to assume that market characteristics and forces are constant across various market entry situations. There is a considerable base of research findings that indicate wide differences in strategic situations created by the stage of market development, the characteristics and requirements of buyers, and the patterns of change over time (see, for example, Lambkin and Day 1989; Robinson and Fornell 1985; Urban, Carter, Gaskin, and Mucha 1986; Aaker and Day 1986).

Figure 16.1
A Framework for Integrating Entrepreneurship Research into the Study of Marketing Strategy

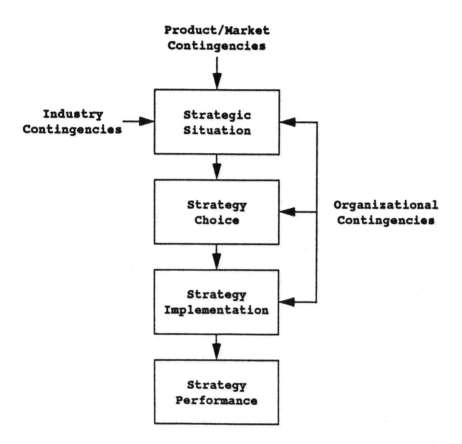

The existence of market entry barriers is an important strategy situation issue. Identification of the types and importance of entry barriers are essential in the entry evaluation decision. The major entry concepts include the cost advantages of incumbents, product differentiation of incumbents, capital requirements, customer switching costs, access to distribution channels, and government policy (Karakaya and Stahl 1989). There are three strategy considerations concerning market entry barriers: (1) identifying the relevant barriers and their strategic and operational importance, (2) estimating the effect of the barriers on entry at different market maturity stages, and (3) examining the differences in entry factors across markets (Cravens 1991, Chapter 8).

Industry life cycle

The effect of industry life cycle on the strategic situation of a firm may be contingent on the firm's stage of development. Several have used the PIMS data base to explore the strategic marketing situations of firms in growth, mature, and declining industries (e.g., Anderson and Zeithaml 1984; Hambrick, MacMillan, and Day 1982). Changanti (1987) noted that PIMS results indicate profitable large firms emphasize resource efficiencies, productivity, and product quality in each industry life cycle stage; only the strength of the relationship between strategies and profit performance varied across industry growth situations.

A replication of the PIMS examination of industry life cycle using a sample of small Canadian manufacturers found the relationship between stage of industry life and small firms to be different than PIMS firms (Chaganti 1987). Profitable small firms required very different marketing strategies across varying situations of industry growth. Profitable small firms in growth industries emphasized sales in local markets at competitively low prices with little new product development, whereas successful small firms in decline industries utilized broad product lines and aggressive marketing expenditures. This finding is consistent with the results of Covin and Slevin (1988). Pricing, advertising, and product line elements of marketing strategy were found to vary across stages of the industry life cycle.

In conclusion, strategic situations defined by industry life cycle appear to influence large and small firms differently in terms of their strategic choices. Among small firms, industry life cycle stages moderate the form as well as the strength of the relationship between strategy and performance.

Organizational characteristics

Entrepreneurship research also suggests marketing strategy should be conceptualized and investigated within the context of the organizational mission. Most marketing strategy frameworks address the role of organizational mission but few empirical investigations actually take mission into account.

Cooper (1979) defines three types of new enterprises and small firms. Because of different organizational goals and missions, each organizational type defines a unique strategic situation. The first group was labeled "mom and pop shops." These firms are extremely small and possess little marketing expertise or resources. The second group are stable, high-payoff companies. These enterprises have achieved some success and may have acquired substantial marketing expertise within a limited market. Such firms have no aspirations for future growth. A third group is composed of growth-oriented small firms. These are new ventures with a mission defined by aggressive growth. These firms often face a strategic situation defined by a high need for outside sources of funding and a marketing situation in a high-growth environment that emphasizes current risk for future growth.

Cardozo (1989) defined a growth trajectories model to underscore the varying profiles of new enterprises. A trajectory is defined in terms of the "source" of the firm (independent or corporate start-ups, turnarounds, and business combinations), whether the new venture is launched with a large or small initial mass, defined in terms of its resource base, and the initial growth and performance path (growing, arrested development, stable, marginally viable). By providing a taxonomy for classifying populations of new businesses, the model can be used to define the strategic situations of small firms.

Industry structure may have an important impact on new and small firm performance. Davig (1986) identified successful strategies within the strategic context of mature, fragmented industries. In a comprehensive examination of new venture success, Sandberg (1986) found strategic situation defined in terms of industry structure and strategy to interact in predicting success. New ventures in industries with heterogeneous products performed best.

Three propositions can be derived from the integration of entrepreneurship issues and marketing strategic situations (see Table 16.2). The propositions add to the dominant conceptualization of strategic situation in marketing strategy by explicitly considering organizational characteristics and their direct and interactive effects on marketing strategy choice.

Marketing Strategy Choice

Cravens (1987) identifies and provides a supporting rationale for four generic marketing strategies. These include market domination in the firm that tries to achieve or hold the dominant competitive position in an industry. A market development strategy seeks to expand market boundaries to generate enhanced performance. A market selectivity strategy is defined as trying to dominate one or a few market segments in heterogeneous markets. Finally, a firm may employ a differential advantage strategy where it seeks to develop and exploit a competitive advantage in a homogeneous market.

Table 16.2
Research Propositions: Organizational Contingencies and Strategic Situation

---

P1:   A firm's strategic situation, defined in terms of developmental traject-
        ories or organizational mission, will strongly influence marketing
        strategy choice.

P2:   The product-market life cycle stage will create a strategic situation
        eliciting a different strategic response in new enterprises versus mature
        firms.

P3:   Industry structure and associated entry barriers will create a strategic
        situation eliciting a different strategic response in new enterprises versus
        mature firms.

Empirical evidence from entrepreneurship research indicates new enterprises may employ any of these four marketing strategies. Initial strategy choices have been described as either specialist or generalist in nature (Tucker, Singh, and Meinhard 1990). McDougall and Robinson (1987) used factor analysis to identify eight strategic orientations chosen by 269 new ventures. A diversity of strategic choices were identified along such dimensions as channels, product line breadth, and promotion expenditures.

Marketing strategy choice is a function of firm stage of development (Drazin and Kazanjian 1990; Miller and Friesen 1984). As firms advance through a life cycle, marketing strategy also evolves. The use of niche strategies, vertical integration, and market segmentation changed as firms developed from new ventures to large, mature organizations. The "strategic brand concept" provides a conceptual framework for marketing strategy design and management over the various product-market life cycle stages (Park, Jaworski, and MacInnis 1986).

The extent to which a marketing strategy should be modified over time is an important strategy choice issue. Despite the uncertainties present in a new industry, growing evidence indicates "that more successful or longer-living firms engage in less change than firms which fail" (Romanelli 1987). Successful enterprises select and retain a strategy on a continuing basis. This issue has critical implications for the new enterprise, particularly when entering a new product-market where the lack of experience in the market provides little or no direction concerning strategy choice.

Entrepreneurship research also provides insight into two important marketing strategy options: strategic alliances and product diversification. Varadarajan and Rajaratnam (1986) developed a model of symbiotic marketing describing the use of cooperative marketing strategies. They presented several examples of symbiotic modes used by two or more large firms. Shan (1990) found small firms are also utilizing collaborative marketing strategies. In an empirical study of entrepreneurial high-technology firms, small firms at a competitive disadvantage with rivals in their industry were likely to utilize joint ventures or other cooperative strategies to launch new products.

Several propositions can be developed to illustrate the research direction provided by integrating entrepreneurship into marketing strategy research (see Table 16.3).

Table 16.3
Research Propositions: Organizational Contingencies and Marketing Strategy Choice

---

P1:   Choice of marketing growth strategy is a function of organizational life cycle stage. Market penetration is most likely in new enterprises with diversification the most often used strategy among mature firms.

P2:   Choice of a new enterprise's initial marketing strategy is a function of strategic situation, organizational characteristics, and entrepreneur motivations.

P3:   Use of collaborative ventures in new enterprises is a function of the competitive position of the firm. As the competitive position of the firm declines, use of collaborative ventures is more likely.

Strategy Implementation

Implementation has received increasing attention as an important determinant of marketing strategy performance. The implementation of marketing planning (John and Martin 1984), interaction of marketing personnel with other functional areas (Ruekert and Walker 1987), and marketing strategy implementation as a make or buy choice (Ruekert, Walker, and Roering 1985) are exemplars of work in this area. Yet, both conceptual and empirical work provides little insight into the potential moderating effect of firm stage of development on implementation.

Results from entrepreneurship research indicate implementation issues are strongly influenced by organizational characteristics. Kazanjian (1988) found that the reported dominant problems of firms were a function of the firm's life cycle stage. Marketing problems occurred most in the firm's growth stage. Marketing is also a commonly reported problem in the firm's initial development (Alpander, Carter, and Forsgren 1990) and product/market problems are cited as major reason for new venture failure (Bruno and Leidecker 1988). The perception of problems is an important indicator of implementation issues.

Control of marketing systems and strategies is an important element of implementation. Empirical evidence that control systems evolve over time within the firm has been reported (Boag 1987). A metamorphosis of marketing control systems was found as firms grew in age and size.

A preliminary integration of implementation research within both fields indicate propositions for future investigation (see Table 16.4). Overall, the propositions suggest no single marketing control system is equally appropriate for all types of tasks, environmental situations, or firms. For example, Ruekert, Walker and Roering (1985) concluded that highly formalized, bureaucratic organizational forms were not appropriate for marketing functions within an environment of high uncertainty. Yet, Boag (1987) reported evidence that the opposite may be true for small, early-growth firms. Formal control systems up to a point may enhance successful implementation even within volatile environments.

Jaworski (1988) has developed a marketing control framework and propositions intended to overcome several limitations in prior research in the control area. It links the environment context, control types, and consequences, showing how these contingencies influence the selection and use of marketing controls. This framework offers useful conceptual material for further development of strategy implementation propositions for emerging enterprises.

Table 16.4
Research Propositions: Organizational Contingencies and Strategy Implementation

---

P1:   The relationship between marketing function organization and performance is a function of firm's stage of development.

P2:   Marketing strategy control systems evolve as a firm develops from new enterprise to mature firm.

P3:   Increasing formal control within early-growth firms in volatile environments positively influences performance, whereas the opposite influence exists when formal control is increased within mature firms.

Strategy Performance

Strategy choice and implementation are the primary determinants of strategy success. The analysis of strategy performance over time provides important diagnostic inputs into the development of strategy choice concepts. The early discussion highlights the importance of matching the strategy choice with the conditions of the environment and the organization's skills and resources. The long-term importance of selecting a sound initial strategy has research support (e.g., Romanelli 1987; Park, Jaworski, and MacInnis 1986).

Lambkin and Day (1989) propose several strategy choice guidelines that offer success potential depending on the type of firm and the stage of market maturity. They suggest that small-scale pioneers are the best performers in embryonic markets, whereas early followers with established businesses in related markets are the most successful organizational forms in developing and maturing markets. Small-scale late entrants may also be successful by occupying narrow market segments in mature markets. Several research findings and case studies provide support for the strategic framework. Illustrative research propositions are presented in Table 16.5.

Table 16.5
Research Propositions: Organizational Contingencies and Strategy Performance

---

P1:   A core strategy concept that is maintained over life cycle stages will be more successful than a strategy concept that is modified over time.

P2:   New enterprises will be most successful when entering emerging markets.

P3:   New enterprise success in maturing markets is heavily dependent on developing a dominant competitive position in a narrow market segment.

CONCLUSIONS

This chapter illustrates how entrepreneurship concepts can be used to enhance our understanding of marketing strategy. It provides a review of empirical research on the strategy issues of new ventures and small enterprises. Evaluating this research against the backdrop of marketing strategy research allows the development of several propositions. These are not meant to be exhaustive but to be illustrative of the contribution of integrating entrepreneurship into marketing strategy research.

REFERENCES

Aaker, D. A., and G. S. Day. "The Perils of High-Growth Markets." *Strategic Management Journal* 7 (1986): 419.

Alpander, G., K. Carter, and R. Forsgren. "Managerial Issues and Problem Solving in the Formative Years." *Journal of Small Business Management* 28 (Apr. 1990): 9–19.

Boag, D. A. "Marketing Control and Performance in Early Growth Firms." *Journal of Business Venturing* 2(4), (1987): 365–79.

Bruno, A. V., and J. K. Leidecker. "Causes of New Venture Failure: 1960s vs. 1980s." *Business Horizons* 3 (Nov.–Dec. 1988): 51–56.

Buzzell, R. D., and B T. Gale. *The PIMS Principles: Linking Strategy to Performance.* New York: Free Press, 1987.

Cardozo, R. N. "Developmental Trajectories of New Businesses." In *Research at the Marketing/Entrepreneurship Interface*, edited by G. E. Hills, R. W. LaForge, and B. J. Parker, 19–32. Chicago: University of Illinois at Chicago, 1989.

Chaganti, R. "Small Business Strategies in Different Industry Growth Environments." *Journal of Small Business Management* 25 (July 1987): 61–68.

Chaganti, R., R. Chaganti, and V. Mahajan. "Profitable Small Business Strategies Under Different Types of Competition." *Entrepreneurship Theory and Practice* 13 (Spring 1989): 21–35.

Cooper, A. "Strategic Management: New Ventures and Small Business." In *Strategic Management: A New View of Business Policy and Planning*, edited by D. Schendel and C. Hofer, 316–38. Boston: Little, 1979.

Cravens, D. W. *Strategic Marketing*, 3rd ed. Homewood, IL: Richard D. Irwin, 1991.

Cravens, D. W., G. E. Hills, R. W. LaForge, and D. A. Lunsford. "Toward a Theory of Marketing Strategy for New Ventures: Some Preliminary Propositions." In *Proceedings of the Winter Educators' Conference.* Chicago: American Marketing Association, 1989.

Covin, J. G., and D. P. Slevin. "New Venture Competitive Strategy: An Industry Life Cycle Analysis." In *Proceedings of the Eighth Annual Babson College Entrepreneurship Research Conference*, 446–60. Wellesley, MA: Babson College, 1988.

Day, G. S. "Diagnosing the Product Portfolio." *Journal of Marketing* 41 (Apr. 1977): 29–38.

Drazin, R., and R. K. Kazanjian. "A Reanalysis of Miller and Friesen's Life Cycle Data." *Strategic Management Journal* 11(4), (1990): 319–25.

Feeser, H. R., and G. E. Willard. "Founding Strategy and Performance: A Comparison of High and Low Growth High Tech Firms." *Strategic Management Journal* 11(2), (1990): 87–98.

Hills, G. E. "Marketing and Entrepreneurship Research Issues." In *Research at the Marketing/Entrepreneurship Interface*, edited by G. E. Hills, 183–286. Chicago: University of Illinois at Chicago, 1987.

Hills, G. E., and R. W. LaForge. "Marketing and Entrepreneurship: The State of the Art." In *The State of the Art of Entrepreneurship*, edited by D. L. Sexton and J. D. Kasarda, 164–90. Boston: PWS-Kent, 1992.

Hisrich, R. D., and M. P. Peters. *Entrepreneurship.* Homewood, IL: BPI/Irwin, 1989.

John, G., and J. Martin. "Effects of Organizational Structure of Marketing Planning on Credibility and Utilization of Plan Output." *Journal of Marketing Research* 21 (May 1984): 170–83.

Karakaya, F., and M. J. Stahl. "Barriers to Entry and Market Entry Decisions in Consumer and Industrial Goods Markets." *Journal of Marketing* (April 1989): 80–91.

Kazanjian, R. "Relation of Dominant Problems to Stages of Growth in Technology-Based New Ventures." *Academy of Management Journal* 31 (June 1988): 257–79.

Lambkin, M., and G. S. Day. "Evolutionary Processes in Competitive Markets: Beyond the Product Life Cycle." *Journal of Marketing* (July 1989): 1–16.

MacMillan, I., and D. L. Day. "Corporate Ventures into Industrial Markets: Dynamics of Aggressive Entry." *Journal of Business Venturing* 2(1), (1987): 29–37.

McDougall, P., and R. B. Robinson, Jr. "New Venture Strategies: An Empirical Identification of Eight Distinct Strategic Orientations." *Academy of Management Proceedings* (1987): 73–77.

McDougall, P., and R. B. Robinson, Jr. "New Venture Performance: Patterns of Strategic Behavior in Different Industries." In *Proceedings of the Eighth Annual Babson College Entrepreneurship Research Conference,* 477–91. Wellesley, MA: Babson College, 1988.

Miller, A. "Entry Order and Its Relationship to Market Share and Competitive Advantage: A Study of New Corporate Ventures." *Academy of Management Proceedings* (1988): 64–68.

Miller, A., W. B. Gartner, and R. Wilson. "Entry Order, Market Share, and Competitive Advantage: A Study of Their Relationships in New Corporate Ventures." *Journal of Business Venturing* 4(3), (1989): 197–209.

Miller, D., and P. Friesen. "A Longitudinal Study of the Corporate Life Cycle." *Management Science* 30 (Oct. 1984): 1161–83.

O'Neill, H. M., and J. Duker. "Survival and Failure in Small Business." *Journal of Small Business Management* (Jan. 1986): 30–37.

Park, C. W., B. J. Jaworski, and D. J. MacInnis. "Strategic Brand Concept—Image Management." *Journal of Marketing* (Oct. 1986): 135–45.

Robinson, W. T., and C. Fornell. "Sources of Market Pioneer Advantages in Consumer Goods Industries." *Journal of Marketing Research* (Aug. 1985): 305–15.

Romanelli, E. "New Venture Strategies in the Minicomputer Industry." *California Management Review* (Fall 1987): 161.

Ruekert, R. W., and O. C. Walker, Jr. "Marketing's Interaction with Other Functional Units: A Conceptual Framework and Empirical Evidence." *Journal of Marketing* 51 (Jan. 1987): 1–19.

Ruekert, R. W., O. C. Walker, Jr., and K. J. Roering. "The Organization of Marketing Activities: A Contingency Theory of Structure and Performance." *Journal of Marketing* 49 (Winter 1985): 13–25.

Sandberg, W. R. *New Venture Performance: The Role of Strategy and Industry Structure.* Lexington, MA: Lexington, 1986.

Shan, W. "An Empirical Analysis of Organizational Strategies by Entrepreneurial High-Technology Firms." *Strategic Management Journal* 11(2), (199): 129–39.

Stasch, S. F., and J. L. Ward. "Some Observations and Research Opportunities Regarding Marketing of Smaller Businesses. In *Research at the Marketing/Entrepreneurship Interface,* edited by G. E. Hills, 82–94. Chicago: University of Illinois at Chicago, 1987.

Tucker, D. J., J. V. Singh, and A. G. Meinhard. "Organizational Form, Population Dynamics, and Institutional Change: The Founding Patterns of Voluntary Organizations." *Academy of Management Journal* 33 (Mar. 1990): 151–78.

Urban, G. L., T. Carter, S. Gaskin, and Z. Mucha. "Market Share Rewards to Pioneering Brands: An Empirical Analysis and Strategic Implications." *Management Science* (June 1986): 645–59.

Wensley, R. "Strategic Marketing: Betas, Boxes or Basics." *Journal of Marketing* 45 (Summer 1981): 173–82.

A BROADER PERSPECTIVE

17

Entrepreneurship in International Marketing: A Continuing Research Challenge

Hans B. Thorelli and George Tesar

INTRODUCTION

International marketing and international business textbooks do not directly address international issues faced by small businesses operated by individual entrepreneurs or by entrepreneurial teams (Thorelli and Becker 1980). The entrepreneurship practiced by small firms active in international marketing, and its role in entering foreign markets remains outside of the mainstream of entrepreneurial and international marketing research (Low and MacMillan 1988).

Small businesses operated by individual entrepreneurs or by entrepreneurial teams tend to differ substantially from the typical small business. Small businesses function in many different ways on many different levels (Tesar 1977). However, it is the entrepreneur who provides a small firm with the unique dimensions that set it apart from any other small firm (Kilby 1971). A similar phenomenon exists among the small businesses operated by entrepreneurs or an entrepreneurial team.[1] These firms differ from the typical small firm in their propensity to explore and undertake opportunities, such as entering foreign markets, that would generally be perceived as involving too much risk (Bilkey 1982; Katz and Gartner 1988). Yet most of the relevant literature addresses firm size rather than new ventures, so small firms receive considerable attention in this chapter.

The concept of entrepreneurship, defined in this presentation as a process of entering foreign markets, is generally accepted in academic research and in practice as a transitional state from entrepreneurial activities to professional corporate management. Once the entrepreneurial effort is completed, foreign market entry activities become more routine (Flamholtz 1986).

This type of entrepreneurship, venturing into international marketing by entrepreneurial firms, is particularly important in the context of export performance of U.S. firms (GAO/ID-83-21 1983). Expansion into foreign markets represents one of the more difficult aspects of entrepreneurship (GAO/NSID-86-43). Our examination of this type of entrepreneurship is based on two important notions: (1) that the apparent chronic U.S. trade deficit is indeed a matter of national concern and (2) that entrepreneurial firms are vastly underrepresented in the effort to reduce the chronic trade deficit.

This presentation poses a series of questions designed to stimulate practical and academic interest. Our purpose is to (1) illustrate some of the concepts that we know and understand and (2) point out areas of new research opportunities.

The cited studies are mainly American, although foreign scholars also have made significant contributions to this literature. Three major reviews of literature indirectly focus on the issues of entrepreneurship and international marketing. Bilkey (1978) addressed the issues of export behavior among smaller firms. Dichtl et al. (1984) examined the export decision of small and medium-sized firms. And, more recently, Aaby and Slater (1989) focused on management influences of export performance among smaller firms. We shall first present a model outlining relationships between entrepreneurial firms and international marketing in order to formulate basic questions and to focus research opportunities.

AN ECOLOGICAL VIEW OF ENTREPRENEURIAL FIRMS IN INTERNATIONAL MARKETING

An ecological approach is useful in examining small firms in international marketing, as illustrated in Figure 17.1. The entrepreneur, the firm, the home country, and the host country environment constitute an open interaction system. The strategies of the firm play the primary role in the interaction; secondary roles are played by a number of other players. The results of the interaction may be more or less successful from the point of view of the firm, the host country, or other institutions or organizations involved (Thorelli 1978, 1987).

The model is largely self-explanatory. The entrepreneur's general background and specific dimensions including the entrepreneur's (1) view of the world, (2) values, and (3) objectives, along with the management type and style, are important. The characteristics that become important for the entrepreneurial firm include: its (1) mission, (2) resource base, (3) competitive posture, (4) differential advantage, (5) distribution strategy, (6) culture, (7) market share, and (8) reward system. From an operational perspective, the salient factors in the home country environment include such marketing variables as (1) number, size, and behavior of consumers; (2) degree of market saturation; (3) stage in the life cycle; (4) generic features of the product; and (5) product-by-product competition. It is also important to recognize that, within the context of the general

Figure 17.1
Ecological Model of Entrepreneurial Firms with International Marketing Component

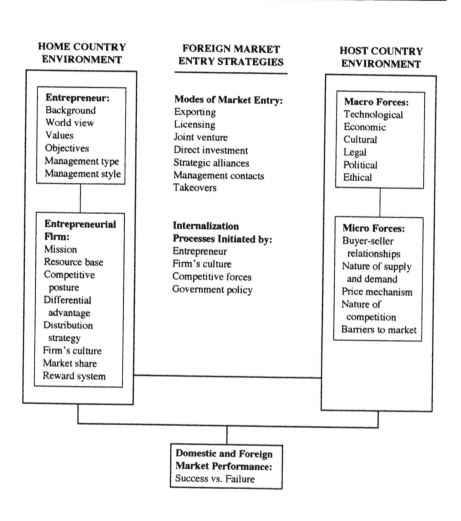

HOME COUNTRY ENVIRONMENT	FOREIGN MARKET ENTRY STRATEGIES	HOST COUNTRY ENVIRONMENT

Entrepreneur:
Background
World view
Values
Objectives
Management type
Management style

Entrepreneurial Firm:
Mission
Resource base
Competitive posture
Differential advantage
Distribution strategy
Firm's culture
Market share
Reward system

Modes of Market Entry:
Exporting
Licensing
Joint venture
Direct investment
Strategic alliances
Management contacts
Takeovers

Internalization Processes Initiated by:
Entrepreneur
Firm's culture
Competitive forces
Government policy

Macro Forces:
Technological
Economic
Cultural
Legal
Political
Ethical

Micro Forces:
Buyer-seller relationships
Nature of supply and demand
Price mechanism
Nature of competition
Barriers to market

Domestic and Foreign Market Performance:
Success vs. Failure

home country environment, the cost of labor, capital, and other factors such as the role of government and public policy need to be considered.

The host country environment presents another set of macro and micro environmental factors. On the macro environmental level, technological, economic, cultural, legal, political, and ethical forces need to be evaluated. On the micro environmental level, the factors become more specific; they include (1) buyer-seller relationships, (2) nature of supply and demand, (3) market price mechanism, (4) nature of competition, (5) barriers to market entry, and (6) nature of distribution.

At the operational level, factors such as (1) soft versus hard currency, (2) exchange rate fluctuations, (3) inflation, (4) tariffs and quotas, and (5) invisible barriers become extremely important. Research suggests that "cultural distance" also presents a major challenge to an entrepreneur assessing the potential of the host market.[2] The notion of "cultural distance" comprises the differences of the host country relative to the home country regarding social values and styles of life, income distribution, attitudes to foreign products, language, legal system, and any other relevant artifacts of culture.

Implicit in the ecological model are three strands of strategy. First, the firm must consider the strategy to enter the host country such as direct or indirect exports, licensing, joint venture, strategic alliance, or direct investment, among others. The mode of entry will generally reflect the degree of commitment of the firm to the host country market. Second, once the firm selects the host market entry mode, it must consider the internal mode of operations. Although internal mode of operations is even less likely to represent a "steady state" abroad than at home, it will typically have some degree of permanence after an initial period of experimentation and securing of a viable market share. The third strand of strategy implied in the model pertains to the overall internationalization process, that is, the critical choice of first country to enter, the selection of additional countries and modes of entry, and operations in each additional country. The gradual transformation of the firm from a parochial to a global outlook with concomitant changes in organization and resource allocation patterns needs to be considered within the context of the outlined three strands of strategy (Thorelli 1966).

The performance resulting from the dynamic interaction of firm and host country market can be measured in terms of the objectives and plans of the entrepreneur or the entrepreneurial firm using conventional financial criteria, but also taking into account the values of distribution channel members, customers, the host country, the home country, and other interested parties (Thorelli 1986).

The ecological model raises many questions; several need to be examined more closely because they form the critical theoretical and conceptual foundation for additional research. These questions are (1) What small businesses engage in international marketing and what are their major opportunities? (2) Why are relatively so few small firms in international marketing? (3) What are the determinants of success or failure? (4) What entry modes are used? (5) What steady-state strategies are used? (6) What is the process of internationalization? Each of these questions will be discussed separately.

WHAT SMALL BUSINESSES ARE IN INTERNATIONAL MARKETING, AND WHAT ARE THEIR MAJOR OPPORTUNITIES?

If estimates by the U.S. Department of Commerce are correct, it seems safe to say that at the very least 15,000 small businesses are engaged in international marketing. To this should be added similarly scaled intrapreneurships in medium and large businesses whose sales are wholly or partly in other countries. Depending on whether or not one wishes to count separately overseas subsidiaries, such intrapreneurships may number anywhere in the range of 1,000 to 10,000 or more. These estimates are not precise. Estimates dealing with consumer versus industrial goods, services versus products, or low-technology versus high-technology involvement of small businesses and their international operations are even less precise. Improvements in the accuracy of these estimates offer major research opportunities.

A combination of country-specific ("comparative") advantages and firm-specific ("differential") advantages may be a prime source of success in international marketing for smaller entrepreneurial businesses. One might postulate that many U.S. entrepreneurs base their success abroad on high-technology specialty niches in such areas as electronics and instrumentation. Although it may be generally true that a large part of the U.S. machine tool industry has lost its competitiveness, machinery and equipment manufacturers and fabricators are well represented in foreign markets according to several recent studies (Johnson and Czinkota 1985; Tesar 1988).

Hundreds of thousands of U.S. small firms are not engaged in international marketing, even though a great number of them are, or soon will be, subject to foreign competition in their own home market (Tesar 1987). Most small firms are almost by definition local or regional due to the inherent nature of their business. The small-town barber shop, most saw mills, the less-than-truckload trucking firm, and the small-time manufacturer of standard nuts and bolts (especially if the standards happen to be inches or fractions thereof!) could hardly be expected to have much interest in export operations.

Generally, makers of standard, low-margin products would not have an easy time, even if they tried. In many instances, transportation and other economies of scale in international operations would work against small firms. The single most important factor in explaining the exclusively domestic orientation of the majority of U.S. small firms is the size of the domestic market. Why take on foreign customers and competitors as long as there is great potential at home? Contrast this with another equally industrialized country, Sweden, whose market may be one-fifteenth that of the United States. Literally thousands of Swedish entrepreneurs simply could not survive without their export markets, which typically account for two-thirds or more of their total sales.

Yet, it does seem reasonable to believe the estimates of the U.S. Department of Commerce that another 25,000 small- and medium-sized U.S. firms could be exporting. Exploring the reasons for their reluctance to export is clearly a priority concern of future research on small businesses and international marketing.

WHY ARE RELATIVELY SO FEW SMALL BUSINESSES IN INTERNATIONAL MARKETING?

This question has been explored by a number of researchers. The first empirical study in this area was presented by Tesar (1975). Subsequent studies on his data base of small- and medium-sized manufacturing firms examined various elements of export behavior, included Bilkey and Tesar (1977); Cavusgil, Bilkey, and Tesar (1979); and Cavusgil and Nevin (1981). Although this research is substantial, significant conclusions regarding the reluctance of small- and medium-sized firms to export can not be reached. Further research focusing particularly on smaller entrepreneurial firms is needed.

Researchers generally agree that the perceptions, values, and background of the entrepreneur play a key role in his/her decision making. Entrepreneurial outlook with regard to exporting is not sufficiently researched. It appears that international marketing involvement requires a different entrepreneurial effort than the traditional technological or marketing entrepreneurial effort. It is generally argued that an innovator in one area may also be an innovator in another area; however, it is not clear that an entrepreneur building a business on a technologically new process will also be likely to develop a new and creative export program.

In order to examine the issues dealing with export program development, it is essential to consider (1) the background of the entrepreneur, (2) the environmental influences in which the entrepreneur operates, and (3) the perceived attractiveness of exporting for the entrepreneur. Some of these concepts have been discussed and researched. For example, the issues dealing with a number of the ambiguous factors in the behavior of entrepreneurs have been discussed by Welch and Wiedersheim-Paul (1980). The environmental influences have been examined by Johnston and Czinkota (1985). Other related issues have been examined by Tesar and Velu (1989). These research results provide a foundation for additional studies in focusing on the relationship between the entrepreneur and the export process.

WHAT ARE THE DETERMINANTS OF SUCCESS AND FAILURE?

Potential determinants of success and failure are presented in Figure 17.1. Few studies have specifically focused on identifying and specifying of these determinants. Some exceptions are studies by Johnston and Czinkota (1987), Johanson and Vahlne (1977), and Tesar (1977).

The causes of entrepreneurial success or failure in international marketing have not been sufficiently researched. Most of the cornerstone studies were conducted in the 1970s and significant follow-up studies have not been done. More and better-formulated empirical research is needed.

WHAT ENTRY MODES ARE USED?

Some small firms begin exporting by filling an unsolicited order from abroad; other firms systematically seek export opportunities. This kind of dichotomy has been examined by several researchers, including Wiedersheim-Paul et al. (1975), Tesar and Tarleton (1982), and Thorelli et al. (1975). The pre-export behavior among entrepreneurs and entrepreneurial firms needs more attention from researchers interested in the theory of international marketing.

Once a small firm makes its commitment to international marketing, it needs to decide on its mode of entry into export operations. An entrepreneur can enter export markets in a variety of ways (Brasch 1978, 1981). Typical indirect modes of export market entry are: export agents, import agents, export management companies, export trading companies, and others. For some firms these options tend to be inefficient and detrimental in the long term because the small business tends not to learn as much about export technology or its export markets.

The advantages and disadvantages of various modes of exporting also need substantially more research. The literature suggests that there might be some advantage for entrepreneurs to enter export markets indirectly in the initial stage in order to simply realize the benefits that exports might contribute to the firm. In the long run, however, the firm must integrate export operations into the mainstream of its operations. The relative advantages and disadvantages of different modes of entry into export markets require in-depth research (Reid 1983).

WHAT STEADY-STATE STRATEGIES ARE USED?

It is popular to use process approaches in analyzing export marketing, be they based on product life cycles, experience curves, or stepwise models. This chapter, for example, is representative of the latter approach in that we are postulating an orderly progression among these strategies: (1) pre-entry, (2) entry, (3) ongoing (steady state), and (4) internationalization process. Because they are inherently dynamic, each of these "stages" can be viewed as a process in itself.

The ecological model presented in Figure 17.1 suggests that there is no single, successful ongoing or steady-state strategy for small firms involved in international marketing. Standardization versus local differentiation is the single most important issue in ongoing international marketing strategy. One may hypothesize that a maker of high-technology equipment and products for industrial customers has the best chance of pursuing a standardized strategy across a variety of cultures.

Although technology would ordinarily include unique prowess in marketing or financial matters, small business strategy would more likely be based on differential advantage in product or process technology and associated pre- and post-service. This contrasts with studies that suggest that imitation is more frequently a viable strategy in domestic marketing for small firms (Biggadike 1979). Alternatively, superior feedback from the marketplace and its use also seems especially relevant to small firms in international marketing (Kirpalani and Macintoch 1980). The superior motivation of distributors and personal contacts with them are related to this factor (Cavusgil 1984).

There are surprisingly few large-scale studies of steady-state strategies of small firms and their involvement in international marketing. None of the preceding literature includes systematic examination of entrepreneurship related to international marketing activities. This is probably due to the large number of variables involved in conceptualizing and formalizing this entire area of research, which, in the future, may yield the greatest understanding of small firm involvement in international marketing.

WHAT IS THE PROCESS OF INTERNATIONALIZATION?

The most significant research dealing with this question suggests that firms grow into international operations on an organic, incremental basis (Johanson and Wiedersheim-Paul 1975). In practice, this means that exporting begins to a country perceived as culturally close. As experience is gained, the firm expands from cultural neighbors to culturally more distant lands. In somewhat parallel fashion, the firm progresses from modest to more ambitious modus vivendi in each country, as follows: (1) fortuitous export, (2) export via agent, (3) export via distribution or sales subsidiary, and (4) production in a foreign subsidiary. Data from various European countries and Canada support these assertions to varying, in some cases substantial, degree.

The internationalization theory has gained considerable prominence (Rugman 1979; Dunning 1980). From this perspective, the behavior of multinational firms can be explained best in terms of desire to preserve control of differential advantage. With regard to mode of entry, this line of reasoning points to the polar ends of commitment, that is, exporting or direct investment in production facilities abroad. In addition to market potential, choice of country market will be governed primarily by the relative opportunity to retain control; cultural differences would be a secondary concern.

Although additional research questions can be formulated in this area, research on actual business experiences is critically needed. Clearly, there may be actual and/or desirable changes taking place in the global outlook of management and in the internal organization of small firms themselves as general internationalization proceeds. This is another unexplored area that affects entrepreneurial activities related to international marketing.

SUMMARY AND SAMPLE PROPOSITIONS

For over a decade, the United States has been faced with a structural trade deficit problem that as yet is nowhere near resolution. At the same time, it is probably true that a smaller percentage of U.S. small firms are engaged in international marketing than in virtually any other industrialized country. Furthermore, a majority of small firms actually engaged in exporting apparently have favorable experiences, both in terms of profitability and managerial challenge. Thus, it is clear that whatever research can be brought to bear on the issues related to small firm participation in international marketing will be of real value to executives and public policy makers as well as academics. Why do some small firms participate in international marketing, whereas others do not? What are the general determinants of success? What overall internationalization process seems most appropriate in different sets of internal and external circumstances? This chapter has pointed to a number of areas in need of research. In closing, we would like to set forth a sample of that which seem especially timely for new research of high quality such as was done in the mid-1970s and early 1980s.

1. A standardized small firm export strategy is more appropriate for high-technology industrial products than for other products.

2. Differential advantages in the product (service) are more important to international marketing success for small firms than for large ones.

3. In the process of expanding international marketing operations, small firms will pursue the incremental approach rather than internalization more often than large businesses.

4. Psychological barriers (beyond those already studied) constitute important deterrents to entrepreneurs' engagement in international marketing.

5. A high proportion of small firm failures in international marketing are due to distribution problems.

6. Locally (regionally) confined small firms are less likely than regional (national) small businesses to engage in international marketing.

7. Entrepreneurs physically located in international marketing centers will more often and more readily engage in international marketing than firms in peripheral locations.

8. Export success in small firms is correlated with the extent of information search prior to the commitment to export.

9. Entrepreneurs who base their export commitment essentially on "impulse selling" fail more often in international marketing than those who engage in planned pre-export activity.

10. Intrapreneurial businesses in international marketing have a longer time perspective on success and failure

than independent entrepreneurial businesses in international marketing.

11. Federal and state international marketing support programs are too diffused among agencies, causing ignorance and/or misinformation and confusion among potential small firm exporters.

12. Export stimulation programs for entrepreneurs should be more concerned with motivation because information is not enough.

The list of studies and methodologies worth exploring is endless. We would like to point out four types of studies that seem to hold special promise today:

1. There is a burgeoning literature on customer and industrial buyer behavior and attitudes. A systematic review of this stream of research would likely yield a host of stimuli for further "seller behavior" and attitude research.

2. Research on networking is a phenomenon of particular relevance to entrepreneurs in international marketing. Of special interest is how international business contacts are established and cultivated.

3. A promising and underused approach is that of entrepreneurial simulation models for study of strategic decision making in international business operations.

4. We need comparative studies across cultures of (a) government export promotional activities, (b) use of trading companies, (c) cooperative arrangements, and (d) perceptions of cultural distances among others.

Of all countries, the United States seems to have the most to gain from further research on what makes small firms operate successfully in international marketing. This is not merely because too few small businesses are currently engaged in export operations. The vast U.S. market has enough regional variation to provide a valuable proving ground for many potential exporters. This review of small firm involvement in international marketing is designed to stimulate additional research to benefit increased involvement in international marketing operations. This chapter is not designed to include all available literature in this field, but rather to include research that has made a significant impact and will serve as a foundation for future research.

NOTES

1. For the purposes of this presentation, small businesses operated by an entrepreneur or by an entrepreneurial team will be referred to as entrepreneurial firms.
2. The so-called Uppsala School (Sweden) of international business researchers pioneered academic attention to this area, dubbing it "psychological distance." We think cultural distances are more telling.

REFERENCES

Aaby, N.E., and S. F. Slater. "Management Influences on Export Performance: A Review of the Empirical Literature 1978–88." *International Marketing Review* 6(4), (1989): 7–25.

Biggadike, R. "The Risky Business of Diversification." *Harvard Business Review* (May–June 1979): 103–14.

Bilkey, W. J. "An Attempted Integration of the Literature on the Export Behavior of Firms." *Journal of International Business* 9 (Spring–Summer 1978): 33–49.

Bilkey, W. J. "Variables Associated with Export Profitability," *Journal of International Business Studies* 13 (Fall 1982): 434–57.

Bilkey, W. J., and George Tesar. "The Export Behavior of Smaller-Sized Wisconsin Manufacturing Firms." *Journal of International Business Studies* 8 (Spring–Summer 1977): 93–98.

Brasch, J. J. "Export Management Companies." *Journal Of International Business Studies* 9 (Spring–Summer 1978): 59–71.

Brasch, J. J. "Deciding on an Organizational Structure for Entry into Export Marketing." *Journal of Small Business Management* (Apr. 1981).

Cavusgil, S. T. "Organizational Characteristics Associated with Export Activity." *Journal of Management Studies* 1 (1984): 3–22.

Cavusgil, S. T., W. J. Bilkey, and G. Tesar. "A Note on the Export Behavior of Firms: Export Profiles." *Journal of International Business Studies* 10 (Spring–Summer 1979): 91–97.

Cavusgil, S. T., and J. R. Nevin. "Internal Determinants of Export Marketing Behavior: An Empirical Investigation." *Journal of Marketing Research* 18 (Feb. 1981): 114–19.

Dichtl, E. M., M. Leibold, H.-G. Koglmayr, and S. Muller. "The Export Decision of Small and Medium-Sized Firms: A Review." *Management International Review* 2 (1984): 49–60.

Dunning J. H. "Towards an Eclectic Theory of International Production." *Journal of International Business Studies* 11 (Spring–Summer 1980): 9–31.

Flamholtz, E. G. *How to Make the Transition from and Entrepreneurship to a Professionally Managed Firm.* San Francisco: Jossey-Bass Publishers, 1986.

Johanson, J., and F. Wiedersheim-Paul. "The Internationalization of the Firm: Four Swedish Case Studies." *Journal of Management Studies,* 3 (1975): 305–22.

Johanson, J., and J. Vahlne. "The Internationalization Process of the Firm: A Model of Knowledge Development and Increasing Foreign Commitments." *Journal of International Business Studies* 8 (Spring–Summer 1977): 23–32.

Johnston, W. J., and M. R. Czinkota. "Managerial Motivations as Determinants of Industrial Export Behavior." In *Export Behavior: An International Context,* edited by Michael R. Czinkota and George Tesar, 3–17. New York: Praeger Publishers, 1987.

Johnston, W. J., and M. R. Czinkota. "Export Attitudes of Industrial Manufacturers." *Industrial Marketing Management* 14 (1985): 123–32.

Katz, J., and W. B. Gartner. "Properties of Emerging Organizations." *Academy of Management* Review 13 (July 1988): 429–41.

Kilby, P. "Hunting the Heffalump." In *Entrepreneurship in Economic Development,* edited by Peter Kilby, 1–40. New York: The Free Press, 1971.

Kirpalani, V. H., and N. B. Macintoch. "International Marketing Effectiveness of Technology-Oriented Small Firms." *Journal of International Business Studies* 11 (Winter 1980): 81–90.

Low, M. B., and I. C. MacMillan. "Entrepreneurship: Past Research and Future Challenges," *Journal of Management* 14 (June 1988): 139–61.

Reid, S. D. "Firm Internationalization, Transaction Costs, and Strategic Choices." *International Marketing Review* (Winter 1983): 153–55.

Report # GAO/ID-83-21. *Efforts to Promote Exports by Small, Non-Exporting Manufacturers.* United States General Accounting Office, Washington, DC, January 18, 1983.

Report # GAO/NSIAD-86-43. *Export Promotion: Implementation of the Export Trading Company Act of 1982.* United States General Accounting Office, Washington, DC, February 1986.

Rugman, A. M. *International Diversification and the Multinational Enterprise.* Lexington, MA: D. C. Heath Publishers, 1979.

Tesar, G. "Empirical Study of Export Operations among Small and Medium Sized Manufacturing Firms," Ph.D. dissertation, University of Wisconsin-Madison, Madison, WI, 1975.

Tesar, G. "Identification of Planning, Attitudinal, and Operational Differences among Types of Exporters" *American Journal of Small Business* 2 (Oct. 1977): 16–21.

Tesar, G. "West European Direct Investment in the U.S." *International Marketing Review* (Spring 1987): 52–60.

Tesar, G. "Strategic Technological and Market Development among Fabricators of Custom Equipment." *Industrial Marketing and Purchasing* 3(10), (1988): 17–29.

Tesar, G. and J. S. Tarleton. "Comparison of Wisconsin and Virginia Small and Medium-Sized Exporters: Aggressive and Passive Exporters." In *Export Management: An International Context,* edited by Michael R. Czinkota and George Tesar, 85–112. New York: Praeger Publishers, 1982.

Tesar, G. and R. Velu. "Technologically Evolving Industrial Equipment Fabricators: Their Foreign Involvement." *R&D Management* 19 (Jan 1989): 3–11.

Thorelli, H. B. "The Multinational Corporation as a Change Agent." *The Southern Journal of Business* (July 1966): 1–9.

Thorelli, H. B. "Management Audit and Social Indicators: The MNC Through the Glasses of the LDC." *Journal of Contemporary Business* (Winter 1978): 75–91.

Thorelli, H. B. "Networks: Between Markets and Hierarchies." *Strategic Management Journal* 7 (1986): 37–51.

Thorelli, H. B. "Entrepreneurship in International Marketing." In *Research at the Marketing/Entrepreneurship Interface,* edited by Gerald E. Hills, 183–204. Chicago: University of Illinois at Chicago, 1987.

Thorelli, H. B., and H. Becker, editors. *International Marketing Strategy,* Part VI. New York: Pergamon Press, 1980.

Thorelli, H. B., H. Becker, and J. Engledow. *The Information Seekers.* Cambridge, MA: Ballinger, 1975.

Welch, L. S. and F. Wiedersheim-Paul. "Initial Exports: A Marketing Failure?" *Journal of Management Studies* 4 (1980): 333–44.

Wiedersheim-Paul, F., H. C. Olson, and L. S. Welch. "Before the First Export Order: A Behavioral Model." Working Paper No. 10, Department of Economics, University of Queensland, Queensland, Australia, 1975.

18

Entrepreneurship in LDCs: Perspectives and Experiences

William Lazer and David K. Hardin

The bulk of the research and literature on entrepreneurship pertains to well-developed capitalistic economies. The important role of entrepreneurs in fostering innovation and creativity, in providing jobs, and in unleashing individual initiatives and talents are highlighted. In the United States, entrepreneurship has been identified as the next stage in its capitalistic evolution, for the entrepreneurial era has begun (Drucker 1985). By contrast, entrepreneurship's meaningful role in non-capitalistic environments, in socialistic or communistic societies, and especially in the lesser-developed countries (LDCs), has largely been neglected.

The entrepreneurial literature related to the LDCs is scarce indeed. It falls into three categories. First, the bulk of it is only peripherally related, pertaining mostly to other disciplines, such as developmental economics, political science, rural sociology and the like. It contains some relevant concept and general ideas, mostly in the nature of background information and perspectives. Second, it is information that has been gathered through research done by a variety of private sources, little of which has been published. It is believed to be in company, government, and association files, generally made available to a limited audience, such as association members.[1] These materials are more germane, they relate to smaller enterprises, but for the most part are still not directly focused on the topic of entrepreneurial ventures and activities in LDCs. Third are data, insights, and information that have been assembled, but not widely distributed by organizations sponsoring and working directly with entrepreneurs and entrepreneurial ventures in LDCs such as OPPORTUNITY International, Grameen Bank, ACCION, and AID. They are the most directly relevant, reflecting a growing body of experience gathered by concerned organizations and individuals and will comprise the core of this chapter.

In LDCs, entrepreneurship offers opportunities for relatively significant economic and social progress. Although no substantive body of pertinent literature exists, a growing body of experience, gathered by concerned organizations and individuals, attests to its significance. Entrepreneurs in LDCs can make very special contributions to social and economic progress. They offer a practical and effective means of attacking such fundamental problems as hunger and unemployment; utilizing the creative energies and talents of native people; serving local markets; and furnishing developing countries with opportunities to help themselves, thereby building dignity and hope.

The entrepreneurs referred to in this chapter are micro entrepreneurs who carry on very small businesses, usually family businesses. They operate in far different settings, and run their businesses in much different ways than their counterparts in more developed economies. They are not the highly educated, sophisticated, high-tech, foreign-trained college graduates. Rather, they comprise the uneducated, underclass, poor entrepreneurs, who need help, and for whom assistance and supporting institutions are not often accessible. As is understandable, the better-educated people want to live in far more comfortable environments than deprived barrios or villages.

This chapter explores some of the pragmatic aspects of encouraging entrepreneurship in LDCs. It investigates opportunities for poor, illiterate entrepreneurs involved with micro businesses to help themselves, their fellow citizens, and their countries. Some of the difficulties in identifying and supporting budding entrepreneurs are noted and the necessary ingredients for success are considered.

Entrepreneurship is presented as a logical and often superior strategy alternative to the usual economic development approaches of making large-scale capital investments, or extending outright economic aid. The special role of the private sector, with an emphasis on entrepreneurial initiatives in market settings, hopefully in consort with local governments, is seen as an engine leading to economic growth, employment, and self-sufficiency.

THE LDC ENTREPRENEUR

Ben Santos, an entrepreneur who manufactures garments in Manila, and others like him, may hold a key to Third-World development.[2] Recently, Ben perceived of a market opportunity and took out a loan of $4,000 to purchase equipment to make stone-washed denims. His marketing instincts were correct, and as stone-washed jeans became popular in Manila, his sales increased 50 percent, his income doubled, and he added 20 workers to handle the increased business.

Ben, who is uneducated, without formal exposure to such business areas as finance and marketing, is, nevertheless, a classic entrepreneur. He got married when he was 16 and provided for his wife and himself by selling underwear from a market stall. He gradually expended into manufacturing various types of garments, demonstrating an ability to capitalize on his innate marketing acumen. He worked his way up from poverty to develop a very successful business, which benefits not only his wife and family but 60 employees.

As an entrepreneur in an LDC environment, Ben shows great concern for his employees. For example, once a month he has a doctor and a dentist visit his plant to check on the workers. In a country where over 50 percent of the population is unemployed, or underemployed, Ben created jobs for 20 people with a loan of $4,000 that was obtained outside the normal band and credit institutions. Ben could not use normal financial channels because he did not meet their standard requirements. Yet, his investment of just $200 per job, provides a lasting source of income for 20 families that, in turn, furnishes food and shelter for about 120 people. This is a fantastic return.

Ben, a very capable entrepreneur and concerned employer, is hardly unique. The Third World contains a large number of capable, budding entrepreneurs who are prepared to sacrifice, work hard, and develop businesses that will meet local needs. In so doing, they can expand the local economy and create jobs. Many very competent people, however, are not as fortunate as Ben. Although they have the talents and ideas, they are not able to obtain credit, which often represents an insurmountable barrier among LDCs, blocking entrepreneurial initiative and ability.

FOREIGN AID THAT GETS REPAID

In LDCs, governments often regulate interest rates, the sources of credit are extremely limited, and banks lend only to their most secure customers. Banks will not make loans to poor, uneducated, struggling entrepreneurs because they lack both the collateral to guarantee loans and the education and skills necessary to fill out the loan applications. Ben Santos' loan did not come from a bank, but from the local partner agency of OPPORTUNITY International, a U.S.-based nonprofit organization that makes small loans to small enterprises sponsored by the poor.

Micro loans, from nonprofit agencies represent a new type of development assistance, a form of foreign aid that not only gets to where it will have great impact by encouraging and supporting struggling entrepreneurs, but that also gets repaid. Micro loans are recycled again and again, having a multiplier effect in providing jobs and income for the poor. They represent one of the best forms of foreign aid: aid that motivates and enables people to help themselves and develop their communities and countries. Micro loans become investments in the ingenuity and entrepreneurial ability of thousands of people around the world who, as a result, will be able to provide for their own families, create jobs for others, and add to general well-being. All they seek is to be given the opportunity. Such loans represent investments in the future with both immediate and long-term payoffs.

ENTREPRENEURSHIP: AMERICA'S GREAT EXPORT

Entrepreneurship is a major means of creating income opportunities and a better life not only in well-developed economies, like the United States, but in poorer countries worldwide. Entrepreneurs can help LDC societies meet pivotal social and economic issues. Its hallmarks are capital and investment rather than handouts, independence and self-development rather than dependence, and hope and pride rather than charity.

Entrepreneurs in LDCs invest in their communities and recycle money so that others can benefit from realizing increasing opportunities. They do not siphon off wealth and ship it overseas, as has often been the case with some of the wealthier people in LDCs. Entrepreneurship in reality is a method of democratizing wealth, distributing income, building individuality, and helping to build a middle class. It is successful in replacing the perspective of just trying to cope with insurmountable adversity and hopelessness of daily existence in LDCs, with an outlook of opportunity, economic growth and improvement of life styles.

The American entrepreneurial experience is now being emulated throughout the world. Countries such as Hungary, China, and Russia are moving forward rapidly with plans supporting entrepreneurial ventures. Fundamental economic and political shifts from socialistic to capitalistic approaches have a very special meaning for entrepreneurship. For example, perestroika embraces entrepreneurial initiative, as Mr. Aganbegyan, an author of recent Russian economic changes, stated in Russia, "We are encouraging people to go into business for themselves. In the past few months, 300,000 people have done it. Soon, new laws will stimulate the process even further" (Wren 1988).

BLOCKS TO ENTREPRENEURSHIP

Unfortunately, too many LDCs explicitly or implicitly limit the potential impact of entrepreneurship. The reality is that LDC situations are vastly different from those of more industrialized countries in at least two dimensions. First, in most, if not all, substantial corruption exists among current institutions and officials, regardless of political orientation. That often results in siphoning off a substantial proportion of foreign investments and financial aid, which in turn puts a damper on potential entrepreneurs. Second, no substantial middle class or mass market exists to drive mass consumption, encourage manufacturing, and stimulate exports.

In LDCs, three institutions, usually closely intertwined, seek to retain their powerful and privileged positions and tend to counter entrepreneurial thrusts: the government, the military, and the oligarchy (or very wealthy). They compromise an unholy trinity in possession of the reins of power. Except for a very small proportion of the population at the very top, people in LDCs generally have exceedingly low standards of living, and illiteracy is rampant. This is coupled with arcane regulations that inhibit entrepreneurial initiative, both directly and indirectly, to discourage the poor from engaging in entrepreneurial ventures.

For entrepreneurial ventures to take hold in LDCs, it is usually necessary to disrupt an existing order, to threaten and even change the status quo, so as to break a repetitive poverty/unemployment cycle. Hernando de Soto (1989) points out, very insightfully, that one way to break the cycle is through the informal sector, those unregulated activities of the urban and rural poor. He found the informal sector to be the most dynamic part of Central and South American economies generating an amazing 60 percent of all employment.

In the past, the poverty/unemployment cycle has sometimes been interrupted by revolution. However, it is possible to interrupt it without great political and social upheavals through the adoption of entrepreneurial approaches. Requisites include making new sources of capital and managerial assistance available to potential entrepreneurs who are poor and uneducated, so as to encourage very small businesses, micro ventures, that will motivate people to release their creativity, energy, and individual initiative.

Entrepreneurial development, particularly the development of micro businesses, means getting capital into the hands of small businessmen at local levels, in the urban shanty towns, in the small villages, and in rural areas. This contrasts with the widely adopted economic development strategies that focus on such large-scale capital investment projects as irrigation dams, hydroelectric plants, railways, major highways, and air and sea ports. Although these projects are certainly needed, and can help LDCs, in general, capital investment approaches to economic development have encountered some difficulties. They present ample opportunities for corruption and the diversion of funds. They assume that the funds invested will reach the poor, those who need help. In reality, little of it reaches people at the lower economic levels where it can make the greatest difference. Some may eventually trickle down, but a lot is inevitably diverted through many creative arrangements devised by the trinity.

By contrast, the grassroots, entrepreneurial-investment approach focuses on micro loans, recognizing that they will have a direct and immediate beneficial impact on poor peoples' lives. They can make a great difference for the majority of people in both the long and short run. They motivate entrepreneurs to create jobs, ameliorate hunger, and furnish hope. Mr. Sewel, the president of the Oversees Development Council, commenting on micro business programs, states:

"These entrepreneurial programs really do demonstrate the magic of the marketplace—[they] clearly deserve to be supported" (Wren 1988, E2).

It must also be recognized that LDC entrepreneurs may be viewed by some entrenched groups as threats to society, rather than as desirable actors. They have the capability, over time, of becoming rather formidable forces that may challenge the existing power structure, be it the military, the oligarchy, dictators, or government officials. Entrepreneurs usually set out to change things, to get things done, often by means other than the traditionally accepted ways. Successful entrepreneurs may not fall into line as readily, and may eventually become strong enough economically, and socially, to withstand the usual pressures and express themselves. They tend to be more independent, to take over some control, and set out to do their own thing. As a result, they may be in the forefront, encouraging the redistribution of power, and supporting individual initiative and choice. They become forces for change, forces that can challenge the dominance of established groups.

SUPPORTING ENTREPRENEURSHIP IN LDCs

The majority of people living in the Third-World countries are not able to earn a living, exist in a morass of deep underemployment, and confront feelings of hopelessness and despair. The financial support of local entrepreneurs can be a low-cost approach to dealing with some of their most basic problems, combatting hunger, and overcoming unemployment.

There are three requisites for encouraging entrepreneurship in LDCs. First is the development of an economic and political environment, which if not outright supportive of individual initiative and private enterprise, is at least neutral, or not actively adversarial. This requires a legal, political, and economic system plus financial policies that encourage risk-taking and investment. The best results occur in a market-friendly environment, and as de Soto noted, democracy is crucial for any government seeking to adapt itself to the emerging markets (de Soto 1989). Although that is a long-range goal which cannot be met by most LDCs in the near future, it does not negate the encouragement and benefits of entrepreneurship in existing LDC environments.

The second requirement is creating indigenous financial institutions and accompanying lending procedures that will stimulate and support capital flows, of small amounts, to uneducated, poor, but promising entrepreneurs. Existing LDC financial institutions and their borrowing requirements lock out the participation of poor entrepreneurs. Many antiquated regulations and requirements often exist that are designed specifically to eliminate or limit entrepreneurial development.

The third requisite is to be realistic in assessing and recognizing the conditions that surround LDC micro businesses and adopting appropriate methods of operation. A lot of the expertise of sophisticated business experts and economic development specialists is superfluous in such settings. The rules are different for micro businesses initiated and operated by illiterate Third-World entrepreneurs. Different approaches, guidelines, and support systems from those used in highly industrialized countries must be employed.

Micro businesses in LDCs usually suffer from a number of real limitations beyond those imposed by the oligarchy. Most have very limited financial resources, cannot capitalize on economies of scale, lack power in the marketplace, cannot afford the help of experiences people, face high loan rates, and are greatly undercapitalized. On the other hand, they also have some advantages. They can capitalize on being close to their markets and customers; on the ease of communicating with them; on having great flexibility and being able to adapt easily; on being able to make decisions readily; and importantly, on the personal touch. In addition, they often enjoy a great advantage, a monopoly position in their local village or barrio. They are free from the impact of competition from chains and other more efficient enterprises, which gives them breathing room and a splendid chance to gain a foothold in the marketplace.

In this regard, a very interesting and unexpected phenomenon has occurred. The American government, and various U.S. charities, intent on helping LDCs, in some instances have actually done unexpected harm by their actions. For example, the United States shipped surplus supplies of grain to Third-World countries. This had the unanticipated effect of bankrupting and discouraging local small farmers. In some villages where small entrepreneurs had established shirt, dress, pant, and shoe factories that seemed to be getting well underway, charity bred disaster. American charities acting out of concern and kindness, seeking to help the less fortunate, collected clothing, sent their bounty to the villages, and thereby destroyed markets and actually forced entrepreneurs to close. This not only had the immediate effect of ruining some enterprises with potential, but also the longer-lasting effect of dampening entrepreneurial enthusiasm; making people more dependent; and destroying self-respect, hope, and pride.

FINANCING

Financing is usually the most immediate and obvious critical need facing micro businesses in LDCs. Indigenous lending institutions willing and able to finance them do not exist (Black 1985). Entrepreneurs are often forced to use local moneylenders who charge such unbelievable rates as 10 percent or more *per week* to finance inventories (Wren 1988). These outlandish rates preclude many potentially viable ventures from earning a profit and becoming successful.

In most LDCs, more than an adequate number of aspiring entrepreneurs with good concepts exist. However, they do not have the equity, assets, or financing to initiate projects. Thus, in the start-up phase, most micro businesses become so highly leveraged that they are pressured to make quick returns to meet loan requirements. This has the disastrous effect of throwing even fine business opportunities into jeopardy. To make the system work more effectively, new sources of financing are mandatory. The traditional bank-financing approach mentioned previously is a road block that will not do the job.

It is also worth emphasizing that LDC business ventures are low tech and unsophisticated. The financing involved comprises micro loans for small amounts such as $500, $800, or $1,000. Starting a clothing factory simply means wiring a home for electricity, putting in sewing machines, irons, a supply of cloth, and miscellaneous items, such as thread, zippers, trim, and buttons. If a factory proves successful, it is largely because of those who initiate the project and work very hard at the business. Interestingly, 40 percent of the loans made by OPPORTUNITY International are made to women who have a knack for an enterprise, start very small, and have the determination and persistence to succeed.

Experience indicates that micro business entrepreneurs usually lack two important skills: finance and marketing. Both can be bolstered through basic seminars and manuals designed for uneducated audiences. Concepts such as cash flow, inventory turnover, fixed cost, break even, and so on can be illuminated by simple explanations, as can methods of marketing products more effectively, gaining market acceptance and expanding markets, and rules of thumb. This very important challenge, if carried out effectively, contributes much to the success of a new venture.

Results in the field indicate that when fairly adequate financing is coupled with good marketing knowledge and assistance, a micro business' chance of success increases manifold. Moreover, as a few new enterprises in a village or barrio actually succeed, a multiplier effect occurs because these successes are visible and encourage other potential entrepreneurs to try their hands. Success generates success, benefiting not only individual entrepreneurs and their families, but their employees, the village or barrio, and the whole society.

In LDC settings, what is very small can really appear relatively large. Very small loans of a few hundred to a few thousand dollars can encourage substantial numbers of people to develop their own enterprises. Relatively small increases in employment, and regularly received modes and incomes can have major impact—they make a large difference.

In most LDCs, a lending logjam confronts potential entrepreneurs and deters them from pursuing viable opportunities. Loans tend to be tightly controlled. Banks, as was noted, will not provide the necessary financing, and have the justification (and excuse) that local entrepreneurs are too small, have no assets, cannot fill in the forms, and hence cannot quality for bank loans. In reality, banks in LDCs have loans available for those businesses that do not need them. Loan sharks, on the other hand, with charges of 10, 15, or 20 percent a week, have financing available at rates that almost automatically ensure failure. Both situations repress entrepreneurship, dampen the self-help approach, and support maintenance of the status quo.

Fortunately, things are changing somewhat, albeit slowly. A few Third-World banks are now beginning to practice micro-lending by extending small loans to selected promising entrepreneurs. In some LDCs, voluntary, nonprofit financial organizations have sprung up to provide some entrepreneurial financing. The basic point is that landless and illiterate people in LDCs possess the entrepreneurial potential to succeed, are worthy credit risks, and, given opportunities, can function readily within existing systems. Normal business approaches, however, work against them. De Soto (1989) explains that the poor are also entrepreneurs so do not say the only way to help them is through Marxist-Leninist means. In fact, the communistic/socialistic approach in LDCs, as in other countries, has failed. East European block countries, and Russia, for example, have had to shift political and economic bases, becoming more market oriented and entrepreneurial.

The support of the U.S. Congress for an entrepreneurial approach was evidenced in a new thrust for the Agency for International Development. Congress directed the Agency to budget $75 million to finance Third-World small credit programs. The amount, although not large, nevertheless lends significant recognition and support to the efficiency of an entrepreneurial approach.

PROVIDING INCOME FOR A LIFETIME

The results of programs aimed at supporting entrepreneurial activities of the poor in LDCs have been most encouraging. For example, OPPORTUNITY International, a private organization concerned with fostering self-help through small ventures, has developed 20 partner agencies in 13 countries. They found that, on the average, every $500 lent creates a new private-sector job. By comparison, in the United States, it takes an estimated average investment of $30,000 to create a new job.

Eight of the 20 OPPORTUNITY International partner agencies are now self-sufficient, able to continue operations through earned interest and their own fund raising activities. The diversity of entrepreneurial ventures they have financed include horse cart maker; egg farmer; manufacturer of false teeth; manufacturer of corrugated boxes; producer of stuffed animals; bakery; tailor shop; shirt, shoe, and dress manufacturers; repair shops; restaurants; and food stalls. In one instance in Pakistan, workers' contracts were bought up to free them from virtual slavery and permit workers to run their own brick factory (OPPORTUNITY International 1989 Annual Report, 6–7).

ACCION International, of Cambridge, Massachusetts, which works in 20 countries in the Americas, has had similar success. In 1987, they provided 3,400 small loans that created 15,000 jobs, and increased the average income of each borrower by 30 percent.

The largest of all the small enterprise lending programs is that of the Grameen Bank in Bangladesh. This, for-profit, locally-owned bank makes about 400,000 loans per year with a total value of $24 million. The average loan size is only $60, an unbelievably low amount. Yet, they have been exceedingly successful in supporting viable ventures and creating jobs.

What rate of repayment can beginning, poor entrepreneurs be expected to realize on their loans? After all, they are not used to handling business loans, have no assets, and are uneducated. Won't they just take the money and default? Experience shows that is not the case. In many instances, it is interesting to note, the poor are actually better credit risks than the wealthy. OPPORTUNITY International, ACCION International, and the Grameen Bank, all report repayment rates of well over 90 percent. Contrast this loan repayment rate with that of lenders in highly industrialized nations, or with the current Savings and Loan debacle in the United States.

Why should poor entrepreneurs be such good credit risks? Why should they repay loans? Why don't they just walk away from such obligations? What is the motivation? For poor people in LDCs access to credit at non-usurious rates is a treasured commodity. They know that if they do not repay their loans, they may never have another opportunity to borrow at normal rates of interest. Moreover, they will spoil the chance for a loan for their fellow villagers, preventing them from success.

A FEW PRAGMATICS

The general loan process pattern in LDCs is as follows: A prospective entrepreneur approaches a lending agency with an idea for starting or expanding a business. The lending institution evaluates it, and should the proposed idea be deemed viable, three practical questions are addressed. How to set up the micro business so that it will function well in a particular environment; how to make the micro business successful within a very short time span, of perhaps months, or even weeks; how to identify the real entrepreneurs, those micro business owners, who will provide a stimulus for longer-run future jobs and benefits from among loan applicants. Let us briefly address each of them.

In industrialized countries, before agreeing to a loan, creditors would expect to see credit references; perhaps draw a Dun & Bradstreet report, or get a bank referral. But how can this be done in an LDC for individuals who are poor, illiterate, and not yet involved in business; in a setting where corruption and authoritarian control usually exist; in societies that may not encourage individual initiative and entrepreneurial ventures?

Micro loan programs may rely on community/peer/superior evaluations to try and get useful information about the likelihood of loan repayment. Lenders often use respected community leaders, religious or otherwise, who have earned "legitimacy," as sources of information about loan applicants. Community leaders have a unique and important role in directing and guiding small business ventures in their local areas. Their insights and advice about applicants can be extremely useful in identifying potential business proprietors and entrepreneurs.

With the primacy of the family, a motivational device often used to encourage loan repayment is to have every member of the family sign for a loan. Thus, they all feel personally responsible and become even more committed and determined to work hard and make the new venture succeed.

Sometimes lending programs organize individual micro borrowers into groups, such as groups of five, who jointly guarantee the individual loans of each of the group members. Thus, if one borrower does not repay his/her loan, the other members of the group have to assume the repayment responsibility. In such programs, neither the individual nor the group is eligible to receive a new loan until the previous loans are completely paid. The pressure of the group on potential individual deadbeats can be great, and the results are very encouraging.

Starting even the simplest manufacturing operation requires realistic evaluations of both the potential market and the kinds and amounts of support that are necessary. Market niches can usually be identified readily in both geographic and need terms, because villages or barrios have natural geographic boundaries, basic unmet needs, and lack of suppliers. As for support, the needs of the total operation must be evaluated clearly and realistically, which potential entrepreneurs often fail to do. To accommodate home production, for example, not only must a hut be wired for electricity, or supplied with water, but selling the products may require delivery and credit, meaning enough financing to purchase bicycles, scooters, or cars.

TRAINING FOR SUCCESS

Experiences show very clearly that training and supportive services are important ingredients in ensuring micro enterprise success. Lenders sometimes provide them. For example, when OPPORTUNITY International extends a loan, it requires that three conditions be met. First, recipients must attend seminars that deal with basic business fundamentals, in very simple terms, so that they can become familiar with such important activities as keeping records and maintaining financial controls. The seminars teach new entrepreneurs to pay attention to critical information and perform tasks with which they may not be familiar.

In this regard, as was briefly mentioned, financial and marketing concepts and guidelines, which are second nature to business administration graduates, such as demand, break even, market potential, inventory management, overhead costs, expense ratios, and the like must be translated into simple, meaningful, really understandable ideas, rules of thumb, and working procedures. They must be presented in such ways that they can be grasped easily and implemented immediately. For instance, simple rules of thumb, such as keeping on hand inventories that are no larger than last week's sales; limiting credit to a specified amount per customer, and total per week; or explaining the idea of break even and the increased profitability of added sales when a certain amount of costs are covered, have proven invaluable. Other topics dealt with during training sessions, included such "how to" aspects as how to price a product, how to expand a market, how to market products and services, how to train employees, how to control inventories, how to control expenses, and so on.

Second, OPPORTUNITY International assists borrowers in developing and maintaining very simple, but very important, business records. This can be a difficult problem for illiterate entrepreneurs. However, data indicate that the absence of written records is one of the major causes of failure among otherwise viable micro businesses. Since an entrepreneur's illiteracy is an inherent problem in keeping records, a solution must be found. Sometimes, sons, daughters, friends, or relatives can be trained to help. With records intact, the results show that illiterate entrepreneurs who have good business sense, are supported in becoming very successful entrepreneurs.

Third, representatives of OPPORTUNITY International visit debtors' businesses on a regular basis, usually every six weeks or so. By so doing, they can see first-hand how the business is doing, what the problems are, and will likely be, and address any emerging difficulties immediately. This provides an opportunity to prevent crises and practice preventive management. OPPORTUNITY International's local staff will make 17,000 on-site consulting visits to small businesses during this year. This hands-on approach, coupled with assistance from able consultants, makes a big difference to the emerging venture.

RATES OF SUCCESS

What proportion of the LDC entrepreneurial ventures can be expected to succeed? How many of the initiators will become entrepreneurs? Statistics relating to OPPORTUNITY International's experience, cutting across many countries, indicate the following: On the average, if 10 business loans are made, one in 10 of the businesses will not exist three years later. Of the remaining nine, seven or eight of them will prove successful in the sense of supporting an immediate or an extended family, and perhaps a few additional employees. They will provide employment and feed and clothe the families. One or two of the 10 initial businesses will be in the hands of entrepreneurs who, like Ben Santos, make things happen. These businesses will take off and grow, extend employment opportunities to many others, and become initiators of social and economic progress. Identifying these potential entrepreneurs and singling them out for special treatment is an important challenge, because they will provide future employment and hope for many others. They are important keys to success in assistance to LDCs.

The credo in Third-World countries must be think small, because it is a matter of starting a very small venture, making small loans, catering to small markets, operating in small villages and barrios, and developing simple support systems that small, illiterate, poor entrepreneurs can understand and use. The paradox is, although while these businesses are indeed small and require only very small amounts of capital, nevertheless, they achieve large benefits for the villagers, and make important permanent differences in life styles.

The magnitude of poverty and hunger problems around the world makes them seem insurmountable, particularly when assessed against the limited development resources available. Such calculations, however, do not take into account a most important resource, the entrepreneurial competence of the poor themselves. People like Ben Santos, able entrepreneurs, are ready to work hard to develop growing businesses and to provide employment for themselves and others, if only given the chance. The determination, creativity, and motivation of potential LDC entrepreneurs is usually left out of the economic development equation. The industriousness of the poor should not be underestimated.

In the LDCs, people are anxious and willing to work long and hard to achieve success. The motivation of poor entrepreneurs in striving to make small ventures succeed is simple and straight forward. Social safety nets do not exist, reliance on self is primary, and those who do not work, do not eat.

The poor in the developing world are not seeking permanent handouts. Rather, they want opportunities—opportunities to use their own capabilities; apply their skills, ingenuity, and enterprise; and support themselves, their families, and others. Toynbee stated that to give a fair chance to potential creativity is a matter of life and death for any society. He goes on to say that this is all important, because the outstanding creative ability of a fairly small proportion of the population is mankind's ultimate capital asset, and the only one with which man has been endowed. This has rich meaning for the LDCs.

Programs that put credit and training in the hands of illiterate, poor entrepreneurs in the LDCs have unleashed individual initiative and creative abilities and have been very successful. They have proven that given opportunities, poor entrepreneurs in LDCs respond by starting and expanding businesses, by providing employment and income for themselves and for others there, by helping overcome hunger and despair. Moreover, they are acutely aware of their obligation to repay loans so that their aspiring fellow entrepreneurs may have similar opportunities. Entrepreneurship has a very special role to play in helping LDCs help themselves. It is a foreign aid strategy with great potential long- and short-run benefits; it is a strategy that works.

NOTES

1. An example is The Canadian Federation of Independent Business Study of entrepreneurs that was carried out in eleven developing and developed countries in 1986/87.

2. This example and references to data and experiences are adapted from the files of OPPORTUNITY International, a private organization dedicated to supporting entrepreneurial ventures in LDCs.

REFERENCES

Black, J. K. "Ten Paradoxes of Rural Development: An Ecuadorian Case Study." *The Journal of Developing Areas* 19 (July 1985): 527–56.

Demsetz, H. "The Neglect of the Entrepreneur." In *Entrepreneurship*, edited by Joshua Ronen, 271–80. Lexington, MA: Lexington Books, 1982.

de Soto, H. *The Other Path: The Invisible Revolution in the Third World.* New York: Harper and Row, 1989.

Drucker, P. F. "The Changed World Economy." *Foreign Affairs* 64 (Spring 1986): 768–91.

Drucker, P. F. *Innovation and Entrepreneurship.* New York: Harper and Row, 1985.

Gough, J. W. *The Rise of the Entrepreneur.* New York: Shocken Books, 1969.

Greenfield, S. M., A. Strickon, and R. T. Aubey, eds. *Entrepreneurs in Cultural Context*, Chapter 1. Albuquerque, NM: University of New Mexico Press, 1979.

Hagen, E. E. *The Economics of Development.* Homewood, IL: Richard D. Irwin, 1968.

Kirzner, I. M. "Entrepreneurs and the Entrepreneurial Function: A Commentary." In *Entrepreneurship*, edited by Joshua Ronen, 281–90. Lexington, MA: Lexington Books, 1982.

Kirzner, I. M. *Perception, Opportunity, and Profit: Studies in the Theory of Entrepreneurship.* Chicago: University of Chicago Press, 1979.

Libecap, G., ed. *Advances in the Study of Entrepreneurship Innovation and Economic Growth,* 2. Greenwich, NC: JAI Press, 1988.

New York Times. "Is This the Second Russian Revolution?" May 29, 1988, F2.

New York Times. "Making Micro-loans to the World's Poorest People." February 21, 1988, F10.

OPPORTUNITY International, 1989 Annual Report: 6–7.

Rohter, L. "A Radical Diagnosis of Latin America's Economic Malaise." *New York Times,* December 27, 1987, E3.

Rosen, S. "Economics and Entrepreneurs." In *Entrepreneurship,* edited by Joshua Ronen, 301–10. Lexington, MA: Lexington Books, 1982.

The Royal Bank Letter, Montreal, December 1987.

Schumpeter, J. A. *Capitalism, Socialism, and Democracy,* Chapter 7. New York: Harper, 1950.

Shapero, A., and L. Sokol. "The Social Dimensions of Entrepreneurship." In *Encyclopedia of Entrepreneurship,* edited by C. Kent, D. Sexton, and K. Vesper, 72–90. Englewood Cliffs, NJ: Prentice Hall, 1982.

Tagliabue, J. "Polish Business Group Gives Up Efforts to Legalize." *New York Times International,* May 22, 1988, Y9.

Tagliabue, J. "East's 'Garbage Can' Economies Get a Whiff of Capitalism." *New York Times,* October 4, 1987, E2.

Thompson, P. Canadian Federation of Independent Business "Characteristics of the Small Business Entrepreneur in Canada." *Journal of Small Business and Entrepreneurship* 4. (Winter 1987).

Unnevehr, L. J., and D. Zain. "Marketing Efficiency, Informal Credit, and the Role of Government Loan Programs: Cassava Trade in Indonesia." *The Journal of Developing Areas* (April 1986): 369–78.

Wren, C. S. "Architect of Perestroika Sells It in The West." *New York Times,* February 28, 1988, E2.

19

The Entrepreneur, The Market Context, and The Venture

Alan L. Carsrud, Robert H. Brockhaus, and Kelly G. Shaver

INTRODUCTION

The blending of entrepreneurship, psychology, and marketing research may be beneficial to all disciplines. Psychology clearly has a valuable impact on marketing and can have the same effect on understanding entrepreneurial behaviors. Likewise, entrepreneurship can provide an applied test for many psychological and marketing theories, such as in the study of small group behaviors or new product introduction. The unique perspective that entrepreneurship provides is that of highly unstable and unstructured groups in rapidly changing markets. This dynamic environment is an excellent counterpoint to the static and artificial conditions all too frequently encountered in traditional psychological and market research.

The Importance of Context

Although it has become increasingly apparent that no simple definition of entrepreneurship is satisfactory (Gartner 1988; Carsrud, Olm, and Eddy 1986), it remains clear that the creation of a new venture is a social phenomenon that exists in a market desiring the output of that venture. In fact, it is nearly impossible to define any *entrepreneurial behavior* without at least an indirect reference to the market or social context in which it occurs. Entrepreneurial behaviors are often viewed as most prevalent in unstable socioeconomic environments, where organizations and society are adapting to rapid change (Carsrud and Johnson 1989).

This conception can be traced back to Schumpeter's (1934) portrayal of the entrepreneur as an agent of "creative destruction" within the market context.

Schumpeter, perhaps the best known twentieth-century student of entrepreneurship, stressed the role of innovation as the distinguishing factor for entrepreneurs. He believed that both managers and entrepreneurs experience risk and held that their challenge is to find and use new ideas. The range of possible alternatives include:

1. Developing new products or services
2. Developing new methods of production
3. Identifying new markets
4. Discovering new sources of supply
5. Developing new organizational forms.

Schumpeter's position was supported later by Kirzner (1982), who felt that the identification of market opportunities is the fundamental function of the entrepreneur.

Recent writers have abandoned the struggle of defining "the entrepreneur." This is because definitions have tended to change as business concepts have evolved and ownership forms have changed. Long (1983) argued that the universal aspects of entrepreneurship involve uncertainty and risk, complementary managerial competence, and creative opportunism. Other writers have characterized entrepreneurial behavior as the pursuit of opportunities for value creation in resource-poor situations. Some propose that entrepreneurial behaviors occur within organizational and market contexts that are resource-tense or strained (Cooper, Dunkelburg, and Woo 1986; Carsrud, Olm, and Eddy 1986). Still others have emphasized that entrepreneurial behaviors are elicited most frequently when and wherever the socioeconomic and market environments are most congenial (Stevenson, Roberts, and Grousbeck 1985). Yet each of these conceptualizations demonstrates that the entrepreneur exists within a complex matrix of social interactions within an even larger context of community, society, and culture (Carsrud and Johnson 1989).

A CONTEXTUAL MODEL

The image of the highly individualistic entrepreneur fascinates even former communists, as Brockhaus (1987) noted in his description of several myths about entrepreneurs and their businesses. In reality, however, even the myth of the individual requires a market environment as the context in which the individual's actions occur. This market context is the "ground" against which the entrepreneur's actions are the "figure." Neither is interpretable without the other.

This social psychological perspective allows access to a rich research literature while providing theoretical linkages among psychology, entrepreneur-ship, and marketing. Given the perspective of a market context, a simple model of entrepreneurial action has three basic components:

1. The entrepreneur's social context
2. The market context
3. The entrepreneurial process.

Although a number of personality and cognitive variables have at one time or another been implicated in entrepreneurial activity (Brockhaus 1987), the contextual model focuses on the entrepreneur's external world. Examples of the entrepreneur's relationships include prescribed roles, role sets, and social networks.

Role Theory and the Entrepreneur

Knowledge and enactment of appropriate roles is important for entrepreneur-ial success as well as understanding consumer behavior in marketing. Roles act as social scripts that dictate how one should act within a given situation or market context (Stryker and Statham 1985). In assuming the role of entrepre-neur, people must be able to exhibit behaviors that are associated with this role. The more the entrepreneur fulfills role expectations, the more likely the individual will be to succeed in that venture (Sexton and Bowman 1985; Aldrich, Reese, and Dubini 1989).

As the markets change, or the venture matures, the *role set* also shifts. To continue successfully, the entrepreneur must adjust to the emerging managerial role by learning new behaviors, such as the delegation of authority, adopting attitudes consistent with the changing role such as becoming a mature family-owned business. Unfortunately, entrepreneurial behaviors that once were adaptive may now interfere with the changed expectations. The resulting conflict may contribute to the downfall of the business venture. On the other hand, successful adaptation to the new role expectations can offer new benefits. One benefit is access to multiple segments of society. These different segments may offer distinct network assets that include resources, monetary (prestige) rewards, and contributions to personal growth and development. In this regard, networks become value-added contacts.

Entrepreneurial Roles in the Market

In their review of a social psychological perspective of entrepreneurial behaviors, Carsrud and Johnson (1989) propose that the social context of entrepreneurial behaviors includes specified *role sets*. These are components of larger social relationships to which the entrepreneur belongs by virtue of a particular status within the social network of the local community. For example, the entrepreneur's role set may include family members, venture capitalists, bankers, investors, partners, distributors, and customers. The entrepreneur's behavior is significantly influenced by the social fabric, or market-oriented network of contacts for both reassurance and for economic motives.

The complexity of this matrix is most obvious when members of the role set have conflicting expectations for the entrepreneur. For example, a partner may expect an entrepreneur to work 12 hours a day, seven days a week, during the venture's early development; this expectation is likely to conflict with the role expectations of the entrepreneur's children, wife, and friends, even if they are involved in the venture.

Alternatively, a positive factor in entrepreneurial behaviors is the "density" of the contacts or social linkages in which the entrepreneur is enmeshed. These social contacts include not only direct, first-level relationships but also other contacts to which these first-level individuals belong. The resulting phenomenon is best described as the "strength of weak ties." As Aldrich and Zimmer (1986) have noted, within a framework of complex relationships, entrepreneurial behaviors are facilitated or constrained by linkages. These linkages are connections between the entrepreneur, resources, and market opportunities. Such linkages are continuing social relationships with ever-changing dimensions and valences. The more extensive and complex the relationships, the greater the access to resources and market opportunities. The less dense the framework of relationships, the less the probability of encountering necessary resources and opportunities. Thus, networks can best be defined as relationships of varying added value.

From such diverse, indirect contacts, the entrepreneur is able to gather the necessary resources and information to ensure the successful development and growth of a new venture within a changing market. The developmental and growth activities would include such things as finding product/service ideas, gaining access to new technology, transferring existing technology, locating capital, collecting current market data, and appraising competition. The direct contacts and far more extensive indirect contacts can significantly contribute to the development and success of the new ventures by actually providing customers for the products and services.

As recent experience in Eastern Europe so dramatically indicates, the creation of new ventures is heavily influenced by the cultural and political context in which that behavior occurs. All managerial problems are inherently social and economic in nature, and the same is true for entrepreneurial activity. There must be political support for innovation, reliable energy supplies, free flow of information, telecommunication infrastructure, and an acceptable medium of monetary or wealth exchange for the creation of new ventures to flourish. This background is to a market system what air is to a human being. It is only noticed in its fatal absence.

Other more noticeable aspects of the day-to-day operation of the market system also contribute to entrepreneurial activity. Population ecologists have noted the importance of a market segment's carrying capacity and degree of differentiation. Students of the labor market have argued that underemployment or unemployment can provide the "push" leading to entrepreneurial activity (Shapero 1975). Finally, on an individual level, dissatisfaction with an existing job may result in reduction of an entrepreneur's willingness to consider the possibility of failure (Brockhaus 1987). Specifically, as many as 60 percent of entrepreneurs decide to start a business before they know what business they will undertake (Brockhaus 1980). For many of these people, job dissatisfaction changes the perceived market for entrepreneurial activity and their perceived intentions for undertaking the entrepreneurial roles (Krueger and Carsrud 1992).

THE ENTREPRENEURIAL PROCESS

Maintaining an Image

Part of the entrepreneur's challenge is to convince the external market to believe in his or her vision. For example, one factor that makes it difficult to obtain capital (not fully secured by collateral) is the perception by the potential providers of these funds that the business will not be successful. Justification for this reluctance can be seen in past studies of discontinuances, which show failure rates to range from 35 percent to more than 70 percent within the first five years (Shapero and Giglierano 1982).

Entrepreneurs, nevertheless, tend to be quite optimistic about their own prospects for success. In a study of almost 3,000 entrepreneurs, Cooper, Dunkelberg, and Woo (1986) found that 81 percent of the respondents perceived that the odds of achieving success for their particular businesses were seven out of 10 or better. For other businesses similar to theirs, however, only 40 percent perceived the odds to be that good. The attribution of success is a very personal, one where the individual entrepreneur's image and confidence are critical.

The keys to selling anything are image and confidence. For the entrepreneur, these may be even more critical with respect to selling herself or himself to significant others such as bankers, investors, and employees. Impression management focuses on the public presentation to others in the environment and involves the internal representation of this public self. In everyday social interaction this self presentation can serve the person's strategic goals (Jones and Pittman 1982). Tactics such as ingratiation and supplication are especially useful for people who find themselves confronting more powerful others. These normal social tactics may be even more highly developed among entrepreneurs, who depend on others not only for social acceptance but also for access to and use of scarce resources.

Entrepreneurial Exchange

The issue then arises as to how the entrepreneur develops and maintains the image required by the market place. As noted early in the study of self-presentation, the maintenance of face requires both a performer and an audience (Goffman 1959). For the entrepreneur, however, the audience is more than a collection of dispassionate observers. If an entrepreneur's venture fails, his or her bankers, employees, and family also suffer. So the success of the entrepreneur's image has economic consequences as well as social consequences. In other words, the entrepreneur and his or her network are *interdependent* in the fashion described by social exchange theory (Thibaut and Kelley 1959; Kelley and Thibaut 1978).

Each party to the interaction seeks to maximize outcomes, whether these be social or economic. But no participant has complete control over the reward system, so each must accommodate the other's expectations. The result, if the interaction is to continue, must be a correspondence of outcomes. The situation has to be "win-win," and the rewards achieved by the entrepreneur and the members of his or her network must exceed a psychological threshold, as well as an economic one, for the relationship to remain stable.

Managing the Networks

As is the case with the entrepreneur's mobilization of resources, the market's influence on new venture development is often transmitted by social contacts, or linkages. The exact effect of these linkages is not always easily identified. For example, in asking entrepreneurs to recount their successes and failures, it is not uncommon for them to emphasize the "know-how" aspects of starting or running a business rather than the "know who" (Peterson and Ronstadt 1987). And indeed some new ventures may not uniformly rely on networks. Carsrud, Gaglio, and Olm (1987) found networks to be unrelated to the success of the initiation process, but potentially very important to success in the growth phase of the venture.

Notwithstanding these exceptions, entrepreneurial networks increasingly have been associated with success. Entrepreneurs count on such connections to cut corners, to pave the way for acceptance, and to enhance image and credibility. Contacts also provide information and support, help avoid costly errors and time-consuming research, help locate resources, and serve as major sources of information about the market. Consequently, entrepreneurs constantly maintain these relationships, so that they are available when needed to provide information and assistance (Birley 1985).

Peterson and Ronstadt (1987) propose a "silent strength" explanation for the tendency of entrepreneurs to avoid talking about their personal networks in terms of their successes and failures. The entrepreneur may wish for these contacts to remain confidential, because if they were revealed, the strength of the network might be weakened or others might have access. It is also possible that entrepreneurs do not emphasize the importance of their networks because the individual wants to receive personal credit for the success of the enterprise, thus maintaining his or her personal attribution of success.

MARKETING—ENTREPRENEURSHIP RESEARCH INTERFACE

Given the importance of the external market in the entrepreneur's social context, the influences of market factors on entrepreneurial activity, and the dynamic exchange between the entrepreneur and representatives from this external community, it is surprising that so little research has yet been done at the interface between entrepreneurship and marketing. This last section builds on the preceding analysis to suggest possible directions for marketing and entrepreneurship research in the future. For example, using social context to describe the marketing—entrepreneurship interface raises a number of interesting research questions:

1. How do effective entrepreneurs recognize and balance the contending, and potentially conflicting, demands of the various constituencies?

2. How does the unique social context of Eastern Europe and the former Soviet Union influence the reactions of entre-preneur to the everchanging market opportunities there? How do these reactions differ from those of entrepreneurs

in the West wishing to enter these markets but not having the same social context?

3. Are the skills involved in maintaining an image the same as, or different from, those involved in managing a network? Are entrepreneurs who are highly successful in maintaining their images and managing their networks better able to *shape* the market context in which their products or services will compete?

Although our analysis suggests that such questions could be fruitful, it also clearly indicates that cause and effect in the market environment of the entrepreneur involves complex relationships. It is possible that simplistically modelled, casual relationships are apt to be misinterpreted. Researchers, the entrepreneurial community, and government policy makers need models that can begin to handle the complexity of this important socioeconomic phenomenon.

The challenge is increased by the fact that researchers and policy makes all too frequently speak different languages. For example, Brockhaus (1988) analyzed entrepreneurial and small business research appearing in the major entrepreneurship journals and conferences in 1986 and compared their topics to the 60 recommendations of delegates to the 1986 White House Conference on Small Business. Only six articles or papers from the 268 examined converged on the central core of concerns of the delegates. Thus, marketing-entrepreneurship research in the future should be more practice-oriented rather than primarily theoretical.

Finally, the potential for interaction among key variables must be recognized. For example, the specific market context may alter the effectiveness of the various entrepreneurial behaviors or governmental policies. What compounds the analysis problem is that every entrepreneur has a unique set of personal constituents and micro-market environments. Such market facts help to explain why entrepreneurial ventures are perceived as being chaotic and disorderly. They also help to explain the seeming inconsistency in the influence of various factors over time. Despite the formidable risks involved in cross-disciplinary endeavors, the market context provides a promising light with which to further illuminate entrepreneurial behavior.

REFERENCES

Aldrich, H., P. R. Reese, and P. Dubini. "Women on the Verge of a Break-through: Networking Among Entrepreneurs in the United States and Italy." *Entrepreneurship and Regional Development* 1(4), (1989): 339–56.

Aldrich, H., and C. Zimmer. "Entrepreneurship Through Social Networks." In *The Art and Science of Entrepreneurship*, edited by D. L. Sexton and R. W. Smilor. Cambridge, MA: Ballinger, 1986.

Birley, S. "The Role of Networks in the Entrepreneurial Process." *Journal of Business Venturing* 1(1), (1985): 107–18.

Brockhaus, R. H. "The Effect of Job Dissatisfaction on the Decision to Start a Business," *American Journal of Small Business* 18(1), 1980: 37–43.

Brockhaus, R. H. "Entrepreneurial Folklore." *Journal of Small Business Management* 25(3), (July 1987): 1–6.

Brockhaus, R. H. "Entrepreneurial Research: Are We Playing the Correct Game?" *American Journal of Small Business* 12(3), (Winter 1988): 55–61.

Carsrud, A. L., C. M. Gaglio, and K. W. Olm. "Entrepreneurs, Mentors, Networks, and Successful New Venture Development: An Exploratory Study." *American Journal of Small Business* 12 (1), (1987): 13–18.

Carsrud, A. L., and R. W. Johnson. "Entrepreneurship: A Social Psychological Perspective." *Entrepreneurship and Regional Development* 1(1), (1989): 21–32.

Carsrud, A. L., K. W. Olm, and G. G. Eddy. "Entrepreneurship: Research in Quest of a Paradigm." In *The Art and Science of Entrepreneurship*, edited by D. L. Sexton and R. W. Smilor. Cambridge, MA: Ballinger, 1986.

Cooper, A. C., W. C. Dunkelberg, and C. Y. Woo. "Optimists and Pessimists: 2,994 Entrepreneurs and Their Perceived Chances for Success." In *Frontiers of Entrepreneurship Research, 1986* (1980): 563–77.

Gartner, W. "Who is the Entrepreneur? Is the Wrong Question." *Entrepreneurship: Theory and Practice* 13(4), (1988): 47–68.

Goffman, E. *The Presentation of Self in Everyday Life*. New York: Doubleday, 1959.

Jones, E. E., T. S. Pittman. "Toward a General Theory of Strategic Self-Presentation." In *Psychological Perspectives on the Self*, edited by J. Sulus, Vol. 1, 231–62. Hillsdale, NJ: Lawrence Erlbaum Associates, 1982.

Kelley, H. H., and J. W. Thibaut. *Interpersonal Relations: A Theory of Interdependence*. New York: Wiley, 1978.

Kirzner, M. (1982). "The Theory of Entrepreneurship in Economic Growth." In *Encyclopedia of Entrepreneurship,* edited by C. A. Kent, D. L Sexton, and K. H. Vesper, 272–76. Englewood Cliffs, NJ: Prentice-Hall, 1982.

Krueger, N., and A. Carsrud. "Entrepreneurial Vision, Intentions, and Self-Efficacy: Applying Ajzen's Theory of Planned Behavior." Presented at the Western Academy of Management, 1992.

Long, W. "The Meaning of Entrepreneurship." *American Journal of Small Business* 8(2), (1983): 47–58.

Peterson, R., and R. Ronstadt. *Developing Your Entrepreneurial Know-Who and Know-How.* London, Ontario: Working Paper Series NC–87–202, National Centre for Management Research and Development, 1987.

Schumpeter, J. A. *The Theory of Economic Development.* Cambridge, MA: Harvard University Press, 1934.

Sexton, D., and N. Bowman. (1985). "The Entrepreneur: A Capable Executive and More." *Journal of Business Venturing* 1(1), (1985): 129–40.

Shapero, A. "The Displaced, Uncomfortable Entrepreneur," *Psychology Today* (Nov. 1975): 83–88.

Shapero, A., and J. Giglierano. "Exits and Entries: A Study in Yellow Pages Journalism." In *Frontiers of Entrepreneurship Research,* 1982 (1982): 113–41.

Stevenson, H. H., M. J. Roberts, and H. I. Grousbeck. *New Business Ventures and the Entrepreneur.* Homewood, IL: Richard D. Irwin, 1985.

Stryker, S., and A. Statham. "Symbolic Interaction and Role Theory." In *Handbook of Social Psychology,* 3rd ed., edited by G. Lindzey and E. Aronson, Vol. 25, 311–78. New York: Random House, 1985.

Thibaut, J. W., and H. H. Kelley. *The Social Psychology of Groups.* New York: Wiley, 1959.

20

Employment Growth in the Decade of the Entrepreneur

Bruce A. Kirchhoff and Bruce D. Phillips

The 1980s were often referred to as the "decade of the entrepreneur." It is easy to see why when one reviews the wide variety of stories on entrepreneurs presented by the news media during the decade. To casual observers, it appears as though entrepreneurship was "invented" during the 1980s. The more sophisticated realize that it has been around for centuries but was only discovered by the press in the 1980s.

On the other hand, it is hard to believe that entrepreneurs could do better in the 1980s than they did in the 1970s. Research by David Birch (1979, 1987) and Kirchhoff and Phillips (1988) shows that small-sized firms created the majority of new jobs in America from 1969 through 1984. The small firm sector's share of net new jobs exceeded its static share of overall wage and salary employment (49 percent) by a substantial margin. Furthermore, small firms created substantial numbers of new jobs during this nation's worst post-World War II recession (1981–82), whereas large firms created a negligible few (Kirchhoff and Phillips 1988).

Although small-firm job creation is not identical to entrepreneurship, detailed analyses of job creation data has shown that new establishment births (entrepreneurship) have dominated new job creation, accounting for three times as many new jobs as establishment expansions. Furthermore, new establishments formed by small firms have accounted for the majority of jobs created by births (Kirchhoff and Phillips 1988). Thus, new small firm births (entrepreneurship) are a most important component of new job creation.

There is also evidence from both the United States and other nations that small firm births vary with the business cycle (Armington 1986). Armington hypothesizes that establishment birth rates rise both during and shortly after periods of economic recession, whereas they fall during the mature, slower growth phases of economic expansion. Gray and Phillips (1983) also suggest that small firm births contribute to the explanation of the fluctuations in overall economic activity, whereas Mills and Schuman (1985) and Smiley and Highfield (1988) also report a cyclical component in small firm births. If these researchers are correct, the 1980s may not have been the decade of the entrepreneur. Although the decade began with a recession (1981–82), it was followed by the longest peacetime expansion ever recorded, an expansion which showed below average growth in gross national product during its last four years. The decade ended with a recession, but the length of the expansion and the low rates of growth experienced during the last four years of the expansion may have significantly reduced the number of new small firm births during the 1980s.

If the "counter-cyclical" hypothesis is correct, small firm birth rates should have risen during the recession of 1981–82 and through the early, high-growth years of the expansion, 1982–86. Thereafter, as the mature growth phase of the expansion continued into 1986–90, small firm birth rates and job creation shares may show a decline.

The purpose of this chapter is to examine the pattern of economic growth and job creation from 1976 though 1988. Using the latest data available from the U.S. Small Business Administration, we will determine whether evidence can confirm or deny the counter-cyclical hypothesis proposed by other researchers. Unfortunately, 1990 data were not yet available at this writing. However, sufficient data are available to disclose additional evidence of counter-cyclical behavior in firm births and job creation.

The evidence reported in this chapter shows that a counter-cyclical phenomena is apparent in the share of net new jobs during the 1980s. More detailed analysis of establishment births and deaths shows that the counter-cyclical pattern is due primarily to the net formation of new establishments owned by the smallest firms. Industrial restructuring changes are taking place among large firms and larger small firms that may overshadow the influence of cyclical phenomena on their birth and death rates. The net effect is a rapid rise in the share of new establishments and net new jobs by large firms during the later stages of the 1980s economic expansion.

SOURCE OF DATA

The U.S. Small Business Administration has constructed a longitudinal data base designed to represent the population of establishments and enterprises with employees in the United States from 1976 through 1988. This data base is called the U.S. Establishment Longitudinal Microdata (USELM) file and includes data on individual establishments identified as such over time. The USELM file is actually a weighted sample of establishments by firm size drawn from the population in the biennial U.S. Establishment and Enterprise Microdata (USEEM) files . As such, the USELM files permit longitudinal analysis of the changes in individual firms and accurately represents the population of firms in each biennial period.[1]

The data for the USELM file is obtained from the commercial data collection activities of the Dun and Bradstreet Corporation (D&B) which assembles the data into a file called the Duns Market Identifier (DMI) file. Occasionally, the data collection procedures for the DMI are changed to enhance the file's value to its primary users—private businesses that use the data for business to business marketing, credit checks, and the like. D&B began a major project to upgrade its coverage in 1986. This major expansion of the DMI file created longitudinal discontinuities in the 1986–88 USEEM file, that is, unexplained changes in the file when compared with the previous 10 years in the USELM file. Because of this, the 1986–88 USEEM files had to be designed differently. To maintain historic comparability, the 1986–88 USEEM files were tied back to the 1984–86 USEEM files. However, the older years of the USELM file could not be adjusted to the 1986–88 USEEM files without considerable imputation, which might damage the representativeness of the USELM business population from 1976 through 1984.

Thus, two versions of the USELM file currently exist: (1) the 1976–86 USELM and (2) the 1984–88 (and beyond as the data becomes available) USELM. Herein, we use the first file to report analysis from 1976 through 1984. The second file is used for analysis from 1984 through 1988.

JOB CREATION SHARES

The first evidence of the counter-cyclical phenomena of job creation appears in the job creation share numbers. The share of net new jobs created by small firms is undoubtedly the most often quoted small firm statistic. Politicians use it; newspapers use it; even academic researchers use it. So we begin by reporting this series.

Table 20.1 shows the share of net new jobs created by firms classified into three size classes based on firm employment at the beginning of each biennial period. The most commonly quoted figures are those shown in the column titled "Less than 500" employees. This is the "small firm" share of net new job formation. During all but two biennial periods, small firms contributed a share of new jobs disproportionately greater than their static share of employment, that is, more than 50 percent. The two periods when this is not the case, 1978–80 and 1986–88, occurred during the mature phase of a business cycle when the gross national product growth rate had declined below its historical average.

It is useful to note that during this entire 12 year period, the static, or cross-sectional, share of total employment held by firms with fewer than 500 employees ranged from 49.5 to 50.9 percent with an average of 50.0 percent.

Table 20.1
Net New Job Creation and Percent Share Contributed by Each Size Class
1976-1988

Firm Size Measured in Number of Employees

Biennial Period	1 to 19	20 to 499	Less than 500	500+	Total Employment Change
1976-78	38.2%	35.0%	-72.7%	27.3%	6,062
1978-80	26.3%	18.8%	45.1%	54.9%	5,777
1980-82	97.9%	-2.4%	95.5%	4.5%	1,542
1882-84	48.8%	27.9%	76.7%	23.3%	4,318
1984-86	35.5%	16.8%	54.3%	47.7%	4,611
1986-88	24.1%	20.8%	44.9%	55.1%	6,169

Dynamic Weighted

| Average | 37.1% | 22.5% | 59.6% | 41.4% | |

| Static Share | 19.4% | 30.6% | 50.0% | 50.0% | |

Ratio of Dynamic

| to Static | 1.91 | 0.74 | 1.19 | 0.83 | |

Source: U.S. Small Business Office of Advocacy, Small Business Data Base, 1976-1986, 1984-1988 USELM files, v.8, respectively, unpublished data.

*Note: Employment changes are in thousands.

Table prepared February 1991.

This is shown as the "Static Share" row near the bottom of Table 20.1. The next row shows the ratio of dynamic to static share, which is 1.19 for the "less than 500" category. This means that on average, the job creation activity of these firms contributed 19 percent more new jobs than their share of employment.

Even more interesting, however, is the extent to which the smallest size class, "1 to 19" employees, dominates the job creation activity of the entire small firm sector. In no period does the share of new jobs created by firms with 20 to 499 employees equal or exceed the share created by the one to 19 class. Furthermore, variations in the one to 19 size class have much more effect on the overall small firm sector share than do the variations in the 20 to 499 class.

The effects of a recession are clearly evident in these results. One recession occurred in 1973–74; this series begins during the expansion which followed that recession with both the one to 19 and the 20 to 499 size classes, showing substantial job creation shares even as the number of new jobs reaches an all time high of over 6 million. Another recession occurs in 1981–82, and the economy expanded continuously thereafter through the end of this series. The greatest share of new jobs provided by small firms occurred in the expansion immediately after the 1973–74 recession (72.7 percent), during the 1981–82 recession (95.5 percent), and in the expansion immediately after (76.7 percent in 1982–84). But, during the 1981–82 recession, all of the employment gains were contributed by the smallest size class, one to 19 employees. Without these smallest of firms, this recession would have been much worse.

Note also that the later years of the economic expansions are characterized by lower rates of overall economic growth and much lower shares of employment growth contributed by small firms. Both 1978–80 and 1986–88 were mature growth periods, and they show below average shares of employment growth, 45.1 and 44.9 percent, respectively. On the basis of the average weighted by the number of jobs created, the small firm sectors' biennial contribution to new job creation is 59.6 percent, significantly greater than its static share of employment (50 percent). But the dynamic-to-static-share ratio for the smallest size class shows that it produces a much greater share of new jobs relative to its share of employment than any other size class. The largest firm size class, on the other hand, produces new jobs at a lesser rate than its static share of employment.

These results provide support for the counter-cyclical hypothesis. And, they also suggest this counter-cyclical job creation phenomena is due to the dynamics occurring within the smallest size class. Many have speculated that the underlying cause is the birth of new small firms and their subsequent growth. However, insufficient data has been available to confirm this hypothesis. The 12 years of data now available allow us to examine this more closely.

DYNAMICS UNDERLYING JOB CREATION— METHODOLOGY EXPLAINED

There are four types of dynamic behavior that can be exhibited by business establishments: (1) birth, (2) death, (3) expansion, and (4) contraction. One additional type of firm behavior exists that is non–dynamic, that is, establishments that do not change. This chapter focuses on the four dynamics that affect growth where growth is measured by changes in employment.

As a brief digression, it is worth noting here that we are using the terms *establishment* and *firm* in very specific ways. An establishment is a place of work—a factory, store, office, shop, and the like—someplace where work is performed. A firm is a unit of business ownership—a corporation, partnership, or proprietorship. Most small firms have only one establishment so we often find the two terms identifying the same thing. The independently owned neighborhood pharmacy is an establishment (store) and a firm typically owned by the pharmacist. But, many firms, especially larger ones, have more than one establishment. Drug store chains, for example, may have several or even hundreds of stores, all owned by the same corporation. In some cases, such stores may exist as separate ownership entities, for example, corporations, but these entities are wholly owned by a parent organization and thus represent only one firm.

Our definition of size is based on the total employment of the ultimate parent (firm) of every establishment. We measure the dynamics of businesses at the establishment level, but relate establishment dynamics back to their owning firms. This is done so that we can determine growth of small firms as distinct from growth of small establishments owned by large firms.

DYNAMICS MEASUREMENT—ESTABLISHMENTS

The share of net new jobs reported in Table 20.1 is derived from all four of the described dynamics. Foremost among these dynamics are the births and deaths of establishments. Earlier research has shown that establishment births account for the greatest percentage of new jobs added during most periods. On the other hand, establishment deaths account for the greatest percentage of jobs lost. Therefore, analysis of the factors underlying net job growth shares shown in Table 20.1 requires an analysis of establishment births and deaths.

TRENDS IN ESTABLISHMENT BIRTHS

Because births and deaths of establishments are so critical to understanding relative shares of employment growth from period to period, it is appropriate to examine the trends in these measures to determine how they change with the business cycle and contribute to the changes in small/large firm shares of new job creation. Figure 20.1 shows the birth rates for each firm size class with the percentage based on the number of establishments in each size class at the beginning of the period. This graph shows that all three small size classes show similar cyclical movements from 1976 through 1984. But, in 1986 and 1988, the 100 to 499 size class shows an increase in birth rates, whereas the other two small size classes show little upward movement. Note that Figure 20.1 clearly shows that the business cycle affects birth rates. Birth rates begin to decline in the mature stage of the expansion in 1978–80. Then, in the recession period of 1980–82, birth rates drop dramatically. The one to 19 size class shows the least percentage decline during the recession. Because establishment formations by such small firms are likely to be firm formations as well, this result suggests that new firm formations are more resistant to the ups and downs of the business cycle than the other size classes.

As the recovery begins (1982–84), all four size classes show rapid return to prerecession birth rates. But, beginning in 1986–88, the two largest size classes show significantly greater establishment birth rates than previously recorded. The largest firm class shows a phenomenal 39 percent increase in establishments.

TRENDS IN ESTABLISHMENT DEATH RATES

Figure 20.2 shows the changes in establishment death rates over time. Note that establishment death rates from 1976 through 1982 for the three smaller size classes varied with birth rates as shown in Figure 20.1. Death rates were lowest in the midst of the 1980–82 recession and highest in the time periods when birth rates were high.

But large firm death rates seem to be on a pattern of their own without regard to the other size classes. Large firms have the highest death rates beginning in 1976–78 and continuing until 1982–84. During these eight years, large firms' death rates started well above other size classes and continuously decreased, reaching the lowest percentage of all size classes in 1984–86. Then, large firm death rates rose to the average of all firms in 1986–88. The high death rates in the late 1970s may be indicative of the restructuring taking place in U.S. industries. Firms were closing plants and transferring work offshore. The decline in death rates may indicate the completion of restructuring. Furthermore, the rise in birth rates in 1984–88 (Figure 20.1) of firms in the

Figure 20.1
Establishment Births by Class Size

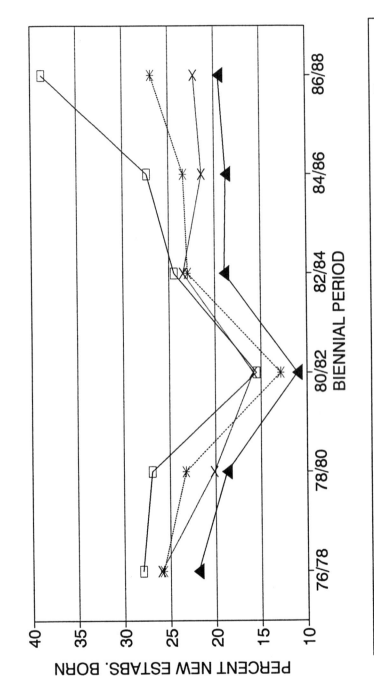

Figure 20.2
Establishment Deaths by Class Size

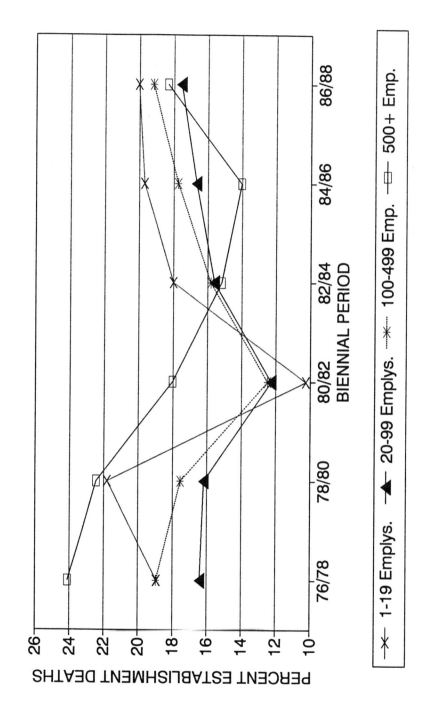

largest size class may indicate that large firms are once again adding new plants and/or acquiring smaller firms to rebuild themselves after restructuring.

The low share of net new jobs reported for large firms in 1980–82 (see Table 20.1) is due to the cyclical decline in new establishment birth rates combined with the continued high level of establishment deaths. The death rate actually exceeded the birth rate for large firms during this biennial period.

NET CHANGE: BIRTHS MINUS DEATHS

The net change due to births and deaths is shown in Figure 20.3. Here the effect of the business cycle is more evident, even for large firms. Note that in spite of their rather constant decline in death rates from 1976 through 1984, the net effect of births and deaths caused an actual decline in total establishments owned by large firms in the recession years of 1980–82. This "negative percentage change" in establishments is also true for the 20–99 size class. A similar effect is evident in the 100–499 size class although the net change is not negative.

Furthermore, the counter-cyclical behavior of the smallest firms is also quite evident. Note that in 1978–80, firms with one to 19 employees had a net decline in total establishments. But, during the recession and the biennial period immediately thereafter, this firm size class shows a positive increase, equal to its growth in the 1976–78 period. And, as overall economic growth tapers off in 1984 through 1988, the percentage increase declines. The smallest firms, then, exhibited counter-cyclical net establishment formation behavior during 1980–82, whereas the other size classes had cyclical behavior. Because these smallest of firms make up over 70 percent of the new establishment formations, their counter-cyclical behavior causes the observed counter-cyclical behavior in net establishment formation.

But this smallest firm counter-cyclical net formation behavior is not due to a major variation in establishment formations. In 1978–80, the decline in net formations is due to a modest decline in birth rate combined with a rise in death rate. In the recession period (1980–82), the surge in net formations is due to a modest decline in birth rate combined with a major decline in death rate. A major increase in the birth rate accompanied by a increase in the death rate caused the rise in net formations in 1982–84. A modest decline in birth rate combined with a modest increase in death rate combined to cause a modest decline in net formations in 1984–86. Stability in both birth and death rates continued this net formation rate in 1986–88. In general, the period-to-period variations in death rates are more significant in determining the net formation rate within this size class than the changes in birth rates.

One characteristic that is not evident but is important is that new establishment formation within the one to 19 employee size class typically represents new firm formations. Thus, births and deaths of these establishments means births and deaths of firms as well, whereas larger firm establishment births and deaths typically do not mean firm births and deaths but only firm expansions or contractions.

What is also interesting is that the range of net establishment change behavior is the same for all size classes except for the largest firm size class in the last three periods. The net changes in the largest firm size class, as shown in Figure 20.3, clearly reflects the unusually high rate of establishment births. All size classes show periods when net formation falls into the 0 to −3 percent range and 5 to 8 percent range. In other words, net establishment formation is a phenomena that has similar magnitudes in all size classes. Large and small firms are approximately equal in the rate of forming new establishments. Interestingly, firms in the 100 to 499 employee size class appear to be the most consistently prolific in net new establishment formations showing the smallest year to year variation.

In summary, the counter-cyclical hypothesis finds support in the net formation rates of the smallest size class. This counter-cyclical behavior is due to a mixture of variations in birth and death rates but the variations in death rates have the most impact. The major increase in establishments occurring during the recession period (1980–82) is due to a major decline in death rates.

Such empirical evidence cries out for explanation. Given the widespread belief that small, start-up businesses are risky and that many fail early in life, it is hard to rationalize why a period of economic adversity is characterized by a decline in establishment deaths. Perhaps small firms are more resilient than we realize. However, it is appropriate to repeat our earlier caution here. All of our conclusions are drawn from data that includes the expansion phase of one business cycle and the recession and expansion phase of a second business cycle. Clearly, this is not adequate evidence from which to draw fully generalizable conclusions. On the other hand, the evidence cannot be ignored either.

MEASURING DYNAMICS—EMPLOYMENT

Table 20.2 shows the employment changes by firm size due to the establishment dynamics of birth, death, expansion and contraction between 1984 and 1988. Small firms' share of overall net job creation for this four-year period is 48.5 percent, below the historical average for small firms shown in Table 20.1 and well below the shares reported for 1976–84 (Kirchhoff and Phillips 1988).

Figure 20.3
Net Establishment Formations

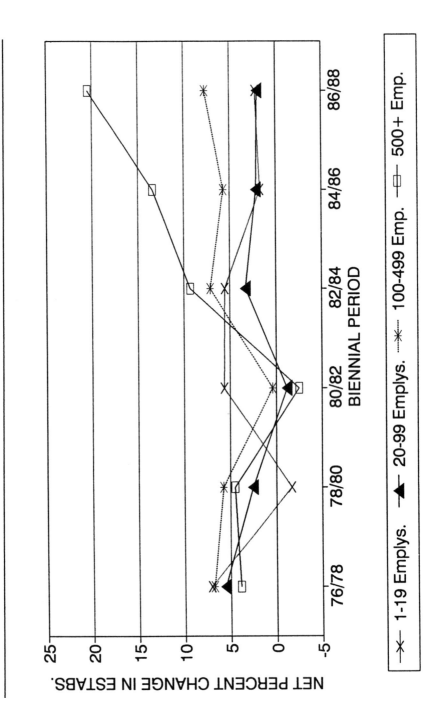

The figures in Table 20.2 show the effect of lower establishment formation rates among small firms during these two biennial periods of slow economic growth. Note that small firms' share of new jobs from establishment births is 46.6 percent, whereas new establishment births by large firms provide 53.4 percent. Comparable figures for the 1976–84 period are 54.6 and 45.4 percent, respectively, essentially a reversal of the 1984–88 period. This difference is due to the lower rate of small firm net establishment formation during this period combined with the high rate experienced by the largest firms. During the 1976–84 period, firms with one to 19 employees accounted for 24.7 percent of new establishment birth jobs. But in 1984–88, they accounted for only 20.3 percent. Firms with 20 to 99 employees accounted for 16.7 percent in 1976–84 (Kirchhoff and Phillips 1988) and only 13.3 percent in 1984–88. At the same time, the largest firm size class increased its share from 45.4 percent in 1976–84 to 53.4 percent in 1984–88. Because establishment births are the largest source of new job creation, the decline in small firms' net rate of establishment formations causes a substantial reduction in the share of net new jobs created by small firms.

The small firm sector's share of job losses due to establishment deaths reflects its average establishment death experience. Table 20.2 shows that small firms account for 53.8 percent of net job losses due to establishment deaths in 1984–88; in 1976–84, small firms accounted for 53.6 percent, a very similar share (Kirchhoff and Phillips 1988).

However, small firm's share of employment gains due to establishment expansions (64.2 percent) was much greater during 1984–88 than large firm's share (35.8 percent). In 1976–84, small firms' share of expansion employment was less than this, 56.8 percent (Kirchhoff and Phillips 1988). Interestingly, the difference in jobs created by expanding establishments is almost entirely in the one to 19 and 20 to 99 firm size classes. In 1976–84, these classes accounted for 25.3 and 13.8 percent shares, respectively. In 1984–88, their shares were 29.2 and 20.6 percent. Apparently, some of the decline in net formations was channeled into expansions within these smaller size classes.

The relative shares of contractions are about equal for small and large firm size classes and very similar to the shares for 1976–84. In the 1976–84 period, large firms had a larger share of contractions (52.1 percent), but not significantly larger than the 1984-88 period's 50.5 percent.

Summarizing the dynamics in 1984-88, the net effect is that small firms' low net rate of establishment formations creates fewer jobs so that small firms' share of net new jobs falls below its historical average. Some of the job creation lost because of low net formation rates is made up by increased small firm expansion activity, but not enough to maintain small firms' share of net new jobs.

Table 20.2
Changes in Establishment Employment by Firm Size: 1984-1988

Firm Size Employees	Births		Deaths		Expansions		Contractions		Total Change	
	Number	Percent	Number	Percent	Number	Percent	Number	Percent	Number	Percent
1-19	5,827	20.3%	-5,004	22.7%	3,336	29.2%	-1,035	15.1%	3,124	28.0%
20-99	3,822	13.3%	-3,604	16.3%	2,348	20.6%	-1,268	18.4%	1,298	11.6%
100-499	3,709	12.9%	-3,262	14.8%	1,638	14.4%	-1,099	16.0%	986	8.8%
<500	13,358	46.6%	-11,870	53.8%	7,322	64.2%	-3,402	49.5%	5,408	48.5%
500+	15,301	53.4%	-10,177	46.2%	4,084	35.8%	-3,473	50.5%	5,735	51.5%
Total	28,659	100.0%	-22,047	100.0%	11,406	100.0%	-6,875	100.0%	11,143	100.0%

Source: Unpublished data from the Small Business Administration's USELM file.

Tables dated November 11, 1990.

To the extent that this low net rate of formations among small firms is business cycle related, one needs to inquire about the role of government actions in "fine tuning" the economy. Some actions in the later half of the 1980s were designed to blunt the tendency toward inflation while avoiding a recession. But by avoiding a recession (and subsequent expansion cycle), small firms did not produce as many net new formations and the accompanying new jobs as expected by historical standards. If long-term growth is a Schumpeterian creative destruction driven process as hypothesized elsewhere (Kirchhoff and Phillips 1988), then the short-term loss of new firms will reduce the long-term growth rate of the economy.

It is useful to look at the size of the numbers that underlie these percentages. For the 1984–88 period, 11 million net new jobs were created (2.75 million annually). To accomplish this, 40 million new jobs were created and 29 million existing jobs were lost. Thus, four jobs were created and three were lost for every one net new job. In the 1976–84 period, 17 million net new jobs were created (2.13 million annually) with three jobs created and two lost for every net new job. In other words, 1984–88 required seven job changes (four created and three lost) to create one net new job, whereas 1976–84 required only five such changes. Apparently, employment turnover rates have increased.

Unfortunately, given the nature of dynamics, one cannot conclude that, on the average, changes were better or worse in 1976–84 than in 1984–88. The different lengths of the time periods and the phases of the business cycle mean that different degrees of employment dynamics have taken place and may merely reflect different degrees of maturity of the new establishments formed. Until we have two equivalent eight-year periods to analyze, we will not have satisfactory answers to the obvious questions derived from these summary comparisons.

INDUSTRY DIFFERENCES AND EXPLANATIONS

This analysis so far has made only cursory references to the shifts in employment that have occurred in the United States during this same time period. It is well known that employment growth has shifted out of manufacturing and into services. Thus, one must consider to what extent such inter-industry shifts have contributed to the dynamics between small and large firms.

To examine this, Table 20.3 shows the "static" employment share in 1984 for small firms and their employment growth share from 1984 through 1988 classified by selected industrial sectors (one-digit SIC). It is immediately apparent that static and dynamic shares are quite different in most industry sectors. In sectors where the two measures are essentially equal, employment distribution by size of firm is relatively stable. However, only two, the transportation, communications and utilities sector and the service sector, show about

Table 20.3
Comparison of Small Firm Static Share and Growth Share of Employment by Major Industry Sector for Two Biennial Time Periods

Industry Sector	1984—1986 Employment		1986—1988 Employment	
	Static Share	Growth Share	Static Share	Growth Share
Construction	80.4%	97.2%	79.2%	138.4%
Manufacturing	35.3%	70.0%	35.6%	42.8%
Transportation, Communications, Utilities	34.4%	33.5%	33.1%	45.7%
Wholesale Trade	72.2%	56.9%	70.5%	52.6%
Retail Trade	63.2%	29.5%	60.1%	26.0%
Finance, Insurance, Real Estate	47.7%	43.8%	45.5%	41.5%
Services	51.3%	49.2%	49.8%	48.1%
Total All Sectors	51.2%	54.3%	50.2%	44.9%

Source: U.S. Small Business Administration, Office of Advocacy, unpublished data from USEEM file, v. 8. Table prepared November 1990.

Note: Employment shares are computed based upon base year's employment. Small firms are those with less than 500 employees.

equal shares. Those sectors with the greatest deviations are construction, manufacturing, retail trade, and wholesale trade.

In industrial sectors where small firms' growth share exceeds their static share, the industrial sector is shifting from one where employment is dominated by large firms to one dominated by small firms. This occurs in manufacturing and construction. These industrial sectors are undergoing major restructuring where large firms are declining and small firms are growing.

In the retail trade and wholesale trade sectors, small firms' growth share is less than their static share. This means large firms are growing while small firms are declining. Retailing, especially, is experiencing a shift from small, independently-owned firms into larger chain stores.

These findings suggest that operating economies often associated with size of business are changing in important ways. For example, computerization of manufacturing processes has become more available and less expensive with the advent of microcomputers. Thus, small manufacturing plants can offer the same manufacturing capability and flexibility previously available only to large plants.

And computerization of retail and wholesale trade is far more advanced than 10 years ago. The major economies derived from computerization of retail involves recording sales, controlling inventory, and automating purchasing/warehousing of merchandise. Thus, computers have routinized processes in ways that previously required active, knowledgeable, and skillful managers at the store level. Achieving the advantages of this sophisticated computerization requires larger retail operations, that is, those with the resources to own and operate complex, integrated warehouse and distribution systems. Thus, small firms that formerly had the advantage of store-level owner managers who delivered personalized service are now at a disadvantage in a price/profit competitive world. Without the advantages of combining retail, wholesale, and distribution profit margins into a single entity, small retailers cannot compete effectively.

In fact, the shift in employment from small to large retailers has been a major factor in the rise in large firm's share of jobs attributable to new establishment formations. This is because the retail trade sector accounts for 25 percent of all small-firm employment. Had small firms created their average share of new jobs in retail trade during the 1984–88 period, the overall job creation share of the small firm sector would have been much closer to its historical average.

In some industries, labor cost reduction has also been a driving factor. In construction, union wage scales have motivated many contractors to avoid hiring union labor by subcontracting work to independent contractors. Many of these independent contractors are former construction workers who have chosen independent contracting as a mechanism to obtain work in a non-union environment. So, a surge of new small firms in construction is indicative of a changing labor environment.

Small firm formations, then, represent (at least in some industries) a mechanism for reallocating resources to their most efficient applications. In other industries, large-firm establishment formations represent the same phenomenon.

CONCLUSIONS

As an overview of economic growth, the 1984–88 period does not look like the "decade of the entrepreneur." Instead, it looks more like the decade of the large corporation. Large firms had a disproportionately greater share of new establishment births and net new job creation from 1984 through 1988.

That large firms have such a large share of net new job creation is evidence supporting the counter-cyclical hypothesis. Further evidence appears in 1980–82, when net establishment changes in the smallest firm size class rose during this recession. But the counter-cyclical hypothesis does not apply to the larger size classes, which show a more conventional cyclical change pattern. The smallest firm counter-cyclical behavior is due to variations in death rates—these declined more than birth rates during the 1980–82 recession period. Such a decline in death rates during a recession is contrary to popular expectations. We cannot explain this phenomenon based on the data analysis herein, and we must leave this explanation to future research. It is, however, an important question because among these smallest of firms, establishment formation equates to firm formation. And new firm formations are the fundamental core of innovation and growth in a capitalist economy characterized by Schumpeterian creative destruction.

Furthermore, the counter-cyclical decline in the smallest firm sector's net establishment formations, and therefore, net firm formations, is evident in the latter stages of the 1982–88 expansion, which is characterized by slow growth in gross national product (GNP). This raises questions about the long-term benefit to be derived from economic policies that choose to avoid inflation without initiating the traditional recession/expansion cycle. Our evidence shows that the recession/expansion cycles measured partially in 1976–78 and 1980–84 generated surges in new firm formations. And historical evidence suggests that such new firms are the core of innovation and long-term growth in a capitalist economy.

The decline in small firm formations' share of net new employment during the later stages of the 1982–90 economic expansion period are partly due to the counter-cyclical phenomenon among the smallest firms. This failure of smaller firm sectors to produce net new establishment formations results in their failure to create sufficient new jobs to produce small firms' "normal" share of net new jobs. Thus, the decline in net new formations is either the cause of or the result of slower overall economic growth. In either case, a large number of new jobs were not created because of the counter-cyclical decline in the smaller firm sectors. On the other hand, this same counter-cyclical phenomena produced a substantial increase in small firms' share of establishment expansions and, at least in 1984–88, a substantial increase in net establishment formations among the largest firms.

Still, the 1984–88 period is unique in economic history. It is a period of below-average growth rate for GNP but above-average growth rate in employment. And, this employment growth occurred through above-average expansions of both large and small firms, whereas net new small firm formations fell below their average. We do not understand what caused this unusual combination of events. We can only identify questions for future research.

The data reported here also show that economic restructuring is not limited to inter-industry shifts in resources. There are also significant intra-industry shifts where employment is moving from and to large and small firms. In construction and manufacturing, changes in scale economies are creating a wealth of new jobs among small firms, whereas declines take place in large firms. On the other hand, in the wholesale and retail trade sectors, changing technologies are shifting employment from small to large firms. Each of these shifts occurs because of economic efforts to bring increased productivity and reduced costs to the industries involved. At the same time, these shifts create huge flows of jobs with four jobs created and three lost for every net new job added to the work force between 1984 and 1988. Clearly, shifts in firm size within industries are important components of the economic restructuring necessary to revitalize the American economy.

Again, our results show that small firms, especially the smallest firms, have significant roles in the U.S. economy. Although long ignored as insignificant individual units, when examined as a sector, these smallest firms become a dominant feature of the dynamics of job creation and industry restructuring. This is especially true of new firm formations, which apparently do much to provide resource mobility, especially job mobility. Overall, U.S. economic growth, both short-term and long-term, depends to a great degree on the behavior of the smallest firm sector, especially births and deaths.

NOTES

1. For further information on these files, see: Office of Advocacy, "The 1976-86 Linked USEEM Users' Guide" (Washington, DC: U.S. Small Business Administration, 1988).

REFERENCES

Armington, C. "Entry and Exit of Firms: An International Comparison."
    Unpublished paper presented at the U. K. Conference on Job Formation
    and Economic Growth, London, England, 1986.

Birch, D. L. "The Job Generation Process" Unpublished paper prepared for the
    Economic Development Agency, U.S. Department of Commerce, 1979.

Birch, D. L. *Job Creation In America*. New York: The Free Press, 1987.

Mills, D. and A. E. Schuman. "Industry Structure with Fluctuating Demand."
    American Economic Review 75(47), (1985): 758–68.

Gray, T. A., and B. D. Phillips. "The Role of Small Firms in Understanding the
    Magnitude of Fluctuations in the U.S. Economy" Paper presented at the
    Atlantic Economics Society Meetings, October 1983.

Kirchhoff, B. A. and B. D. Phillips. "The Effect of Firm Formation and Growth
    on Job Creation in the United States" *Journal of Business Venturing* 3
    (1988): 261–72.

Smiley, R. and R. Highfield. "New Business Starts and Economic Activity: An
    Empirical Interpretation" *International Journal of Industrial Organiza-
    tion* (1988): 51–66.

Index

About the Editor and Contributors

Zenas Block founded the New York University Center for Entrepreneurial Studies where he is a Clinical and an Adjunct Professor teaching courses in entrepreneurship in the MBA and Executive MBA programs. He has been involved in the formation of 28 businesses, most of them corporate ventures, during a fifty-year period as a lead technical person, corporate executive and corporate and independent entrepreneur. Dr. Block and Dr. Ian MacMillan are co-authors of "Corporate Venturing: Creating New Businesses Within the Firm," published in 1993 by the Harvard Business School Press.

Robert H. Brockhaus, Coleman Foundation Chair in Entrepreneurship, is the Director of the Jefferson Smurfit Center for Entrepreneurial Studies at Saint Louis University. Prior to this appointment, he held the L. L. McAninch Chair of Entrepreneurship at Kansas State University. He was a Fulbright Fellow in Entrepreneurship at the University of Waikato in New Zealand and the Schoen Professor of Private Enterprise and Entrepreneurship at Baylor University in Texas.

Ernest R. Cadotte is a Professor of Marketing at the University of Tennessee. His specializations include market opportunity analysis, survey research, distribution planning, and customer satisfaction. Dr. Cadotte has been a consultant to the Oak Ridge National Laboratories (ORNL) where he has conducted more than 50 market opportunity analyses.

Alan L. Carsrud is Visiting Associate Professor in the Entrepreneurial Studies Center at the Anderson Graduate School of Management at UCLA, where he is Chair of the Family Business Program. He serves as Editor of the *UCLA Frontiers of Family Firm Research* and Associate Editor of *Entrepreneurship and Regional Development*.

Peder Smed Christensen is currently an economist with the EC-Commission in Brussels, Belgium and formerly worked as controller for Mercedes-Benz in Germany.

Neil C. Churchill is the Paul T. Babson Professor of Entrepreneurship and Director of the Center for Entrepreneurial Studies at Babson College and a Visiting Professor of Entrepreneurship at INSEAD in France. He has published numerous articles and books, is a member of the boards of directors of several entrepreneurial companies, and is on the editorial boards of six entrepreneurial and small business journals.

David W. Cravens holds the Eunice and James L. West Chair of American Enterprise Studies in the M. J. Neeley School of Business at Texas Christian University. He has written more than 100 articles and papers and is the author of *Strategic Marketing*.

Charles H. Davis is Dean of the School of Business and Economics at Fayetteville State University. He has published in the *Journal of Small Business Management, International Small Business Journal*, and the *International Journal of Management*.

John B. Eighmey is a Professor of Advertising at the University of Alabama. Previously, he was Senior Vice President and Manager of Creative Services at Young & Rubicam in New York. Dr. Eighmey has also served at the Federal Trade Commission in Washington, D.C., as Deputy Assistant Director for national advertising.

Rae K. Eighmey is a specialist in developing marketing and communication plans for small to mid-size companies as well as government agencies and charitable organizations.

David M. Gardner is Professor of Marketing at the University of Illinois at Urbana-Champaign. He has studied, taught and published on the subjects of consumer behavior, marketing strategy and entrepreneurship. His current work on the marketing of high technology products addresses his long-term commitment to understanding the rapidly-growing firm.

William B. Gartner is Visiting Professor in the Henry W. Simonsen Chair in Entrepreneurship at the University of Southern California. His research in new venture development has been published in the *Academy of Management Review*, *Journal of Business Venturing* and *Entrepreneurship: Theory and Practice*. In 1983 Dr. Gartner received the Heizer Award for Outstanding Research in New Venture Development from the Academy of Management and in 1988 he won the Best Article Award from *Entrepreneurship: Theory and Practice*. He served two years as Chairperson of the Entrepreneurship Interest Group of the Academy of Management. Dr. Gartner will be joining the Entrepreneur Program at the University of Southern California as a Visiting Professor in the Henry W. Simonsen Chair in Entrepreneurship beginning during 1993-94.

David K. Hardin is President of the Chicago Sunday Evening Club, a weekly PBS program devoted to ecumenical religious thought. He is also Vice Chairman of OPPORTUNITY International which creates jobs in the Third World as the most effective way of relieving poverty and starvation. He is the former CEO of Market Facts, Inc. and also served as President of the American Marketing Association.

Gerald E. Hills is holder of the Coleman/Denton Thorne Chair in Entrepreneurship and Professor of Marketing at the University of Illinois at Chicago. Dr. Hills has written and edited 15 books and written more than 70 articles in the *Journal of Marketing, Business Horizons, Journal of Technological and Social Change, Journal of Small Business Management, International Journal of Small Business, Journal of Business Venturing,* and in publications of the American Marketing Association. He is Past-President of the International Council for Small Business, and was first President of the United States Association for Small Business and Entrepreneurship. Dr. Hills directs the annual Research Symposium on Marketing and Entrepreneurship and last year was President of the American Marketing Association Academic Council, with more than 3,500 members. He also served as Chairperson of the National Small Business Development Center Advisory Board in Washington. Dr. Hills worked with Xerox Corporation during its early growth stage and has served on the boards and as a consultant to several firms.

Robert D. Hisrich holds the A. Malachi Mixon III Chair of Entrepreneurial Studies and is Professor of Marketing at Case Western Reserve University. He is the author of seven books and his articles have appeared in the *Academy of Management Review, Journal of Marketing Research, Journal of Marketing,*

Journal of International Business Studies, Journal of Business Venturing, Sloan Management Review, Journal of Small Business Management, Columbia Journal of World Business, and *Strategic Management Journal.* Dr. Hisrich has consulted with numerous small and large corporations and has twice been a Fulbright Professor in Hungary. He is currently establishing a business school in Moscow.

Jonathan C. Huefner is currently in the Psychology Department at California State University, Bakersfield. Dr. Huefner has authored entrepreneurship papers appearing in *Entrepreneurship Theory and Practice, Journal of Small Business Management* and *Research at the Marketing Entrepreneurship Interface.* He has authored marketing papers appearing in the *Journal of Consumer Satisfaction, Dissatisfaction and Complaining Behavior.*

H. Keith Hunt is Professor of Marketing and Entrepreneurship at Brigham Young University. He has been elected president of the Association for Consumer Research (1979) and the American Academy of Advertising (1982-83) and Fellow of the American Academy of Advertising (1987). He served as editor of the *Journal of Advertising* (1978-1982), *Advances in Consumer Research* (1977) and, since 1987, as coeditor and publisher of the *Journal of Consumer Satisfaction, Dissatisfaction and Complaining Behavior.*

Thomas N. Ingram is the holder of the Chair of Excellence in Sales at Memphis State University. He has been honored as Marketing Educator of the Year by Sales and Marketing Executive International (SMEI). Dr. Ingram serves as Chair of the SMEI Accreditation Institute, which is responsible for executive certification programs in sales and marketing management.

Bruce A. Kirchhoff is Professor of Entrepreneurship at New Jersey Institute of Technology. He has served as Chief Economist for the U.S. Small Business Administration and as Associate Director of the Minority Business Development Agency in the U.S. Department of Commerce. His book, *Dynamic Capitalism* (1993), describes how small firms contribute to economic growth.

Raymond W. LaForge is the Brown-Forman Professor of Marketing at the University of Louisville. His research interests are in the sales management and marketing strategy/entrepreneurship areas with publications appearing in a number of journals including the *Journal of Marketing Research, Journal of*

Marketing, Journal of the Academy of Marketing Science and many others. He is co-author of *Sales Management: Analysis and Decision Making* (1992).

William Lazer is Professor Emeritus, Michigan State University, and Principal, Lazer Associates International. He is a former President of the American Marketing Association and has published 16 books and more than 150 marketing/business articles. Dr. Lazer was a member of the Presidential Blue Ribbon Committee on GATT Negotiations.

Dale A. Lunsford is Assistant Professor of Marketing at the University of Tulsa. A section editor of the *Marketing Education Review*, he has published research on marketing strategy in emerging firms. Dr. Lunsford has been a leading contributor to the annual UIC/AMA Research Symposium on Marketing and Entrepreneurship.

Ian C. MacMillan is the Executive Director of the Sol C. Snider Entrepreneurial Center and George W. Taylor Professor of Entrepreneurial Studies at the Wharton School. He has been a director of several companies and has extensive consulting experience, having worked with such companies as General Electric, IBM, DuPont, GTE, Citibank and Metropolitan Life. He is editor of the *Journal of Business Venturing*. Dr. MacMillan's articles have appeared in the *Harvard Business Review. The Sloan Management Review* and *The California Management Review*. Dr. MacMillan and Dr. Zenas Block are co-authors of "Corporate Venturing: Creating New Businesses Within the Firm," published in 1993 by the Harvard Business School Press.

Ole Ohlenschlaeger Madsen is a Professor in Managerial Economics and Business Policy at the Institute of Management, University of Aarhus, Denmark. He has published articles on strategic management in small companies, business venturing and the use of competitor analysis.

Michael H. Morris holds the Fletcher Jones Chair in Entrepreneurship at the University of the Pacific. He is currently Chair of the Task Force on Marketing and Entrepreneurship, of the American Marketing Association. Professor Morris is the author of two books and more than 30 journal articles, a number of which focus on applications of entrepreneurship within marketing theory, education and practice.

Daniel F. Muzyka is an Assistant Professor and Director of Entrepreneurship Programs at INSEAD in France. He teaches and conducts research in both entrepreneurship and corporate strategy, especially as it applies to growing businesses. Dr. Muzyka has previous experience in finance and corporate strategy at the General Electric Company, with Braxton Associates, and has also been involved in starting an entrepreneurial business.

Rein Peterson is Professor and Director of Entrepreneurial Studies at York University, Toronto, Canada. Through the Centre of Entrepreneurship he encourages companies in the former Soviet Union, the Baltics and Central Europe to do business in Canada by bringing opportunities to Canadian firms. His research interests include strategic alliances and international entrepreneurship.

Bruce D. Phillips has been Director of Data Base Development for the Office of Advocacy of the U.S. Small Business Administration since 1986. He is the author of more than 30 articles and chapters in books, including an annual chapter in *The State of Small Business*, an annual report from the president to the Congress on economic conditions in the small business sector. He has also been senior lecturer in the School of Business Administration at Georgetown University in Washington, D.C. since 1987.

Mohammed Y. A. Rawwas is an Assistant Professor of Marketing at the University of Northern Iowa. He has published in the *Journal of Business Ethics*, *Journal of Hospital Marketing*, and *Medical Marketing and Media*.

Robert G. Schwartz is Professor of Marketing at Mercer University in Atlanta. He is considered one of the country's small business development experts through his many years of business incubator related studies. Dr. Schwartz teaches the entrepreneurship courses at Mercer and practices as part-owner of a moderate-sized electronics firm.

Kelly G. Shaver is Professor of Psychology at the College of William and Mary. Professor Shaver has been Program Director for Social and Developmental Psychology of the National Science Foundation, served on the editorial boards of the *Journal of Personality and Social Psychology,* and the *Journal of Personality*, and currently serves on the Program Committee of the Eastern Psychological Association and the editorial boards of the *Journal of Applied Social Psychology*, *Entrepreneurship Theory and Practice*, and *Entrepreneurship* *and Regional Development.* He is the author of three books, co-author of two others, and is author or co-author of more than 80 papers and research articles on attribution processes, psycholegal issues, and entrepreneurship.

Stanley F. Stasch taught at the Kellogg Graduate School of Management, Northwestern University, from 1963 to 1977. Since 1977 he has been the Charles H. Kellstadt Professor of Marketing in the School of Business Administration, Loyola University of Chicago, and has published extensively in new product development and entrepreneurship.

Richard D. Teach is a full Professor in both Marketing and International Affairs in the Ivan Allen College of Management Public Policy and International Affairs at Georgia Institute of Technology. He has published more than 50 peer-reviewed articles, delivered more than 40 invited academic papers and lectures and more than 50 competitive papers throughout the United States, as well as in Austria, Canada, England, France, Germany, Italy, Japan, Scotland, the Netherlands, and Romania.

George Tesar is Professor of Marketing at the University of Wisconsin-Whitewater where he lectures on international marketing, corporate marketing planning, and product policies and strategies. Dr. Tesar's research focuses on globalization of small and medium-sized high technology firms, their growth, and market strategy development. Since the 1989 transitions in Eastern Europe, Professor Tesar has lectured at the Czechoslovak Management Center in Celakovice and conducted seminars for executives in Bratislava, Budapest, Prague and Warsaw.

Hans B. Thorelli is Distinguished Professor of Business Administration (Emeritus) at Indiana University. He directed the development of International Operations Simulation Mark 2000 (INTOPIA), perceived by INTOP, a game used by more than 200 universities, companies and consultants around the world. He is a Fellow of the Academy of International Business, and holds an honorary Ph.D. from the University of Gothenburg, Sweden.

Jeffry A. Timmons is internationally recognized for his work in entrepreneurship and is first to hold a joint appointment at the Harvard Business School, as the first MBA Class of 1954 Professor of New Ventures, and at Babson College, where he was the first to hold the Frederic C. Hamilton Professorship. He is co-founder, investor and director of several companies, is an advisor to a $285 million growth capital fund, and Ernst & Young's National Entrepreneurial Services Group. He also serves as a Trustee of Colgate University.

Robert B. Woodruff is Professor of Marketing at the University of Tennessee. He has co-authored four books and more than 30 articles which have been published in various journals and proceedings. He is also an officer of the Academy of Marketing Science and a frequent reviewer for journals and proceedings.